The Specter of Dido

JOHN WATKINS

The Specter of Dido
Spenser and Virgilian Epic

Yale University Press   New Haven and London

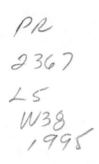

Frontispiece: One of twenty-four engravings by P. Galle illustrating Virgil's *Aeneid* dedicated by Aemilius Gandinus to Albert, Archduke of Austria. Printed on silk, c. 1595, in Antwerp. Courtesy of the Bodleian Library, Oxford.

Published with assistance from the Elizabethan Club, Yale University

Set in Bembo type by Rainsford Type, Danbury, Connecticut.
Printed in the United States of America by Book Crafters, Inc., Chelsea, Michigan.

Library of Congress Cataloging-in-Publication Data
Watkins, John, 1960–
The specter of Dido : Spenser and Virgilian epic / John Watkins.
p.   cm.
Includes bibliographical references (p.   ) and index.
ISBN 0-300-05883-7 (alk. paper)
1. Spenser, Edmund, 1552?–1599—knowledge—Literature.
2. Spenser, Edmund, 1552?–1599–Characters—Queens.   3. Dido
(Legendary character) in literature.   4. Epic poetry, English—Roman
influences.   5. Queens in literature.   6. Virgil—Influence.
7. Virgil. Aeneis.   I. Title.
PR2367.L5W38   1995
821'.3—dc20   94-33643
                                                                              CIP

A catalogue record for this book is available from the British Library. The paper in this book meets the guidelines for permanence and durability of the Committee on Production Guidelines for Book Longevity of the Council on Library Resources

10   9   8   7   6   5   4   3   2   1

For
John Allen Watkins, 1922–1993
Rita McClard Watkins, 1921–1992

ᘛ CONTENTS ᘚ

CONTENTS

⟪ ACKNOWLEDGMENTS ⟫

I n acknowledging those who have influenced this book, I am reminded of Spenser's own "endlesse worke" of numbering "the seas abundant progeny." I am especially grateful to John Pitcher of St. John's College, Oxford, for first sparking my interest in the relationship between the Renaissance and classical antiquity. This particular study began as a doctoral dissertation directed by John Hollander, who has long encouraged and inspired my work on poetic origins.

Several scholars have commented valuably on chapters at different stages of composition: Carolyn Asp, Marie Borroff, Leslie Brisman, Ralph Hexter, G. K. Hunter, Tim Machan, Lawrence Manley, Michael McCanles, Lawrence Rhu, William Sessions, James Stephens, and Jennifer Wagner. I am grateful to the Spenser Society and to the Spenser at Kalamazoo Committee for opportunities to present my work at Kalamazoo and at the Toronto meeting of the Modern Language Association. My three Kalamazoo respondents—Donald Cheney, Craig Berry, and Mihoko Suzuki—offered me excellent suggestions for revision. I have also benefited from conversations with Albert Ascoli, Christopher Baswell, John Carey, Rita Copeland, Karen Ford, Carol Kaske, Kevis Goodman, A. Kent Hieatt, Claudia L. Johnson, William J. Kennedy, Christine Krueger,

Charles Ross, and David Wallace. At a crucial point in the project's reconception, Theresa M. Krier read and commented on every detail of the manuscript. I will always be grateful to her for asking me questions that radically transformed my understanding of Spenser's relationship to classical antiquity. As a reader for Yale University Press, William Oram offered invaluable suggestions for final revision.

I owe a special debt to my students and colleagues at both Marquette University and the University of Minnesota for their suggestions and encouragement. Galina Yermolenko at Marquette was a superb research assistant, and Ruth Jeffries at Minnesota an indefatigable fact-checker, proofreader, and volunteer copy editor. Jonathan Brent, Elaine Maisner, and Jane Hedges guided the manuscript through its final stages at Yale University Press.

Grants from the Mrs. Giles Whiting Foundation, the Newberry Library, and Marquette University have supported my research. The Elizabethan Club at Yale University contributed generously toward the book's publication. I am grateful to the *Journal of Medieval and Renaissance Studies* for permission to incorporate portions of my article on Virgilian *ekphrasis* in the second and sixth chapters of this book. To avoid publication conflict, Arthur Kinney allowed me to withdraw a version of my fourth chapter slated to appear in *English Literary Renaissance*. The Bodleian Library granted me rights to reproduce Galle's 1595 engraving of Aeneas's meeting with Dido.

While writing this book, I often wished that someone had written a comprehensive survey of medieval responses to Dido. On the day I began marking my final proofs, I received my fresh copy of Marilynn Desmond's 1994 *Reading Dido: Gender, Textuality and the Medieval* Aeneid. It is a superb book, and I regret that it did not appear in time to influence my discussions.

Andrew Elfenbein has supported my work on Spenser and Virgil from its inception. He has read countless drafts and helped me to refine both individual readings and central arguments. To him and to my parents, who died just before this work was accepted for publication, I owe my greatest debts.

R eferences to Spenser are to *The Works of Edmund Spenser: A Variorum Edition,* ed. Edwin Greenlaw et al., 9 vols. (Baltimore: Johns Hopkins Press, 1932–49). References to the *Aeneid* are to *P. Vergili Maronis Opera,* ed. R. A. B. Mynors (Oxford: Clarendon Press, 1969); English references are to *The Aeneid of Virgil,* trans. Allen Mandelbaum (New York: Bantam, 1981). I am grateful to these presses for rights to quote from their editions. Since Mandelbaum's line numbers do not correspond to the original Latin, I include citations to both Mynors and Mandelbaum at the end of quotations. The Mandelbaum citations are marked with an "M."

The Specter of Dido

Ever since E. K. first compared *The Shepheardes Calender* and the *Eclogues*, critics have judged Spenser's poetry by its fidelity to Virgilian models. While contemporary admirers hailed Spenser as the English Maro, later neoclassical detractors condemned him for violating decorums supposedly observed by Virgil himself. In a preface to *Prince Arthur, An Heroicke Poem* (1695), Sir Richard Blackmore laments that he abandoned the Virgilian conception of epic as a unified account of a single hero's career: "But *Ariosto* and *Spencer*, however *great Wits*, not observing this judicious Conduct of *Virgil*, nor attending to any sober Rules, are hurried on with a *boundless, impetuous* Fancy over Hill and Dale, till they are both lost in a Wood of Allegories,— Allegories so *wild, unnatural*, and *extravagant*, as greatly displease the Reader."[1] Adopting an image from *The Faerie Queene* itself, Blackmore derides Spenser's poetic by associating him with his own wayward knights. Like Verdant or Redcrosse, he neglects the sober rule of reason and abandons himself to the wanderings of an undisciplined imagination. The wood of moral error into which Redcrosse first strays returns in Blackmore's critique as an image of Spenser's aesthetic error, his flight from Virgil's judicious guidance into a wood of fantastic, Italianate allegories.

I

In likening *The Faerie Queene*'s composition to an epic adventure, neoclassical critics invariably cast Ariosto as the arch-enchanter luring Spenser from Virgilian perfection. Joseph Spence complains that if Spenser had "formed his allegories on the plan of the antient poets and artists, as much as he did from Ariosto and the Italian allegorists, he . . . would not have wandered so often, into such strange and inconsistent imaginations."[2] While crediting Spenser with "a large spirit, a sharp judgment, and a *Genius for Heroic Poesie,* perhaps above any that ever writ since *Virgil,*" Thomas Rymer regrets that he "lost himself by following an unfaithful guide," the Italian poet Ariosto: "They who can love *Ariosto,* will be ravish'd with *Spencer;* whilst men of juster thoughts lament that such great Wits have miscarried in their Travels for want of direction to set them in the right way. . . . We must blame the *Italians* for debauching great *Spencer's* judgment."[3] Rymer condemns Italian influences on Spenser's technique through a sexual metaphor implicitly present in Blackmore's and Spence's critiques. For all three, Ariosto is not just an enchanter but a seducer who debauches Spenser's masculine, Virgilian judgment and effeminizes him as effectively as an Acrasia or a Radigund.

Modern Spenserians tend to dismiss Blackmore's, Spence's, and Rymer's comments as evidence of how neoclassical readers failed to appreciate *The Faerie Queene.*[4] But their remarks reveal an uncanny awareness of how Spenser uses erotic temptation as a metaphor for literary influences that might compromise his identity as a laureate in the Virgilian tradition. The neoclassical critics did not invent the figure of Ariosto as a false guide or seductress *ex nihilo.* They found it in *The Faerie Queene* itself. The triumphs of heroes like Redcrosse and Guyon over temptresses like Duessa and Acrasia signal Spenser's own resistance to romance conventions that might subvert his aspirations "to fashion a gentleman or noble person in vertuous and gentle discipline" ("A Letter of the Author to Sir Walter Raleigh").

This book explores the intertextual phenomenon that so intrigued *The Faerie Queene*'s eighteenth-century critics: its portrayal of seductive women as figures for debasing generic influences. Spenser repeatedly dramatizes his struggle to construct a Virgilian identity at a time when the nature of Virgilian writing was subject to extensive debate. Throughout the Middle Ages, courtly and clerical cultures endowed works ranging from allegorical commentaries to vernacular romances with an aura of Virgilian authority. But by the early sixteenth century, the humanist emphasis on the author as the originator of specific texts rather than of general story lines or moral programs led to a more precise association of Virgil with discrete works like the *Eclogues* and the *Aeneid.* Although publishers continued to reprint allegorizing commentaries alongside Virgil's poetry, they also included commentaries focusing primarily on the grammatical and rhetorical details of his language.

Yet this greater attention to Virgil's text did not necessarily lead to a consensus about the elements guaranteeing a new poem's claim to Virgil's cultural authority. Arguments over the relative merits of the *Orlando Furioso* and the *Gerusalemme Liberata*, for instance, focused on which was truer to the *Aeneid*'s spirit. Whereas some critics condemned Ariosto's multiple heroes, interlaced plots, and narrative digressions as incompatible with Virgilian decorum, others defended them for enhancing what they saw as the heroic poem's primary task, its readers' moral edification. For the latter, the essence of Virgilian writing lay not so much in specific structural criteria as in fidelity to the Horatian principle of instruction through aesthetic delight.

When Spenser began his career, the *Furioso* provided an obvious, although controversial, model of how Virgilian conventions might be adapted to contemporary European culture. Fashioning himself as Virgil's English heir, he had to contend with Ariosto and later with Tasso in deciding what themes, styles, narrative structures, and didactic agendas were appropriate to epic. The more freely he followed the continental poets in departing from the specific precedents of the *Aeneid,* the more easily he might bridge the ideological gaps distinguishing Elizabethan from Augustan culture. Virgil's pagan poem, with its conspicuous opposition to female sovereignty, was an unlikely model for a tribute to the Virgin Queen. But the more Spenser embraced influences that might resist this antifeminism, such as Petrarchan panegyric or Italian romance, the more vulnerable he became to critics who defined epic in more conservative terms.

Throughout *The Shepheardes Calender* and the 1590 *Faerie Queene,* Spenser represents the difficulty of achieving a stable, Virgilian identity through his heroes' resistance to female characters embodying idioms stigmatized as impediments to his laureate vocation. Since he continually reinterprets the nature of that vocation, he varies the specific influences associated with these temptresses from one poem, and from one section of a single poem, to the next. Colin's love for Rosalind, for example, indicts Petrarchanism as a threat facing young poets hoping to write verse of public, high moral significance. Acrasia's punishment distances a more mature Spenser from Tassean romance, recalled as a poetry of pleasant, sensuous effects lacking didactic purpose.[5] At times, Spenser even reclaims previously stigmatized discourses as essential components of a redefined Virgilian identity. By reversing Acrasia's binding, Amoret's release signals a more comprehensive view of the heroic poem that can encompass the *romanzi*'s reconciliation of love with noble enterprise.

The centrality of abandoned temptresses to Spenser's Virgilian self-presentation derives from the significance that Renaissance commentators attributed to Dido's abandonment. For them, the episode demonstrated Virgil's prowess as a moralist. Aeneas's willingness to sacrifice the woman he loves to fulfill the gods' commands inspired readers to emulate his self-denying commitment to duty. Throughout the period, debates over the humanist defense of poetry on didactic grounds were inseparable from debates over Aeneas's repudiation of Dido. Writers rejecting the commentators' confidence in poetry's ability to edify its audience voiced their skepticism by defending Dido or by parodying the Virgilian episode. Those who espoused poetry's didactic defense imitated Aeneas's sacrifice in their relationship to their poetic precursors. Episodes like the Bower of Bliss inculcate Virgilian self-denial on both a fictional and a metafictional level. Spenser not only applauds Guyon's resistance to Acrasia but upholds his own resistance to Tassean romance as a lesson in temperance.

My investigation of Spenser's temptresses joins recent work on the topos of female abandonment by Lawrence Lipking, Mihoko Suzuki, and Barbara Pavlock. For Lipking, the presence of abandoned women in the art of every human society defies universal explanation. Their significance varies "with the minds that conceive them, the needs that they serve in different times and cultures, the poetic forms that contain them, the languages in which they have their being."[6] Lipking raises two points that help us identify the larger literary conditions underlying Spenser's repudiation of temptresses like Duessa, Phaedria, Acrasia, and Malecasta. As Lipking suggests, characters from Ariadne and Dido to Gretchen challenge canonicity itself through their kinship with other women not only in high art but also in such popular forms as ballads and folk songs. Because of their long-standing association with alternative, often noncanonical literary modes, the topos of female abandonment offered Spenser a perfect site to explore styles and genres threatening his identity as a writer on the exalted Virgilian order. Throughout his major works, he links the repudiated lover to influences as socially and aesthetically diverse as Chaucerian fabliau, Petrarchan complaint, and Ariostan romance.

Lipking also suggests that representations of abandoned women resist the Aristotelian rule of action, the notion that a literary work moves through its episodes toward a particular end. The inertia inherent in their anguish poses an alternative poetic grounded in a private, meditative stasis incompatible with public accomplishment. In dynastic epics like the *Aeneid* or *The Faerie Queene,* their association with personal rather than national aspirations necessitates their repudiation. For Spenser, who repeatedly sees the poet's task of educating people in virtue as a type of imperial labor, temptresses like Phaedria and Acrasia appear foremost as artists whose productions end in sensual delight rather than moral instruction. Their conspicuous association with a particular literary mode underscores its didactic failure. Only a poet committed to the Virgilian task of disciplining a nation can overcome its ethical and aesthetic insufficiencies.

Pavlock and Suzuki have addressed the particular case of abandoned women in epic from more pointedly historical perspectives. For Pavlock, the abandoned woman and the night raid constitute the two primary topoi through which epic poets foreground conflicts between erotic and heroic values.[7] Suzuki treats Helen, Dido, and their literary descendants as evidence of the dominant, patriarchal culture's need to validate itself through the victimization of women and minorities.[8] Both critics heighten our understanding of epic as a genre privileging the exclusion, repudiation, and sacrifice of women. My own work suggests that rejections and abandonments within epic fictions form part of the larger process through which epic writers paradoxically aggrandize influences they proceed to stigmatize as hindrances to their vocations. Just as Virgil endows Dido with an allure that makes Aeneas's obedience to duty seem all the more painfully achieved, he invests his own departures from Homer with a pathos of loss measuring the strength of his Augustan commitment. In depicting a world dominated by imperial urgency, Virgil cannot allow his hero to spend years luxuriating in the arms of nymphs and goddesses. But he persistently recalls the leisure of Homeric romance as something he must struggle to renounce.

In championing the novel as the dialogic form par excellence, Mikhail Bakhtin describes epic as a quintessentially monologic genre excluding all discourses except those sanctioned by the dominant culture.[9] My account of the strategies by which writers like Spenser fashion their Virgilian identities challenges Bakhtin's views. Epic in the Virgilian tradition does not succeed in excluding alternative discourses but instead thematizes its author's never fully successful struggle against them.[10] Just as an epic hero must have an antagonist to prove his valor, the epic poet must always have dangerously compelling influences to resist. Instead of actually excluding subversive styles, modes, and narrative techniques, the poet continually evokes them as threats that can be overcome by his or her artistry alone.

By introducing alternative idioms as influences to be abandoned and voices to be silenced, each poet lays the foundation for the next stage of epic history. Whatever idioms early writers may affirm as essential to their epic visions may well be rejected by later writers as an impediment to their aesthetic quest. I have chosen the 1590 *Faerie Queene* as this study's primary focus because it marks a crisis in the development of Virgilian and post-Virgilian epic as a genre resisting degenerate influences. Since individual epic writers often sanctioned narrative structures and rhetorical stances that other writers rejected, there was never any consensus as to what forms were necessarily incompatible with heroic decorums. Nevertheless, poets before Spenser were relatively consistent in their own choices and exclusions. Virgil never reversed his initial stance toward Homer, and Dante stigmatized courtly romance throughout the *Commedia*. Even when Tasso changed his mind about the compatibility of romance with Virgilian *gravitas,* he recast the *Liberata* as the *Conquistata,* a completely new poem.

By contrast, Spenser continually revises his understanding of his Virgilian identity within the context of a single poem. As I will argue, the 1590 *Faerie Queene* develops as a series of exclusions and later recuperations of influences whose Virgilian affinities were contested throughout the Renaissance. Questions of structure and allegorical consistency raised by generations of Spenserians can be resolved into the single, albeit complex question of what particular understanding of epic in the Virgilian tradition dominates a given book or canto. If the notorious flatness of the Medina and Alma episodes owes something to the Fulgentian canonization of Virgil as a moralist advocating erotic restraint, Book III's more positive presentation of desire, as well as its more conspicuous digressiveness, revises the *Aeneid* along lines first established by Ariosto.

In emphasizing this instability of both "Virgil" and "Virgilian epic" as cultural categories, I hope to overcome certain impasses that have characterized earlier work on Spenser's relationship to classical antiquity. Since the publication of Merritt Y. Hughes's *Virgil and Spenser* in 1929, critics have stereotyped Spenser as a syncretist who juxtaposed various sources with no regard to their original aesthetic or ideological context.[11] But in dismissing Spenser as a poor classicist who failed to grasp the "essential nature" of Virgilian poetry, they fail to historicize their own understanding of Virgil and his legacy. The melancholy Virgil esteemed by nineteenth- and twentieth-century critics would seem as fundamentally un-Virgilian to Renaissance readers as the Neoplatonic Virgil hailed by Cristoforo Landino would seem to us. Instead of condemning Spenser for his insensitivity to a Virgil that none of his contemporaries necessarily recognized, I want to explore his artistry in bringing the diverse Virgilian legacies available to his culture into intertextual dialogue.[12]

This book begins with an analysis of the *Aeneid* as the first epic to establish its canonicity by distancing itself from influences unsuited to its imperial character through a fiction of female abandonment. A particular coincidence of antifeminism and Hellenophobia at the Augustan court encouraged Virgil to present Dido's repudiation as an image of his ambivalence toward Homer. Just as Aeneas reveals his *pietas* by abandoning Dido, Virgil establishes himself as Augustus's laureate by stigmatizing Homer's indulgence toward Odysseus's affairs, his championship of ingenuity over truth, and his narrative digressiveness as incompatible with Roman values.

6

Virgil's struggles against Greek influence underlie the contradictions inherent in the *Aeneid*'s later reception that I examine in the second chapter. Ovid vents his nostalgia for the Homeric romance that Virgil discredited by championing Dido over Aeneas. In contrast, allegorists like Fulgentius and Bernard praise Aeneas as a Christian Everyman renouncing carnality in his growth toward spiritual perfection. The moral argument that they discovered in the *Aeneid* paved the way for its Renaissance canonization as the paradigmatic didactic epic. The chapter focuses on how diverse perceptions of Dido's tragedy inspired Dante's, Chaucer's, Ariosto's, and Tasso's divergent representations of their relationship to Virgil's cultural authority.

With chapter 3, I turn specifically to Spenser's appropriation of the hermeneutic and imitational modes mediating Virgil's early modern reception. As an imitation of the *Eclogues, The Shepheardes Calender* announces his intention to join the Virgilian succession. By modeling Colin's infatuation with Rosalind on Aeneas's with Dido, Spenser questions whether Petrarchanism and Chaucerian fabliau can satisfy epic decorums. While the plaintive eclogues discredit Petrarchan complaint as a Dido vitiating epic's didactic commitment, "April" and "November" recuperate Petrarchan epideictic as a medium of moral instruction by evoking the Renaissance distinction between the chaste Dido of history and Virgil's concupiscent queen. Chaucer, praised by John Lydgate and Thomas Hoccleve as a second Virgil but condemned by Sir John Harington for "flat scurrilitie," appears as an even more ambiguous influence. Although Spenser hails him as the English "Tityrus," the moral eclogues condemn his fabliaux for violating Virgilian ideals.

The fourth chapter argues that Book I of *The Faerie Queene* enlists Protestant theology against Italian romance's challenge to epic's exaltation as a didactic form. Ariosto's digressiveness is the structural correlative to suspicions that humanity cannot overcome its passions. Just as characters like Ruggiero depart from Aeneas's example in lapsing not once but multiple times into concupiscence, Ariosto's narrative repeatedly defies the *Aeneid*'s comparative linearity. As a Protestant, Spenser has his own misgivings about the Neo-Latin commentators' view that Aeneas surmounts temptation through unaided natural virtue. But when he recasts Aeneas's truancy in Carthage as Redcrosse's dalliance with Duessa, he asserts that moral reformation is possible through divine guidance. Like his epic precursors, Spenser uses a fiction of female abandonment to define himself against poetic forms that might thwart his Virgilian aspirations. If grace redeems Redcrosse from Duessa's wiles, a commitment to Protestantism redeems Spenser from the skepticism underlying the *Furioso*'s tangled plots.

With Book II's shift to a more temporal perspective, Spenser finds a new counter to Italian romance in the queen's virginity. Elizabeth stands as living proof that passion can be mastered through the discipline and restraint that commentators found extolled in the *Aeneid*. Book II dispels epic's long-standing anxieties about female magistracy by recasting the Renaissance distinction between the chaste and concupiscent Didos as a contrast between Italianate temptresses like Phaedria and Acrasia and surrogates of the Virgin Queen like Medina, Alma, and Belphoebe. Competing versions of Dido's career establish temperance as both a moral and an aesthetic category. By privileging starkly allegorical places of instruction like Medina's Castle and the House of Alma over the luxuriance of the Bower of Bliss, Spenser establishes himself as a writer of explicitly didactic verse in contrast to Ariosto's and Tasso's luxuriance.

In my sixth and final chapter, I argue that Book III transcends the debate over the compatibility of romance and epic conventions by defining epic as a genre foregrounding confrontations between antithetical influences. Recasting the story of Dido's abandonment in Britomart's encounters with Malecasta and Hellenore, Spenser recuperates several modes previously discredited as incompatible with Virgilian decorum. By the end of Book III, Busirane, the sorcerer who reads classical narratives only as antierotic exempla, replaces Acrasia, the temptress who embodies romance, as the hero's primary antagonist. As a reversal of Dido's abandonment, Amoret's liberation from Busirane dissociates epic from the exclusion and repudiation of alternative voices. This revision alters the terms of epic's canonization as a didactic form. Although Spenser never abandons the belief that epic can inspire virtue, he sees it increasingly as a genre exploring the diversity of moral experience rather than prescribing a single mode of behavior.

ONE

From Homeric Romance to Augustan Epic:

Virgil's Revision of the *Odyssey*

A t the center of the *ekphrastic* shield
that Vulcan forges for Aeneas, Virgil commemorates Antony and Cleopatra's
defeat at Actium. The battle appears not just as a military conflict but as a cultural
crisis, a struggle to preserve ancient norms and social practices against foreign
influence. Whereas the monstrous, animal-headed gods of Egypt accompany
Antony and Cleopatra, Augustus enlists all the patriarchal authorities of Rome,
"the senatorial fathers and the people, the gods of individual hearths and the
great gods" (*cum patribus populoque, penatibus et magnis dis,* VIII.678, translation
mine).¹ In contrast to its Egyptian antitype, Roman culture is masculine and
patrilineal. Throughout the battle, Augustus is abetted by his comrade-in-arms
Agrippa and by the numinous presence of his adoptive father, Julius Caesar,
whose star gleams upon his head. In contrast, Antony, charged with "barbarian
wealth" (*ope barbarica,* 685) and followed shamefully by his "Egyptian bride"
(*sequiturque [nefas] Aegyptia coniunx,* 688), abandons himself to Hellenistic deca-
dence. His defeat at Augustus's hands preserves and justifies the Roman ideals
of frugality, perseverance, devotion to the Olympian gods, male sovereignty,
and female subjection.

Aeneas's shield reinforces a larger cultural project, the *renovatio rei publicae,* by which Augustus repeatedly cast himself as the defender of Republican values against foreign decadence.[2] For at least two centuries, Roman expansion throughout the Mediterranean world had drastically altered the economic, social, and political basis of traditional life in the city-state itself. Contact with Greece and Ptolemaic Egypt introduced new gods, new models of government, new art forms, and new attitudes toward women, sexuality, and marriage. For several generations, these innovations alarmed conservatives like Cato and Scipio the Younger, who idealized the Old Republic's austerity and alleged stability. Augustus exploited these fears in portraying himself as a Catonian patriot saving his people from Hellenistic demoralization. In an ostensible effort to revive traditional Roman values, he rebuilt temples to the old gods, restored priesthoods, enacted sumptuary legislation, punished adultery severely, and restricted the greater freedom women had enjoyed since the Second Punic War.

As most historians now agree, Augustus's social program constituted less a sincere attempt to restore Republican mores than a disguise for his own radical departures from Roman precedent. In fact, his despotism was just as alien to ancient principles as Cleopatra's female sovereignty. Its material basis lay in the same military, economic, and imperial expansion that had eroded traditional life. The larger the empire grew, the more impossible it was to govern by the institutions of a city-state. Dictatorship filled the political vacuum left by an increasingly untenable Republican administration. By assuming the title *Divi Filius,* familiar enough in Hellenistic and Eastern courts, Augustus would have appalled a Cato or a Cicero. But by stigmatizing changes in religion, family structure, inheritance patterns, and sexual behavior as threats to the nation's moral fiber that must be resisted at all costs, he justified his assumption of autocratic power. Paradoxically, cultural developments that were no more innovative or foreign than his own rule became the scapegoats proving his commitment to ancient, indigenous ideals.

Throughout his career, Augustus's self-presentation as a champion of Republican mores depended on portraying select social groups and cultural practices as inimical to traditional Roman life.[3] As Virgil's recollection of Actium suggests, foreigners, effeminate men, and women who assumed an active role in public life became particularly vulnerable targets. Imperial propagandists evoked Cleopatra, a Greek-speaking queen who unmanned a Roman hero, to confirm long-standing anxieties about Hellenistic influence in particular.[4] Long after Cato lambasted Greek literature, Romans feared that Hellenic sophistication in the arts of rhetoric, poetry, and music would emasculate their youth.[5] Scipio Aemilianus condemned his contemporaries for adopting Greek customs that would have shocked their Roman ancestors.[6] A letter to Julius Caesar generally attributed to Sallust complained that "manliness, vigilance and industry are wholly lacking" among the Greeks.[7] Since the Hellenistic world was simultaneously notorious for the liberties it granted its aristocratic women, Virgil could enlist well-established popular prejudices in celebrating his emperor's defense of manliness, vigilance, and industry against Ptolemaic decadence.

Yet Virgil honors Augustus for resisting Graeco-Egyptian contamination in an epic based conspicuously on the Greek poetry Cato despised. Paradoxically, the shield that he fashions as a tribute to Augustus's triumph over foreign influences imitates the one forged by Hephaestus for Achilles in the *Iliad*. Nor is such imitation atypical. As Virgil's readers have recognized since antiquity, the *Aeneid* resounds with Iliadic and Odyssean echoes.[8] Throughout the poem, Virgil heightens rather than dispels this contradiction between his debt to Greek models and his ideological commitment to the *renovatio* by presenting Greek art as a temptation that the Trojans must resist. Sinon's oratory leads them to national disaster by persuading them to bring the Trojan horse into their city. Later in Book VI, the Sybil cautions Aeneas not to be distracted by the Greek carvings he discovers at Cumae: "This is no time to gape at spectacles" (*non hoc ista sibi tempus spectacula poscit,* VI.37 [M:53]). Writing in Cato's spirit, Virgil associates Greek art with an indolence fundamentally opposed to the *labor* of founding an empire.

I now want to examine how Virgil established himself as Augustus's laureate by distancing himself from aspects of Hellenic writing that were incompatible with Roman ideals. Just as Augustus disguised his violations of Republican principles by posing as the enemy of foreign innovation, Virgil overcame anxieties about his poetry by casting it as a correction of decadent Greek models. Instead of deleting his precursors' objectionable characteristics, he recalled them throughout the *Aeneid* as foils to his own project of praising Augustus and inspiring his audience to imperial service. Virgilian poetry and Augustan politics share a fundamental representational strategy. In much the same way that Augustus constructed sexual deviance, female participation in public life, and luxurious living as justifications for repressive legislation, the *Aeneid* discredits its Greek sources as threats to be resisted through what Thomas Greene calls "heuristic imitation."[9] Whenever Virgil models his poetry on a conspicuous Greek passage, he transforms it so that it will uphold the values of the *renovatio*.

Aeneas's shield exemplifies the discipline that Virgil imposes on his Greek sources in accommodating them to Augustan ideals. With its depictions of wedding feasts, market places, wars, hunts, festivals, pastures, vineyards, sheepfolds, dancing floors, heavenly bodies, and oceans, Achilles's shield attempts to represent the totality of human and natural experience. Aeneas's shield, by contrast, provides a survey of Roman history from its legendary origins to Augustus's triumph at Actium. As Philip Hardie has argued, the cosmos Virgil depicts is one "pervaded by Roman power or by powers favourable to Rome."[10] But Virgil does not simply endow the topos with a nationalistic agenda absent in Homer. Noting that the shield recounts "the generations of / Ascanius, and all their wars, *in order*" (*genus omne futurae / stirpis ab Ascanio pugnataque in ordine bella,* VIII.628–29 [M:814–15], emphasis mine), he implicitly corrects Homer's lack of any apparent organizational scheme as if it were an aesthetic shortcoming. By dismissing Homer's plenitude of representation as haphazard cataloging, he presents himself as a guardian of order and narrative coherence against chaos.

By the end of the *ekphrasis,* Virgil has developed a compelling analogy between Actium and his own revisionary enterprise. Like Antony's subservience to a Hellenistic queen and her bestial gods, Homer's indiscriminate storytelling disregards natural hierarchies. But just as Augustus's victory establishes Rome's divinely ordained hegemony over the world's barbarian peoples, Virgil's imperial vision organizes Homer's disjointed vignettes of fighting and feasting, labor and diversion. From an Augustan perspective, these activities are no longer part of an enduring, but ultimately meaningless, cycle. All wars culminate in Actium and all celebrations end in Augustus's final, quasi-apocalyptic triumph.

As a heuristic imitation of Homer, Aeneas's shield associates Augustus's triumph over the Greek-speaking Cleopatra with Virgil's correction of his Greek precursor's moral and aesthetic shortcomings. But Cleopatra is just one of several Virgilian females who threaten Rome's imperial future. Throughout the *Aeneid,* the portrayal of women and goddesses hindering Aeneas's career reinforces the *renovatio*'s devaluation of women's status. In the process, it provides Virgil an opportunity to reinforce his own identity as a proponent of Roman values against Hellenic decadence. More often than not, figures like Juno, Dido, Amata, and even the notoriously ambiguous Venus become apotropaic embodiments of the Greek past that Virgil repudiates in defining himself as an imperial poet. In the remainder of this chapter, I want to examine this phenomenon with respect to three episodes that later poets often imitated in attempting to appropriate Virgil's cultural prestige: Aeolus's encounter with Juno, Aeneas's later encounter with Venus, and his tragic affair with Dido. In these three episodes, the conflict between genres and cultures, between Hellenic romance and Roman epic, appears as a conflict between genders. Aeolus and Aeneas differ radically at first from their Odyssean models, but they are lured into a closer identification with them by females who are already more fully associated with the Homeric past. As the narrative unfolds, feminine allure becomes the dominant metaphor for Homeric romance conceived as an attractive but ultimately misleading influence.

The Wiles of the Hellenic Gods: Juno and Venus

In modeling the first encounters of Juno with Aeolus and of Venus with
Aeneas on Odyssean subtexts, Virgil debases Homeric virtues into vices symp-
tomatic of Greek decadence. As a rewriting of Odysseus's visit to Aiolia, Juno's
conversation with Aeolus reduces his Homeric counterpart's procreative energy
to a dangerous vulnerability to concupiscence. Venus's disguise as a Punic hunt-
ress similarly discredits Odysseus's and Athena's characteristic ingenuity as deceit.
This stigmatization of Homeric values sets off in turn the moderation, restraint,
and sincerity exemplified by Aeneas as Augustus's progenitor. It also establishes
Virgil as the ideal imperial laureate who overcomes the moral imperfections of
Greek poetry while enlisting its forms to serve the *patria*.

From the moment that Odysseus and his men arrive on Aiolos's island, Ho-
mer upholds the god as a veritable patron of generation:

> We came next to the Aiolian island, where Aiolos
> lived . . .
> . . . twelve children were born to him in his palace,
> six of them daughters, and six sons in the pride of their youth, so
> he bestowed his daughters on his sons, to be their consorts.
> And evermore, beside their dear father and gracious mother,
> these feast, and good things beyond number are set before them;
> and all their days the house fragrant with food echoes
> in the courtyard, but their nights they sleep each one by his modest
> wife, under coverlets, and on bedsteads corded for bedding.
> (x.1–12)[11]

Neither the fertility nor the endless feasting characterizes the Aiolians as intem-
perate. The image of Aiolos's twelve sons sleeping "each one by his modest /
wife" suggests security and contentment rather than dissipation. As the sign of
a well-ordered household, Aiolian sexuality is inseparable from Aiolian gener-
osity. The god's procreative powers are synecdochic of the general abundance
that he shares with the weary voyager who strays onto his shores.

When Virgil recasts Aiolos as Aeolus at the opening of the *Aeneid*, he trans-
forms the generative energies privileged by Homer into chaotic forces needing
restraint:

> Then—burning, pondering—the goddess reaches
> Aeolia, the motherland of storms,
> a womb that always teems with raving south winds.
> In his enormous cave King Aeolus
> restrains the wrestling winds, loud hurricanes;

13

he tames and sways them with his chains and prison.
They rage in indignation at their cages;
the mountain answers with a mighty roar.
Lord Aeolus sits in his high citadel;
he holds his scepter, and he soothes their souls
and calms their madness.

Talia flammato secum dea corde uolutans
nimborum in patriam, loca feta furentibus Austris,
Aeoliam uenit. hic uasto rex Aeolus antro
luctantis uentos tempestatesque sonoras
imperio premit ac uinclis et carcere frenat.
illi indignantes magno cum murmure montis
circum claustra fremunt; celsa sedet Aeolus arce
sceptra tenens mollitque animos et temperat iras.

(I.50–57 [M:75–85])

In the *Aeneid*, frenzy supplants the *Odyssey*'s serenity of erotic experience. Whereas Homer associated procreation with generosity, Virgil links it to primal, inherently anarchic impulses by figuring Aeolia not as an island but as a womb-like cave "pregnant with the raging southwinds" (*feta furentibus Austris*, translation mine). Aeolus himself shares nothing with his Homeric prototype but a common authority over the winds. Profusion and abundance were the hallmarks of Aiolos's benevolence, whereas discipline and restraint reveal Aeolus's commitment to proto-Augustan ideals. Instead of depicting him as the progenitor of multiple offspring, Virgil upholds him as a repressive agent who "tames," "soothes," "restrains," and even "sways [the winds] with his chains and prison."

Virgil's assault on idyllic, Odyssean eros culminates in Juno's offer of a lovely nymph to bribe Aeolus into destroying the Trojans. For Virgil, the procreative impulses that Homer celebrated become vulnerabilities for the agents of chaos and irrationality to exploit against Roman civilization. Whereas Aeolus contrasts markedly with his Homeric prototype, Juno's treachery identifies her with Hera, whose similar offer bribes Sleep into a conspiracy against Zeus in the *Iliad*. As Robert Lamberton has argued, Hera's corruption of Sleep and her subsequent seduction of Zeus were cited throughout the ancient world as instances of Homer's irreverence toward the gods.[12] Virgil's recalling the episode at this point in the *Aeneid* reinforces his retrospective association of Aiolian sexuality with degeneracy. Juno's promise to make Aeolus the father of fair sons (*pulchra faciat te prole parentem*, I.75) tempts him with nothing more than the opportunity to become a famed progenitor like his prototype. But in this revised ideological context, assuming such a role would compromise his identity as an Augustan jailor.

When Aeolus agrees to assist Juno, his words suggest that he succumbs less to her bribe than to her superior authority:

> O Queen, your task
> is to discover what you wish; and mine,
> to act at your command.

> tuus, o regina, quidoptes
> explorare labor; mihi iussa capessere fas est.
>
> (I.76–77 [M:110–12])

Since Virgil typically leaves open questions about his characters' motivations, we never know whether Aeolus's acknowledgment of subservience masks sexual and paternal ambitions. Perhaps he is so committed to the Olympian order that he would have obeyed Juno even without her Hellenizing promises. But by associating eros with Juno's treachery, Virgil denigrates it as an inherently subversive force. While endorsing its Iliadic construction as a medium of deception, he excludes its Odyssean portrayal as an innocent pleasure. Throughout the *Aeneid,* he presents it both as a threat to Roman civilization and as one of the primary evils that civilization exists to combat.

On an intertextual level, Virgil's story of how a conspicuously Homeric Juno lures a conspicuously un-Homeric Aeolus into a closer identification with his lusty Homeric prototype characterizes Hellenic romance itself as dangerously seductive. Nothing in the Aiolos episode threatened Virgil more than its failure to present sex as a physical, moral, or political threat. Homer raises the possibility of a sexuality that does not need to be suppressed to preserve the social order. Were Virgil to endorse Homer's view of eros as a morally positive force, he would undermine the grounds for Augustus's antierotic strictures: the innocent pleasures enjoyed by Aiolos and his sons hardly justify despotism as a defense against degeneracy. But Virgil resists the Homeric lure precisely by associating sexuality with rebellion and corruption. Throughout the *Aeneid,* he characterizes it as something so inherently destructive that it warrants constant vigilance and restraint.

A common anxiety about Greek influence underlies the formal parallels linking Juno's conversation with Aeolus to Venus's with Aeneas. Although Venus wants to promote rather than impede Aeneas's mission, she too resorts to arts and stratagems linking her conspicuously to the Hellenic past. As Barbara Bono has suggested, Venus apparently calculates her account of Dido's exile to make the exiled Aeneas vulnerable to her charms.[13] Whereas Juno promised Aeolus a nymph to bribe him into attacking Aeneas's fleet, Venus draws Aeneas into a relationship with Dido that will presumably protect him during his stay in Carthage. But if Venus's scheme raises the possibility of using Greek devices to abet rather than to hinder imperial enterprise, her plans backfire in ways that reaffirm Virgil's stigmatization of Hellenic culture. Dido and Aeneas's mutual infatuation ultimately poses a greater threat to his mission than Aeolus's storm. Despite Venus's best intentions, Hellenic scheming remains incompatible with the *labor* of empire.

Whereas the Aeolus episode demonizes Odyssean sexuality, the Venus episode overturns Homer's portrayal of artifice and tale-spinning as commendable, aristocratic talents. Virgil centers this particular turn against Greek romance around two Homeric incidents foregrounding discursive indirection: Odysseus's flattery of Nausicaa and Athena's disguise as a Phaeacian subject. In the first episode, the shipwrecked hero asks Nausicaa for help in what the epic narrator calls "words of blandishment":

> So blandishingly and full of craft he began to address her:
> "I am at your knees, O queen. But are you mortal or goddess?
> If indeed you are one of the gods who hold wide heaven,
> then I must find in you the nearest likeness to Artemis
> the daughter of great Zeus, for beauty, figure, and stature."
>
> (vi.146, 148–52)

Odysseus knows that Nausicaa, who resembles Artemis in her chastity rather than in her divinity, is not a goddess. On a practical level, he flatters her so that she will overcome her embarrassment in seeing a naked man and give him food and clothing.

But the obliqueness characterizing their subsequent conversation cannot be explained solely in terms of practical necessity. In her own way, Nausicaa is just as cunning as the hero. When she explains her anxieties about being seen with him by gossipy townspeople, she not only returns his flattery but hints about her marriageability:

> ... see how one of the worse sort might say when he met us,
> "Who is this large and handsome stranger whom Nausikaa
> has with her, and where did she find him? Surely, he is
> to be her husband, but is he a stray from some ship of alien
> men she found for herself, since there are no such hereabouts?"
>
> (vi.275–79)

Their mutual indirection becomes the unlikely basis for mutual trust and esteem. Each discovers in the other's charismatic wit proof of a common, aristocratic heritage. Nausicaa knows immediately that Odysseus is no common sailor but someone versed in the courtly graces her potential suitors must possess.

In the second Homeric scene that Virgil imitates, Athena disguises herself as a Phaeacian girl and directs Odysseus to Alcinous's palace. Never realizing that the helpful child is really a divine being, the wily hero stands tricked at last by his even wilier patroness. When Athena finally abandons her disguises later in the poem, she describes her relationship with Odysseus as a bond of mutual deception: "you and I both know / sharp practice" (xiii.296–97). Once more, Homer develops a curious ethos in which the most intimate personal relationships are cultivated through disguises, indirections, and outright lies. Athena and Odysseus can trust each other because they are both inveterate liars.

When Virgil revises these passages, he discredits as Hellenic fraud Odysseus's witty, aristocratic versatility. Like Athena, Venus disguises herself as one of the natives and offers her son directions to the local ruler. When she steps out of the forest, her huntress apparel makes her look like the goddess Artemis–Diana to whom Odysseus compared Nausicaa. The pressure of the Homeric subtext mounts when Aeneas's salutation echoes Odysseus's words to Nausicaa:

> I have not seen or heard your sister, maiden—
> or by what name am I to call you, for
> your voice is not like any human voice.
> O goddess, you must be Apollo's sister
> or else to be numbered with the nymphs!

> nulla tuarum audita mihi neque uisa sororum,
> o quam te memorem, uirgo? namque haud tibi uultus
> mortalis, nec uox hominem sonat; o, dea certe
> (an Phoebi soror? an Nympharum sanguinis una?)
>   (I.326–29 [M:462–66])

Unlike Odysseus, Aeneas hails Venus as a goddess not because he wants to ingratiate himself with her but because he genuinely perceives her divinity beneath her disguise. As a revision of Odysseus's conversation with Nausicaa, the Virgilian passage emphasizes the Augustan hero's sincerity as opposed to his Hellenic predecessor's wiliness. As a revision of Odysseus's encounter with the disguised Athena, it upholds Aeneas's greater perspicacity. He might mistake Venus for Diana, but he nevertheless recognizes her as a divine being.

But if Aeneas represents a new kind of hero, Venus, like Juno, retains the artifice and indirection of her Greek prototypes. Once more, Virgil presents the conflict between Greek and Roman culture as a confrontation between a male representative of Augustan virtue and a goddess whose behavior exemplifies the seductiveness of Hellenic influence. While Venus's interest in protecting Aeneas from hostile natives recalls Athena's concern for Odysseus, her probable match-making links her to both the Homeric and the Apollonian Aphrodites. Despite her superficial resemblance to Diana, she remains a goddess of love. Although the extent to which her schemes jeopardize Aeneas's mission becomes apparent only later, her disguise itself torments him by the episode's conclusion:

> When she turned,
> her neck was glittering with a rose brightness;
> her hair anointed with ambrosia,
> her head gave all a fragrance of the gods;
> her gown was long and to the ground; even
> her walk was sign enough she was a goddess.
> And when Aeneas recognized his mother,
> he followed her with these words as she fled:
> "Why do you mock your son—so often and
> so cruelly—with these lying apparitions?
> Why can't I ever join you, hand to hand,
> to hear, to answer you with honest words?"

> Dixit et auertens rosea ceruice refulsit,
> ambrosiaeque comae diuinum uertice odorem
> spirauere; pedes uestis defluxit ad imos,
> et uera incessu patuit dea. ille ubi matrem
> agnouit tali fugientem est uoce secutus:
> "quid natum totiens, crudelis tu quoque, falsis
> ludis imaginibus? cur dextrae iungere dextram
> non datur ac ueras audire et reddere uoces?"
> (I.402–9 [M:573–84])

On an intertextual level, Aeneas's desire to hear and answer his mother with "honest words" (ueras . . . uoces) suggests a desire to escape the chicanery characterizing relationships between gods and mortals in Homeric romance. While Athena's stratagems established a bond between her and the equally cunning Odysseus, Venus's "lying apparitions" only heighten Aeneas's sense of an ultimately insurmountable gap between divine and human experience. If Homer equated artifice with urbanity, Virgil censures it as inadvertent cruelty.

The more Virgil figures his relationship to his precursor through an intersection of divine and human planes, the more he endows the Hellenic past with a plenitude and intimacy he must sacrifice to imperial concerns.[14] Pathos rarely characterizes exchanges between the Virgilian gods. While Juno's encounters with Aeolus and Allecto associate the Greek past with corruption, they do not treat it as something whose abandonment entails a tragic loss. But Aeneas's long-ing for a more candid relationship with his mother constitutes a perpetually frustrated longing for the trust finally achieved by Odysseus and Athena. As a model Augustan hero retaining neither Odysseus's cunning nor his verbal dex-terity, Aeneas has little in common with his persistently Homeric mother. Their alienation remains unresolved throughout the poem. At a later divine council, Venus even offers Aeneas as a sacrifice to fortune, provided that Ascanius can live out his days in peace.[15]

By denying Aeneas a relationship comparable to Odysseus's with Athena, Virgil reveals the costs of abandoning the Homeric past. Were the Hellenic ethos inherently repulsive as well as incompatible with Roman ideals, renounc-ing it would not demonstrate heroic self-denial.[16] Virgil makes it seem as alluring and consoling as possible to stress how difficult it is to reject. This nostalgia does not constitute a covert critique of Augustus; Virgil evokes it to make his achieve-ment of the *renovatio* seem all the more difficult. From a Roman perspective, facile consolations merely cheapen heroic sacrifice. Virgil systematically repu-diates the ease with which Homer's characters find compensations for the losses entailed by their destinies. In abandoning Dido, Aeneas sacrifices the woman he loves for an imperial future in which he does not have a personal stake. This sacrifice transforms epic into a more rigorous genre that demands self-denying commitment to duty.

Dido's Abandonment: The Price of Augustan Laureateship

Throughout the *Aeneid*'s reception history, controversy over the Dido epi-sode has served as a synecdoche for larger questions about Virgil's relationship to Augustus and the *renovatio*. Lillian Robinson has drawn suggestive parallels between contemporary Roman anxieties about female sexuality and Virgil's characterization of Dido as an impediment to Aeneas's mission.[17] Mihoko Suzuki sees Dido as a "sacrificial victim" whose death marks an attempt to exorcise the irrationality and chaos threatening a "rational, orderly, and masculine *fatum*." But Suzuki also maintains that the *Aeneid* is a divided and self-contradictory text whose sympathetic characterization of Dido indicates Virgil's own ambivalence toward the power structure he ostensibly celebrates. Barbara Pavlock reaches similar conclusions about Virgil's ambivalence toward Dido and toward Augus-tan ideology in discussing the poem's conflicts between erotic and heroic values. Drawing on work by Putnam and Johnson, Sarah Spence maintains less tenta-tively that Dido's tragedy constitutes a thinly veiled critique of Augustus and his official myth of history.[18]

The Dido episode's apparent subversion of Virgil's ideological project actually advances and reinforces it: the more sympathetic Dido appears, the more Aeneas's rejection of her proves his exemplary commitment to duty.[19] As the narrative unfolds, her abandonment figures Virgil's own repudiation of several features of Homeric romance that made Odysseus's parallel abandonments of Circe and Calypso less controversial. Above all, transforming Odysseus's private quest for Ithaca into Aeneas's public quest for Latium sacrifices the ethos of leisure underlying the *Odyssey*'s characteristic digressiveness at every level of poetic structure. The *fatum* governing the *Aeneid*'s imperial vision allows no time for diversion. Just as Virgil rejects Homer's typically noncorresponding similes, whose extended vehicles mark absolute deviations from the central narrative, Virgil stigmatizes Aeneas's neglect of his future destiny for a passing moment's satisfaction.[20]

As in the other episodes I have examined, Virgil figures the conflict between Greek and Roman attitudes as a confrontation between a female character associated with Hellenic decadence and a male representative of Augustan virtues. But in contrast to Juno and Venus, whose identity with their Homeric prototypes is immediately apparent, Dido becomes a type of Circe and Calypso only after Cupid kindles her love for Aeneas. More like Aeolus, she first appears as a temperate and effective magistrate. She only becomes a threat to Aeneas's quest and an avatar of the Greek past that Virgil repudiates when she too succumbs to an external power. Elsewhere in the poem, Virgil presents the reversion to behavior associated with Homeric characters as moral corruption. The Dido episode complicates this paradigm by figuring the return to Homer as tragic. Dido's eventual identification with Circe and Calypso, recalled through the mediation of Apollonius's and Euripides's Medeas, leads not only to Aeneas's truancy but to her own destruction.

Aeneas's first glimpse of Dido distinguishes her as an exemplar of such proto-Roman virtues as vigilance and industry by revising Odysseus's encounter with Nausicaa.[21] Just as Homer compared Nausicaa to Artemis, Virgil compares Dido, the royal stranger who promises shelter to the shipwrecked hero, to Diana. In Homer, the Artemis simile principally underscores Nausicaa's vitality:

> But when she and her maids had taken their pleasure in eating,
> they all threw off their veils for a game of ball, and among them
> it was Nausikaa of the white arms who led in the dancing;
> and as Artemis, who showers arrows, moves on the mountains
> either along Taÿgetos or on high-towering
> Erymanthos, delighting in boars and deer in their running,
> and along with her the nymphs, daughters of Zeus of the aegis,

range in the wilds and play, and the heart of Leto is gladdened,
for the head and the brows of Artemis are above all the others,
and she is easily marked among them, though all are lovely,
so this one shone among her handmaidens, a virgin unwedded.

(vi.99–109)

Homer creates an impression of youthful exuberance by structuring the passage
around images of free, almost random activity and motion: the maids throw off
their veils and dance, boars and deer run across the landscape, arrows shower,
and Artemis herself moves with her nymphs along the mountains and ranges in
the wilds. As in the shield ekphrasis, Homer emphasizes plenitude and imme-
diacy of experience.

Virgil's simile, unlike Homer's, endows Dido with mature authority.[22]
Whereas Odysseus discovers Nausicaa dancing with a ball, Aeneas sees Dido
supervising the construction of her new city:

> And just as, on the banks of the Eurotas
> or through the heights of Cynthus, when Diana
> incites her dancers, and her followers,
> a thousand mountain-nymphs, press in behind her,
> she wears a quiver slung across her shoulder;
> and as she makes her way, she towers over
> all other goddesses; gladness excites
> Latona's silent breast: even so, Dido;
> so, in her joy, she moved among the throng
> as she urged on the work of her coming kingdom.

> qualis in Eurotae ripis aut per iuga Cynthi
> exercet Diana choros, quam mille secutae
> hinc atque hinc glomerantur Oreades; illa pharetram
> fert umero gradiensque deas supereminet omnis
> (Latonae tacitum pertemptant gaudia pectus):
> talis erat Dido, talem se laeta ferebat
> per medios instans operi regnisque futuris.
>
> (I.498–504 [M:702–11])

The random energy of the Greek subtext yields to more concentrated enterprise.
By deleting references to showering arrows and running deer, Virgil focuses the
simile exclusively on the goddess and her nymphs. Diana appears less as a fellow
reveler with her band than as their commander "inciting" or "training" (*exercet*)
them in their dancing. For a brief moment, the simile aligns Dido, standing

among her followers and directing the work of her coming kingdom, with Virgil himself, disciplining the Homeric celebration of youthful diversion into a tribute to imperial *labor*.

When Virgil first recast Odysseus's meeting with Nausicaa, the conflict between Venus's Hellenic duplicity and Aeneas's Augustan sincerity reinforced the alienation inherent in relationships between gods and mortals. Here Homeric indirection disappears altogether. Neither Aeneas nor Dido tries to manipulate the other's feelings. At this point in the poem, Dido embodies the same proto-Roman values as Aeneas. By living less in the present than in recollections of past tragedy and in hopes of an imperial future, she shares with him what Angus Fletcher calls the burden of Virgilian prophecy.[23] Whereas mutual aristocratic dissimulation laid the basis for Odysseus and Nausicaa's trust, Dido and Aeneas are joined in their mutual commitment to their people.

Ironically, the same values that establish a rapport between Dido and Aeneas also prevent a more permanent union. This impasse lies at the heart of Virgil's revisionary project. As a romance hero, Odysseus can toy with alternative careers without compromising his ultimate destiny. Homer repeatedly interrupts his return home to let him sleep with a nymph or disguise himself as a shepherd. Rather than betraying sacred trusts, such adventures heighten Odysseus's heroic stature by making him seem all the more superhuman and intriguing. Virgil challenges Homer by defining Aeneas's heroism exclusively in terms of *pietas*, his responsibility in fulfilling one historical destiny. Under the burden of an imperial *fatum*, Aeneas is not free to linger for months or years on an enchanted island. Nor is Dido free to pursue a relationship with him. Her distinction as a proto-Roman heroine is inseparable from her status as *femina univira*, a widow faithful to her husband's memory.[24]

Barring divine interference, Dido and Aeneas presumably would never consummate their mutual attraction. Like Odysseus and Nausicaa, they would part without succumbing to desires incompatible with their respective destinies. But once again, Virgil rejects the possibility of innocent desire by recalling the *Odyssey* through a mediational Greek source casting eros in a negative light. Just as Juno uses an Iliadic bribe to lure Aeolus into a closer identification with his Homeric prototype, Venus adopts an Apollonian strategem to transform Dido into a second Circe or Calypso. As commentators have noted for centuries, Virgil models Cupid's corruption of Dido on Book III of the *Argonautica*, where Eros infects Medea with her destructive passion for Jason. Like his Iliadic recharacterization of Aiolos, his Apollonian recharacterization of Circe and Calypso completely suppresses the idyllic nature of Odyssean sexuality.

Odysseus's experiences on Aeaea and Ogygia challenged Virgil's Augustanism by yet again associating sex with hospitality and gracious living. Despite subsequent allegoresis, Circe's magic poses a physical rather than a moral threat to Odysseus and his men. On an ethical level, it is more akin to the Cyclops's brute strength or the Laestragonians' appetites than to Dido's erotic intensity. Even though Odysseus's men "took on the look of pigs," Homer insists that their "minds within them stayed as they had been / before" (x.239–41). Nothing in the poem suggests that their metamorphosis is a punishment or outward manifestation of lust. Hermes's instructions include divinely sanctioned sex with Circe as one of the conditions Odysseus must fulfill to rescue his shipmates: "Do not then resist and refuse the bed of the goddess, / for so she will set free your companions, and care for you also" (x.297–98). Odysseus not only sleeps with her once to fulfill Hermes's injunction but stays with her for a year. During this time, her sinister aspects fade into insignificance and her sexual favors to the hero typify her fundamental generosity. After he has enjoyed months of feasting on her island, his decision to return home marks not the choice of good over evil but the choice of one particular good—his own family, property, and native culture—over another, Aeaea's exotic attractions.

Calypso's rage over Odysseus's departure might suggest that love has a darker, more possessive character on Ogygia than on Aeaea or Aiolia. But the episode ultimately recuperates love's association with benevolence and generosity. As Knauer has observed, Tiresias's prophecies during the *Nekyia* cast a pall over the Calypso episode that distinguishes it from the Circe idyll.[25] By the time Odysseus reaches Ogygia, he knows about the suitors ransacking his property. Whereas his sailors had to urge him to leave Circe, he wants to leave Calypso and return as soon as possible to Ithaca. Calypso's reluctance to let him go makes her a more obvious prototype of Dido than Circe was, but nothing in the episode suggests that their sexual involvement has been itself immoral. Nor does Hermes's command that Calypso free Odysseus prevent them from enjoying one last night together:

> . . . the sun went down and the darkness came over.
> These two, withdrawn in the inner recess of the hollowed cavern,
> enjoyed themselves in love and stayed all night by each other.
>
> (v.225–27)

Such lovemaking is not emblematic of lassitude, heroic truancy, or fierce possessiveness. It expresses instead mutual gratitude and forgiveness for the past seven years.[26]

Although commentators from antiquity to the present have noted that Aeneas's relationship with Dido reenacts Odysseus's with Circe and Calypso, Virgil replaces Homer's erotic graciousness with an Apollonian emphasis on love's destructiveness. In contrast to the candor of Odyssean sexuality, Virgilian love is clandestine and dangerous. From the moment that Venus commissions Cupid to infect Dido with desire, Virgil adopts Apollonius's metaphors of poison and hidden fire to suggest its treacherous nature:

> . . . when she
> embraces you, and kisses tenderly,
> your breath can fill her with a hidden flame,
> your poison penetrate, deceivingly.

> cum dabit amplexus atque oscula dulcia figet,
> occultum inspires ignem fallasque ueneno.
>   (I.687–88 [M:959–62])

Once such passion becomes public, its social disruptiveness jeopardizes Dido and Aeneas's heroic identities. In contrast to her Homeric prototypes, Dido becomes an object of shame when she stops building her city and races through its streets in her mad longing for Aeneas. Aeneas disgraces himself by neglecting his own vocation for the false destiny of sharing Dido's kingdom on the North African plains.

Whereas affairs with exotic hostesses enhance Odysseus's stature as a hero of romance, Aeneas's involvement with Dido subverts his identity as a prototype of Augustus. Recasting Hermes's visits to Aeaea and Ogygia as Mercury's descent to Carthage, Virgil repudiates Homer's indulgence of Odysseus's escapades. The appearance of a divine messenger is a Hellenic topos, but the values informing Virgil's particular use of it are insistently Augustan.[27] When Mercury discovers Aeneas wearing the Carthaginians' effeminate garb and directing their city's construction, his castigations overturn Hermes's sanction of Odysseus's relationship with Circe:

> Are you
> now laying the foundation of high Carthage,
> as servant to a woman, building her
> a splendid city here? Are you forgetful
> of what is your own kingdom, your own fate?
> . . .

> What are you pondering or hoping for
> while squandering your ease in Libyan lands?
> For if the brightness of such deeds is not
> enough to kindle you—if you cannot
> attempt the task for your own fame—remember
> Ascanius growing up, the hopes you hold

for Iülus, your own heir, to whom are owed
the realm of Italy and land of Rome.

>   tu nunc Karthaginis altae
> fundamenta locas pulchramque uxorius urbem
> exstruis? heu, regni rerumque oblite tuarum!
> . . .
>
> quid struis? aut qua spe Libycis teris otia terris?
> si te nulla mouet tantarum gloria rerum
> nec super ipse tua moliris laude laborem,
> Ascanium surgentem et spes heredis Iuli
> respice, cui regnum Italiae Romanaque tellus
> debetur.
>   (IV.265–67, 271–76 [M:353–57, 362–69])

Transforming Odysseus's leisurely stay in Aeaea into an act of criminal truancy, Virgil exposes Aeneas's love for Dido as a threat to the hierarchies underlying Roman civilization. Through the subversive agency of desire, men become servants to women, private loyalties subvert patriotic commitments, and passing satisfactions supplant an imperial future.

In his account of Mercury's descent, Virgil presents Odysseus's unrestricted libido as an affront to Roman values of *labor, vigilantia,* and *virtus* that must be countered through heuristic imitation. He also resists a Homeric tendency toward consolation that mitigates Odysseus's sacrifice in renouncing the pleasures of Aeaea and Ogygia. In the *Odyssey,* Hermes never decrees anything contrary to Odysseus's wishes. As we have already seen, he explicitly encourages Odysseus to accept Circe's overtures. When Hermes descends on Ogygia, his commands accord with Odysseus's own desire to return home and vanquish the suitors. Although the message thwarts Calypso's hopes, even she finds some consolation in knowing that Zeus's will cannot be resisted. After a short outburst about the gods' peevishness in resenting liaisons between nymphs and mortals, her anger subsides and she assists Odysseus in his preparations for his voyage.

By juxtaposing elements from Hermes's two Odyssean descents in a particularly volatile combination, Virgil heightens the bitterness distinguishing Aeneas's departure from Odysseus's. As in the Circe episode, Mercury reveals the gods' will to the hero rather than to his hostess; as in the Calypso episode, the message ends their affair. But in contrast to Odysseus, Aeneas does not want to leave Dido. As he confesses to her shade in the underworld,

>   I was
> unwilling when I had to leave your shores.

> But those same orders of the gods that now
> urge on my journey through the shadows, through
> abandoned, thorny lands and deepest night,
> drove me by their decrees.
>
> . . . inuitus, regina, tuo de litore cessi
> sed me iussa deum, quae nunc has ire per umbras,
> per loca senta situ cogunt noctemque profundam,
> imperiis egere suis.

(VI.460–64 [M:605–10])

By reversing the Calypso episode's gender configuration so that Mercury delivers Jupiter's orders to the hero rather than to the woman he abandons, Virgil emphasizes Aeneas's sudden moral reformation, his renewed obedience to divine decree over his own desires. His stoical devotion to duty precludes even the momentary complaints that Calypso raised when she first heard the gods' decrees: he only admits his pain in leaving Dido after he has brought his ships safely to the Hesperian shores.

Since Aeneas never voices his own suffering, Dido's lamentations alone measure the cost of his imperial commitment. Once more reversing Homer's gender configurations, Virgil heightens her anguish to underscore the experience of loss validating Augustan heroism. Since Calypso learns firsthand that Zeus wants Odysseus to return home, she vents her anger on the gods rather than on the hero. Fate's sheer inexorability offers her some comfort, and her rage soon subsides into melancholy submission. Virgil denies Dido this consolation by making her learn about the divine decrees only through Aeneas's secondhand account. Since Mercury never addresses her directly, she is left to suspect Aeneas of fabricating the whole story. Whereas Calypso could satisfy her rage by lambasting the gods, Dido can vent hers only on Aeneas and herself. By appealing once more to Apollonian and Euripidean models, Virgil subverts the comparative securities of Odyssean romance: what might have been a reenactment of Calypso's surrender to fate mounts into tragic, suicidal frenzy.

When Aeneas and Dido first meet, they both exemplify Augustan values; after their romance begins, they appear as Homeric lovers cast in a world that no longer sanctions their desires or indulges their disregard of public commitments. While Dido's association with Greek decadence persists, however, Aeneas resumes his status as a proto-Roman hero by resuming his quest for Italy. His submission to fate reestablishes Virgil's earlier association of specific genders with particular national and generic characteristics: as in Juno's opening confrontation with Aeolus or in Venus's appearance to Aeneas, a female linked to the Greek genres of romance and tragedy sets off an epic hero's *pietas*.

Even after Dido's death, her memory continues to reinforce Virgil's turn away from Homeric consolations. In commanding Calypso to release Odysseus, Hermes promises that he will once more "see his dearest, and walk on his own land" (vi.78). Although Odysseus abandons an island paradise and rejects Calypso's offer of eternal life, he finds compensation in his own recovered possessions and in the love of his faithful wife. Aeneas, by contrast, must abandon Dido for the shadowy promises of fate. Transforming the Homeric *nostos* into the quest for a New Troy, Virgil suppresses the comforts of familiarity and restored acquaintance awaiting Odysseus in Ithaca. Throughout the *Aeneid*'s second half, fulfilled omens and prophecies replace Odyssean recognition scenes. Discovering a white sow and her thirty offspring on the long-awaited site of Alba might confirm Aeneas's faith in destiny, but it lacks the warmth of Odysseus's encounter with the dog he has not seen in twenty years.

Virgil's reluctance to grant Aeneas personal consolation for losing Dido appears more striking than ever in the contrast between Penelope and Lavinia. Although classicists have stressed how the *Aeneid*'s last six books reenact the *Iliad* by casting Lavinia as a second Helen, they also reenact the *Odyssey* by casting her as Penelope with Turnus as a rival suitor.[28] Penelope reveals the same verve and sophistication that Odysseus found in his more exotic lovers. Although she is mortal rather than divine, her intelligence, vitality, and proven devotion to Odysseus make her a formidable rival to Circe and Calypso. But as an embodiment of Augustan restraint who hardly speaks, Lavinia pales beside Dido.[29] Her most memorable act is blushing when her mother begs Turnus not to confront the Trojans. Her blush is so inscrutable that classicists still debate whether it reveals her love for Turnus or her embarrassment over her mother's hysterics.[30] Her *pudor* makes her an appropriate ancestor for Augustus, but it can never be as engaging as Dido's passionate intensity.

After a series of recognitions assures Penelope of Odysseus's identity, their embrace confirms the higher good for which he rejected the pleasures of Aeaea, Ogygia, and Phaeacia:

> . . . her knees and the heart within her went slack
> as she recognized the clear proofs that Odysseus had given;
> but then she burst into tears and ran straight to him, throwing
> her arms around the neck of Odysseus, and kissed his head.
>
> (xxiii.205–8)

Nothing so intimate awaits Aeneas. Although Renaissance critics argued that Virgil's failure to depict Aeneas's marriage to Lavinia indicated the *Aeneid*'s incompletion, its abrupt ending reinforces a more rigorous ethos distinguishing it from the *Odyssey*.[31] Just as Aeneas renounces individual fulfillment in committing himself to a future empire he will never personally know, so Virgil denies his readers a gratifying ending in order to teach them hard lessons in self-sacrifice.

By writing an epic that achieves its canonicity through the aesthetic sacrifice of Homer, Virgil laid the basis for later critical controversy. More often than not, objections to his moral and political vision have centered around his apparent sanction of Dido's abandonment. Much of the pity felt for her over the centuries arises from her status as a victim of the gods: Venus inflames her with the passion that destroys her solely to protect Aeneas during his stay in Carthage. Because Dido rages under Cupid's spell, her anguish cannot be seen as a justly deserved punishment for intemperance.[32]

Even at the height of Dido's identity with everything inimical to the values of the *renovatio*, Virgil himself never holds her accountable for any crime. Mercury censures Aeneas for his truancy, but no one condemns Dido for her love, her vindictive fury, or her suicide. Proserpina's hesitation in releasing her soul from her body foregrounds uncertainties about her culpability:

> For as she died
> a death that was not merited or fated,
> but miserable and before her time
> and spurred by sudden frenzy, Proserpina
> had not yet cut a gold lock from her crown,
> nor yet assigned her life to Stygian Orcus.

> nam quia nec fato merita nec morte peribat,
> sed misera ante diem subitoque accensa furore,
> nondum illi flauum Proserpina uertice crinem
> abstulerat Stygioque caput damnauerat Orco.
> (IV.696–99 [M:958–63])

Since her death can be attributed neither to fate nor to her own merits, it defies ethical assessment. Virgil refrains from judging it and emphasizes instead its tragic, pitiable (*misera*) character.[33] When Juno finally sends Iris to cut Dido's locks, her primary motivation is also pity for her "long sorrow and hard death" (*longum miserata dolorem / difficilisque obitus,* IV.693–94 [M:956]). The same rationale underlies Dido's consignment not to the grove of the suicides who "took death by their / own hands" (*qui sibi letum / . . . peperere manu,* VI.434–35 [M: 574–75]) but to the mournful fields with those whom "bitter love consumed" (*quos durus amor . . . peredit,* VI.442 [M:584]).

Although Virgil's sympathetic treatment of Dido's death has been taken as a critique of the imperial values necessitating her abandonment, it actually enhances rather than subverts his didactic project. The more we sympathize with Dido, the more we identify with Aeneas in confronting the exacting nature of destiny. As a fundamentally didactic work, the *Aeneid* challenges its readers to explore their emotional responses to the fiction in terms of higher truths. But as I will argue in the next chapter, not every reader has met that challenge in the same way.

CHAPTER TWO

Remembrances of Dido:
Medieval and Renaissance
Transformations of the *Aeneid*

As medieval and Renaissance commentators, allegorists, editors, homilists, storytellers, poets, painters, illustrators, and tapestry-makers judged Dido's abandonment, diverse and often competing notions of what constituted Virgilian writing developed. By the late sixteenth century, imitations of her tragedy responded not only to Virgil's text but to the long history of its cultural reception. A complete reconstruction of that history would constitute an enormous study in itself.[1] This chapter concentrates on those writers and commentators who adopted the topos of female abandonment to stigmatize specific poetic and exegetical traditions as incompatible with their aesthetic, religious, or political commitments.

I begin by examining two writers, Ovid and Augustine, who established their own careers in self-conscious reaction against Virgilian authority. Their revisions of the Dido episode expose the ethical limitations of such Augustan values as Aeneas's defining *pietas*. The next section demonstrates how their anti-Virgilian narrative strategies paradoxically acquired an aura of Virgilian authenticity among medieval authors, who transformed the *Aeneid* into vernacular romances and Christian allegories. Poets as late as Chaucer and Dante respond as much to these mediational discourses as they do to Virgil's own text. Renaissance humanists were more emphatic about essential differences between the *Aeneid* and works derived from it. But by debating whether narrative practices that lacked a specific precedent in Virgil's poetry were necessarily incompatible with Virgil's didactic ideals, they preserved a certain aesthetic and ideological flexibility in the potentially monolithic notion of "Virgilian authority." My final section addresses the complex and often contradictory conceptions of Virgilian poetry adopted by Spenser's immediate precursors, Ariosto and Tasso.

Classical and Late Classical Confrontations: Ovid and Augustine

Although Ovid and Augustine approach the *Aeneid* from antithetical cultural perspectives, they both refute the Augustan vision of history that it reinforces. In the *Heroïdes* and the *Metamorphoses,* Ovid dismisses Virgil's evocation of an inexorable destiny culminating in the *Pax Augustana* as a fiction imposed on inchoate human experience. Retold from Ovid's alternate point of view, Dido's repudiation constitutes an act of treachery rather than of heroic sacrifice. The imperial future for which she dies marks only a passing instant in the universal flux of nature. Augustine joins Ovid in rejecting Virgil's confidence in an *imperium sine fine*, but he exposes its illusoriness from the perspective of eternity rather than that of an ever-changing, capricious present. The rhetorical strategies through which these writers defined their opposition to Virgil—Ovid's recuperation of Homeric digression and Augustine's implicit allegorization of Aeneas's quest—established the terms of the *Aeneid*'s later assimilation into Christian culture.

In the *Epistulae Heroïdum,* Ovid transfers Dido's story from an account of Rome's imperial origins to a collection of letters written by classical heroines lamenting erotic betrayals. A more intimate, cyclical view of history as repeated instances of male treachery replaces Virgil's portrayal of it as a linear progress from Troy to Actium. From this feminine perspective, the crucial events are not the rise and fall of empires but the births, deaths, and love affairs of private individuals. By disregarding Aeneas's public accomplishments, Ovid undermines the official justification for Dido's abandonment. If Aeneas is a hero according to one account, he is a traitor according to the other.

Ovid's principal revisionary strategy lies in recasting Dido's story as her own first-person narrative. By eliminating the divine decrees and the epic narrator's presumably objective pronouncements, he suppresses the means by which Virgil justified her abandonment.[2] In the *Heroïdes,* no other voices challenge her diatribes against Aeneas by insisting on his *pietas*. By letting us hear everything from her perspective, Ovid invites us to share her doubts about his motives. When

Virgil's Dido accuses Aeneas of fabricating the gods' command that he depart,
Mercury's descent exonerates him. But when Dido makes the same charges in
the *Heroïdes,* no celestial councils or divine messengers refute her. What Virgil
honored as a denial of private desire for the greater good of the *imperium* appears
retrospectively as a cad's excuse for inconstancy.

Ovid increases our sympathy for Dido by suppressing the vindictiveness that
characterizes her in the *Aeneid.* There her Euripidean fury reinforces Virgil's
portrayal of love as dangerously volatile:

> And could I not
> have dragged his body off, and scattered him
> piecemeal upon the waters, limb by limb?
> Or butchered all his comrades, even served
> Ascanius himself as a banquet dish
> upon his father's table?
>
> non potui abreptum diuellere corpus et undis
> spargere? non socios, non ipsum absumere ferro
> Ascanium patriisque epulandum ponere mensis?
> (IV.600–602 [M:826–31])

By contrast, Ovid's Dido never wishes Aeneas any harm. Throughout her epis-
tle, she stresses her continued love for him despite his cruelty in deserting her:

> . . . however ill his thought of me, I hate him not, but only complain of
> his faithlessness, and when I have complained I do but love more madly
> still.
>
> non tamen Aenean, quamvis male cogitat, odi,
> sed queror infidum questaque peius amo.
> (VII.29–30)[3]

Whereas Virgil's Dido conjures the waters to overwhelm Aeneas and his de-
parting fleet, Ovid's Dido worries that the sea will exact "the penalty for
[Aeneas's] faithlessness" (*perfidiae poenas,* VII.58).[4] Even in charging him with
infidelity, she shows a tenderness that makes her repudiation seem all the more
cruel and unjustified.

The increased sympathy with which Ovid depicts Dido culminates in his
most startling departure from Virgil, his hint that she is pregnant with Aeneas's
child:

> Perhaps, too, it is Dido soon to be mother, O evil-doer, whom you
> abandon now, and a part of your being lies hidden in myself.

Forsitan et gravidam Didon, scelerate, relinquas,
parsque tui lateat corpore clausa meo.

(VII.133–35)

By portraying Dido as a mother worrying about her unborn child, Ovid coun-
ters her Virgilian fantasies of butchering Ascanius for his father's supper. Now
Aeneas seems to be the one lacking parental feeling. In the *Aeneid*, Dido ex-
plicitly states that she bears no "little Aeneas"; if Virgil's Aeneas deserts the
woman who loves him, he does not abandon his own child. Ovid's Aeneas, by
contrast, deserts both Dido and "a part of [his own] being" in his indifference
to natural affection.

Dido's emphasis on Aeneas's disregard for her and her unborn child arises
from a private, feminine perception of experience that defies the *Aeneid*'s cel-
ebration of history as an unbroken, patriarchal succession. From Virgil's per-
spective, the crucial relationships in Aeneas's life are those with Anchises and
Ascanius, the male figures linking him respectively to the heroic past and to the
imperial future.[5] But if Virgil grounds Aeneas's *pietas* in his responsibility toward
men, Ovid exposes *crudelitas* in his characteristically discontinuous relationships
with women. Aeneas proves disloyal not only to Dido but even to his own
divine mother. As Dido charges in the *Heroïdes*, Aeneas's willingness to sacrifice
her violates his identity as Venus's son: *matris ab ingenio dissidet ille suae* (VII.36).
Only an inexorability altogether foreign to the tender goddess of love could
underlie his indifference to her pleas.

Whereas the *Heroïdes* counters Virgil's imperial vision by retelling Aeneas's
career from Dido's perspective, the *Metamorphoses* challenges it by subsuming
Rome's seemingly linear political history in a larger pattern of universal trans-
formation. As Barbara Bono has observed, the *Metamorphoses* stands as "a kind
of anti-*Aeneid* that ironically recounts the erotic descents of the gods and the
hubristic aspirations of men, and ultimately conflates them all in a vast cosmic
naturalistic cycle."[6] Pythagoras's climactic sermon implies the radical instability
of any goal pursued in a world characterized by endless variation: if the *Heroïdes*
indicts Aeneas's sacrifice of Dido for its cruelty, the *Metamorphoses* arraigns it for
its vanity. By positing mutability as the fundamental ground of history, Ovid
insists that the *imperium* for which Dido suffers is not a final, perfect, and en-
during state. It constitutes simply one more episode in the ongoing cycles of
human experience.

In the *Metamorphoses*' final books, Ovid undercuts the Augustan myth of
history by retelling Aeneas's career in ways that diminish its original, imperial
significance.[7] In his revisionary *Aeneid,* urgency yields to leisure. His Aeneas
seems no more anxious to reach his new home than Ovid himself seems to

33

finish his tale. In contrast to Virgil, Ovid is an irrepressibly digressive narrator. He continually passes over the main events of Virgil's poem to dwell on minor episodes; while he barely mentions such a politically crucial event as Turnus's death, he lingers over the Trojan ships' transformation into nymphs. A fascination with self-contained instances of metamorphosis rather than with the final conquest of Latium governs his narrative. At points, he introduces characters that do not appear in the *Aeneid,* such as the Greek Macareus, who interrupt the action with their own stories about people turned into animals, monsters, or features of the landscape.

Macareus's sudden appearance proclaims Ovid's allegiance to the Homeric aesthetic that Virgil repudiated. Rejecting the *Aeneid*'s disciplined, teleological structure, Ovid presents his own fragmentary plot as a recuperation of the *Odyssey*'s digressiveness. As it turns out, Macareus is one of Ulysses's own sailors who vividly recounts his visits to Aiolia, Laestrygonia, and Aeaea. What Richard Lanham terms Ovid's "rhetoricity," his delight in storytelling as an end in itself, conspicuously recalls Homer's constant interruptions of his main narrative for yarns, flashbacks, songs, and fables.[8] Most of the tales punctuating Ovid's account of Aeneas's travels involve Homeric characters and locations that the Trojans bypass in the *Aeneid.* Whereas Virgil's heroes avoid Scylla and Charybdis, for example, their Ovidian counterparts' passage through them occasions a long, digressive account of how Circe first transformed Scylla into a monster. Although Aeneas scrupulously avoids Circe in the *Aeneid,* she figures prominently in Macareus's recollections. By incorporating her legacy in Dido's characterization, Virgil associates her with the dangerous allure of digressive, metamorphic narration. Defying Virgil, Ovid recovers her as his muse, the goddess presiding over a poem portraying history itself as endless digression.

Writing long after the *imperium* that Virgil celebrates had fallen into political and economic chaos, Augustine also repudiated Virgil's historical vision.[9] But the four centuries intervening between Ovid and Augustine witnessed the canonization of Virgil's poem as a secular classic, a text excerpted by grammarians, memorized by students of rhetoric, and imitated by poets like Statius.[10] Although Augustine vehemently rejected its celebration of an earthly kingdom as the end of human *labor,* he did not disregard its cultural authority. In the *Confessions,* he adopts it as the principal model for his spiritual autobiography. Whereas Ovid countered Virgil's imperial model of history with a private, feminine view of time in the *Heroïdes* and with a cyclical, quasi-Lucretian one in the *Metamorphoses,* Augustine subsumes it in the Christian view of historical experience fulfilling God's eternal decrees.

When Augustine recalls reading the *Aeneid* at school, he contrasts its falsehoods with Christian truths:

. . . I was forced to learn all about the wanderings of a man called Aeneas, while quite oblivious of my own wanderings, and to weep for the death of Dido, because she killed herself for love, while all the time I could bear with dry eyes, O God my life, the fact that I myself, poor wretch, was, among these things, dying far away from you. . . .

I wept for dead Dido "who by the sword pursued a way extreme," meanwhile myself following a more extreme way, that of the most extremely low of your creatures, having forsaken you, and being earth going back to earth.

. . . quibus tenere cogebar Aeneae nescio cuius errores oblitus errorum meorum et plorare Didonem mortuam, quia se occidit ab amore, cum interea me ipsum in his a te morientem, deus uita mea, siccis oculis ferrem miserrimus.
. . . flebam Didonem extinctam ferroque extrema secutam, sequens ipse extrema condita tua relicto te et terra iens in terra.

(I.13)''

With one word, *errores,* Augustine rejects the teleology governing Virgil's narrative and subverts his imperial theme. In the *Aeneid,* the hero's wanderings (*errores*) end with the conquest of Italy. But like its English cognate, the Latin word *error* can be read in an intellectual or moral as well as a physical sense. From Augustine's Christian perspective, nothing that Aeneas accomplishes is anything but error. Since the only truly significant conquest is victory over sin, his triumphs in Latium prove as vain as his truancy in Carthage.

At first, Augustine seems to follow Virgil in only one thing, the use of Dido's tragedy to repudiate influences contrary to his moral and spiritual commitments. Ironically, just as Virgil created Dido to distance himself from Homer, Augustine evokes his own youthful sympathy for her to distance himself from Virgil. He now recognizes such sympathy as an effect of Virgil's seductive, pre-Christian influence. In the same way that Dido blinded Aeneas to dereliction of duty, Augustine's pity for her blinds him to his alienation from God in preferring secular fictions to divine truths. By recalling the intensity of his response to the *Aeneid,* he makes classical poetry seem all the harder, and all the more necessary, to renounce as a distraction from the City of God. In the process of rejecting Virgilian fictions, he leaves intact only the Virgilian notion that virtue defines itself through sacrifice and renunciation: salvation necessitates abandoning what one loves most. For Augustine, that means repudiating his own Graeco-Roman cultural inheritance.

As an alternative to Virgil's dangerously alluring poetry, Augustine advocates the rudimentary studies of grammar and mathematics, which are "undoubtedly better, because more reliable." His boyhood preference for poetry strikes him retrospectively as evidence of a fundamentally fallen nature:

> At that time "One and one make two; two and two make four" was a horrible kind of singsong to me. What really delighted me were spectacles of vanity—the Wooden Horse full of armed men, the Burning of Troy, and "there the very shade of dead Creüsa."

> iam uero unum et unum duo, duo et duo quattuor odiosa cantio mihi erat et dulcissimum spectaculum uanitatis equus ligneus plenus armatis et Troiae incendium atque ipsius umbra Creusae.

(I.13)

This passage's dichotomies and antitheses imply a rigorously straightforward approach to Virgil and classical poetry: just as Aeneas abandoned Dido for Rome, Augustine ought to abandon Virgil for truth in all its mathematical purity. The opposition between literature's emotional richness and the abstraction of grammar or arithmetic transforms the contrast between Dido and Lavinia into a conflict between antithetical disciplines. Augustine privileges mathematics over tragic narrative precisely because the former fails to satisfy humanity's fallen identification with operatic passion over reason.

But as straightforward as these dichotomies might seem, Augustine's own Virgilian allusiveness dismantles them. The passage's central paradox lies in its conspicuous appropriation of classical fictions to renounce classical influence. For all Augustine's talk about rejecting Virgil, the *Aeneid* provides him a narrative for understanding and describing his spiritual autobiography. He does not absolutely abandon Dido but translates her into an image of classical culture; he adopts Aeneas's wanderings as a trope for his own alienation from God. As Andrew Fichter has remarked, Augustine not only identifies himself with Aeneas in rejecting something he loves but also with Dido in his previous "spiritual suicide" (48). If he plays Aeneas the Virgilian hero in his abandoning pagan fictions, he plays Aeneas the Ovidian traitor in having first abandoned God.

Throughout the passage, allegorical interpretation spares Augustine the necessity of absolutely renouncing his Virgilian inheritance by transforming the seemingly unbridgeable gap between truth and fiction into the dialectic of tenor and vehicle, parable and interpretation. The moment Augustine recalls his own turn from pagan learning to Christianity, *allegoresis* emerges as the aesthetic equivalent of religious conversion. Just as the old Adam is not left to pursue "a way extreme" but to be born again in Christ's image, the old texts and topoi are not completely cast aside but reread and rewritten in the light of Christian revelation. On a literal level, history had already refuted Virgil's prophecy of

Rome as an *imperium sine fine*. But taken allegorically as a promise of Christian salvation, the prophecy might be revived and Virgil's cultural prestige preserved. After rereading the *Aeneid sub specie aeternitatis*, Augustine incorporates it as the *Confessions'* principal subtext. As several critics have observed, Aeneas's wanderings underlie not only individual episodes but Augustine's general progress from North Africa and Carthage to Italy: the quest for a future *imperium* becomes the quest to transcend time altogether and to enter the City of God.[12]

This tendency toward the Christian recuperation of classical influence manifests itself in a number of passages challenging the Dido episode's tragic finality. As Bono (46) has noted, Monica's anguish when Augustine secretly departs Carthage for Rome recalls Dido's. But their separation is only temporary: unlike her Virgilian prototype, Monica later rejoins Augustine and nurtures his conversion. Book VIII recounts his final commitment to Continence by transforming Dido's abandonment into an image of his struggles against concupiscence:

> Toys and trifles, utter vanities had been my mistresses, and now they were holding me back, pulling me by the garment of my flesh and softly murmuring in my ear: "Are you getting rid of us?" and "From this moment shall we never be with you again for all eternity?"

> Retinebant nugae nugarum et uanitates uanitantium, antiquae amicae meae, et succutiebant uestem meam carneam et submurmurabant: "dimittisne nos?" et "a momento isto non erimus tecum ultra in aeternum?"
>
> (VIII.11)

On one level, the passage recalls Virgil's portrayal of women and erotic desire as threats to be resisted. But it departs from Virgil in figuring Continence herself as a generative female presence:

> In the direction toward which I had turned my face and still trembled to take the last step, I could see the chaste dignity of Continence; she was calm and serene, cheerful without wantonness, and it was in truth and honor that she was enticing me to come to her without hesitation, stretching out to receive and to embrace me with those holy hands of hers. . . . With her were so many boys and girls, so much of youth, so much of every age, grave widows and women grown old in virginity, and in them all was Continence herself, not barren, but *a fruitful mother of children*.

> aperiebatur enim ab ea parte, qua intenderam faciem et quo transire trepidabam, casta dignitas continentiae, serena et non dissolute hilaris, honeste blandiens, ut uenirem neque dubitarem, et extendens ad me suscipiendum et amplectendum pias manus. . . . ibi tot pueri et puellae,

ibi iuuentus multa et omnis aetas et graues uiduae et uirgines anus, et in omnibus ipsa continentia nequaquam sterilis, sed fecunda mater filiorum, gaudiorum de marito te, domine.

(VIII.11)

Fichter has suggested that Augustine's marriage to Continence parodies Aeneas's destined marriage to Lavinia (52). But Continence is a more vital, actively loving figure than Lavinia. Whereas Lavinia's *pudor* could never compensate for Dido's passionate intensity, Continence offers an emotionally richer experience than the erotic vanities that Augustine renounces.

Once more, Dido is not absolutely abandoned. Something of her first appearance at Juno's temple with a retinue of noble youths informs the gracious image of Continence herself. At that point in Virgil's story, Dido too might be described as "calm and serene, cheerful without wantonness." Just as Dido shelters Aeneas after the opening storm, Continence provides Augustine a harbor from his passions. Dido's serenity was short-lived, and the harbor that she offered Aeneas proved as much a threat to his mission as the storm itself. But in this redeemed *Aeneid,* Continence grants Augustine a true and lasting defense against his enemies.

The Medieval Dido: Dante and Chaucer

Ovid and Augustine bequeathed two different, but equally influential revisions of the *Aeneid* to later writers. From the antithetical perspectives of an ever-varying present and of an eternity set apart from time altogether, both challenged Virgil's championship of a future *imperium* over individual longing. But over the next several centuries, the notion of literary authority shifted. As A. J. Minnis has suggested, readers and commentators from late antiquity through the thirteenth century located a work's *auctoritas* more in an abstract truth it presumably embodied than in its actual language.[13] This hermeneutic readily assimilated the ancient texts to changing cultural conditions: objectionable features of Virgilian writing could simply be dismissed as extrinsic to whatever an interpreter believed to be the *Aeneid's* central intention. For Fulgentius and Bernard Silvestris, for example, the pagan myth that appalled Augustine was merely an *integumentum* concealing truths consistent with Christianity. Paradoxically, greater interpretive flexibility attributed Virgilian authority to the very rhetorical strategies that Ovid and Augustine adopted to reject Virgilian ideals. Vernacular romances juxtaposed passages from the *Heroïdes* and the *Aeneid* without recognizing their ideological and aesthetic incompatibility.

This less explicitly confrontational stance toward Virgil manifests itself in the way a commentator like Fulgentius accommodates the *Aeneid* to Christian culture. Augustine's implicit allegorization of Virgil marked the end of a complex, agonizing revisionary encounter. He could not recuperate the *Aeneid*'s basic narrative of renunciation and perseverance until he had first repudiated Virgil's fictions as incompatible with Christian truth. Writing a century later, Fulgentius too acknowledges that Virgil, as a pagan, could not fathom the truths of Christianity.[14] But for him, this does not mean that the *Aeneid* is a dangerously seductive influence that must be renounced; on the contrary, Fulgentius maintains that its fictions depict, under an allegorical cover, whatever moral principles might be available to pagan reason unilluminated by Christian grace. Aided by the precedent of an earlier tradition of allegorizing Homer, he discovers in the *Aeneid* an account of an individual's growth toward moral perfection. For Fulgentius, this account is not imposed on Virgil's text but underlies it as its fundamental truth and the source of its *auctoritas*.[15]

Perhaps the absence of any need to reject Virgil explains an anomaly that distinguishes the allegorical tradition running from Fulgentius through the commentary commonly ascribed to Bernard Silvestris—its comparative inattention to Dido's abandonment.[16] Since their *allegoresis* could assimilate any pre-Christian work to Christian belief, these commentators never thought of prior literary influences as threats to be renounced for the sake of truth.[17] Not having to abandon the poetry they loved, they did not identify with Aeneas in sacrificing his lover to duty. For Fulgentius, Book IV stands simply as an exemplum on youthful concupiscence:

> In book 4 the spirit of adolescence, on holiday from paternal control, goes off hunting, is inflamed by passion and, driven on by storm and cloud, that is, by confusion of mind, commits adultery. Having lingered long at this, at the urging of Mercury he gives up a passion aroused to evil ends by his lust. Mercury is introduced as the god of the intellect: it is by the urging of the intellect that youth quits the straits of passion. So passion perishes and dies of neglect; burnt to ashes, it disintegrates. When it is driven from the heart of youth by the power of the mind, it burns out, buried in the ashes of oblivion.[18]

> Feriatus ergo animus a paterno iudicio in quarto libro et uenatu progreditur et amore torretur, et tempestate ac nubilo, uelut in mentis conturbatione, coactus adulterium perficit. In quo, diu commoratus Mercurio instigante libidinis suae male praesumptum amorem relinquit; Mercurius enim deus ponitur ingenii; ergo ingenio instigante aetas deserit amoris confinia. Qui quidem amor contemptus emoritur et in cineres exustus

emigrat; dum enim de corde puerili auctoritate ingenii libido expellitur, sepulta in obliuionis cinere fauillescit.[19]

Dido is not even mentioned by name. Treating her only as a silent ethical category, a love "aroused to evil ends," Fulgentius never mentions the agonies of her suicide. He recalls her pyre only as an emblem of lust's disintegration before the higher power of reason. In "quitting the straits of passion" Aeneas does not have to surrender anything more alluring than the "storms and clouds" of a confused mind. After elaborating slightly on Fulgentius's exposition of the storm, Bernard repeats his final assessment of Dido as "abandoned passion" that "ceases and, consumed by the heat of manliness, goes to ashes, that is, to solitary thoughts" (*Desueta enim libido defficit et fervore virilitatis consumpta in favillam, id est in solas cogitationes, transit*).[20]

Whereas the allegorical commentators underplayed Dido's anguish, vernacular writers brought it to the center of twelfth- and thirteenth-century romances based on the *Aeneid*. Works like the *Eneas*, the *Primera Crónica General*, Simon Aurea Capra's *Ilias Latina*, and *I Fatti d'Enea* retell her tragedy predominately in terms of human and personal rather than supernatural and political motivations.[21] As in the *Heroïdes*, Cupid does not infect Dido with desire and Mercury rarely orders her abandonment. By drawing on Ovid as well as on Dares and Dictys, whose Trojan histories condemned Aeneas as a political traitor, the romances often present her death as testimony to Aeneas's villainy. They also join Ovid in suppressing the vindictiveness that mars her character in the *Aeneid*. Their Dido is a passive, preeminently sympathetic martyr. In the *Eneas*, she pardons her betrayer with her dying words: "He has killed me most wrongly, but I here pardon him my death. In the name of peace and reconciliation I kiss his clothes upon his bed."[22]

But despite the centrality of Dido's abandonment in the vernacular romances, their authors do not evoke it as a figure for their departures from their precursors. Although they follow Ovid in minimizing supernatural machinery, in characterizing Aeneas as a scoundrel, and in sympathizing with Dido as love's martyr, they do not adopt his overtly agonistic stance toward the *Aeneid*. When Ovid transforms Mercury's descent into Aeneas's *claim* that the gods have ordered his departure, he implicitly challenges Virgil's conception of *fatum* and the political establishment that it underwrites. By contrast, the author of the *Primera Crónica General* leaves out the descent because he is writing for an audience more interested in human drama than in supernatural wonders.[23]

Just as Fulgentius and Bernard presented their allegorical interpretations as the true *intentio* of Virgil's text rather than as corrections of its pagan errors, the author of a work like the *Eneas* thinks of himself as retelling and augmenting

Virgil's story rather than challenging its fundamental values. If Virgil's *auctoritas* lies in an abstract moral truth for the allegorists, it lies in his *materia,* his general subject matter, for the writers of the romances. Since Virgilian authority could be defined in a variety of ways and attributed to a range of hermeneutic and imitational practices, no one interpreting or retelling the story of Aeneas's adventures seemed to be concerned with fidelity to one moral or aesthetic perspective privileged as authentically Virgilian. Neither the Neo-Latin allegorists nor the vernacular authors define themselves as Virgil's true heirs in opposition to any other available mode of "Virgilian" composition. The vernacular writers show no consciousness of the allegorists and the allegorists have no interest in challenging the romances. This absence of competition reflects in part the different audiences for which the clerkly allegorists and the courtly writers of romance composed their works. But it also attests to the fluidity and polyvalence characterizing the culture's perception of Virgil and the Virgilian.

Although something of this fluidity persisted into the Renaissance, writers began to question it during the thirteenth century. It gradually yielded to a more integrated sense of the author as a particular personality associated with a particular text.[24] The moment poets like Dante and Chaucer started to hierarchize, or even to see the possibility of hierarchizing, alternative literary modes in terms of greater or lesser authority, Dido's abandonment began to figure again as a topos of poetic self-definition. The mounting tension between the clerks' Latinity and the courtiers' vernacularity, which culminated in works like *Confessio Amantis* and *The Legend of Good Women,* heightened this renewal of interest in her tragedy.[25] The question of her identity as a pitiable victim or as an embodiment of concupiscence ultimately engaged the larger question of which writers, vernacular poets or academic commentators, were authorized to bring classical works to a contemporary audience.

Critics have often discussed how the Paolo and Francesca episode revises Book IV of the *Aeneid.* But Dante shows as much concern over the fluidity of Virgil's cultural reception as over the letter of Virgil's text.[26] The conflict between Dante the Pilgrim's and Dante the Poet's responses to Francesca's confession foregrounds contradictions between the romances' sympathy for Dido and the commentaries' contempt for her as embodied concupiscence. In the course of the episode, the Poet dismisses the romances' pity toward passion-driven women as a failure of ethical discrimination. But at the same time, he figures his own attraction to the genre through the Pilgrim's intense sympathy for Francesca. Just as Aeneas's love for Dido provided Virgil an image of his problematic susceptibility to Homer, the Pilgrim's fascination with Francesca presents courtly romance as a powerfully alluring but ultimately pernicious influence that the Poet must resist.

The Poet figures the dangers of the romances on two narrative levels, both in Francesca's confession itself and in the Pilgrim's response to it. As Renato Poggioli has remarked, Francesca's account of her tragedy dramatizes the ways in which literature mediates desire: her downfall occurs when she tries to pattern her erotic life on the romances that she and Paolo have read.[27] According to her own narrative, their affair began when the description of Lancelot and Guinevere's first kiss inspires Paolo to kiss her. But that kiss is only a synecdoche for their overall surrender to the romance ethos, with its insistent portrayal of love as a force that cannot be resisted. Francesca specifically recalls the Lancelot story as an account of erotic compulsion: "We read one day for pastime of Lancelot, how love constrained him" (*Noi leggiavamo un giorno per diletto / di Lancialotto come amor lo strinse,* V.127–28).[28] In describing her own relationship with Paolo, she adopts this view of love as a tyrannical master to absolve them of responsibility for their actions. *Amor* first "seized" (*prese*) Paolo and then "Love, which absolves no one beloved from loving, seized [her]" (*Amor, ch'a nullo amato amar perdona, / mi prese,* V.101, 103–4).

Although the specific text that Francesca reads is a book about Lancelot and Guinevere, the personification of love as a tyrant paralyzing the will recurs throughout vernacular retellings of the *Aeneid.* The Guinevere story serves as a metonomy for the vernacular accounts of Dido's tragedy that had been popular in Europe for over a hundred years. They typically emphasized her inability to resist the emotions driving her to her death. The *Eneas,* for instance, minimizes the role of the Virgilian gods in recounting Aeneas's adventures; nevertheless, it follows Virgil with comparative fidelity in insisting that Venus inflames Dido with her destructive passion. Denied the exercise of free will, she cannot be blamed for her actions. As in the *Aeneid* itself, her death appears as pitiable rather than as justly merited.

Dante further discredits the romances in recounting the Pilgrim's susceptibility to Francesca's view of love. Just as the romances blinded her to the sinfulness of her involvement with Paolo, the pathos of her suffering blinds the Pilgrim to her status as an adulteress. Because she patterns her own biography on those of heroines like Guinevere and Dido, her confession becomes a *Galeotto* deflecting him from his development as a Christian. He sees her tortures neither as a punishment nor as a warning to other sinners but as a "martyrdom" that makes him weep with sorrow and commiseration (*Francesca, i tuoi martiri / a lacrimar mi fanno tristo e pio,* V.116–17). His nearly blasphemous misinterpretation of her torments exposes the extent to which the pity stirred by the romances precludes sound moral judgments.

But if Dante the Pilgrim falls under Francesca's spells, Dante the Poet retains his full moral awareness. He frames Francesca's narrative with reminders of the sinfulness that both she and the Pilgrim overlook. The inhabitants of the Second Circle might be pitiful in their suffering, but the Poet charges them with responsibility for their own damnation. From his perspective, they are not the victims of Love's tyranny but "carnal sinners" who willfully surrender reason (*i peccator carnali, / che la ragion sommettono al talento,* V.38–39). Although the Inferno's inhabitants typically fail to grasp their sin's true character, Dante particularly stresses Francesca's blindness not as a consequence but as the essence of her crime. Her inability to discern right from wrong is inseparable from *luxuria*'s definitional submission of reason to passion.

While the Francesca episode focuses explicitly on the seductions of vernacular romance, its indictment of *pietà* implicitly criticizes Virgil's own sympathetic treatment of Dido. Although Dante never foregrounds his contention with Virgil in the same way that he challenges courtly romance, the Second Circle revises the *lugentes campi* where Aeneas encounters Dido wandering among other souls "whom bitter love consumed with brutal waste" (*quos durus amor crudeli tabe peredit,* VI.442 [M:584]). Virgil's personification of *durus amor* anticipates Francesca's displacement of responsibiity for her adultery onto *amor*. When Dante rewrites Virgil's passage, he abandons its delicate ambivalences and characterizes Dido both as a suicide and as a post-mortem adulteress, "she that slew herself for love and broke faith with the ashes of Sychaeus," (*che s'ancise amorosa, / e ruppe fede al cener di Sicheo,* V.61–62). Above all, he rejects her daimonization by Cupid: his Dido is unquestionably responsible for her own crimes and fully deserves her eternal torments.

Giuseppe Mazzotta has suggested that Dante adopts a more conciliatory stance toward Virgil and pagan antiquity that distinguishes him from Augustine (165–70). But the contrast that Mazzotta describes exists less in Augustine's and Dante's actual attitudes toward Virgil than in the way they figure their similar resistance to his influence. The *Aeneid*'s subtextual presence throughout the *Confessions* contradicts Augustine's overt repudiations. At the same time, the respect that Dante pays Virgil as his beloved guide and master disguises his moral and spiritual dissent from the *Aeneid*'s central values. In actual practice, he insists as much as Augustine on assimilating Virgilian fictions to Christian doctrine. But by substituting a romance for the *Aeneid* itself as the *Galeotto* misleading its readers, he displaces any opprobrium that might redound to Virgil onto the genre into which his epic had been debased. For Dante, although the romances must be condemned even as Francesca is consigned to hell, the *Aeneid* can be embraced as a positive and empowering influence as long as Christian revelation expands the limits of its pagan vision.

Dante privileges the Neo-Latin commentators' view of Dido's tragedy as an exemplum about concupiscence over the vernacular sentimentalization of it as an engaging love story. By rejecting the hierarchization of one view over another, Chaucer defines himself in opposition to Dante. He foregrounds the contradictions between them to challenge the belief that any single moral perspective on her abandonment can prove authoritative.[29] This new stance toward Dido arises from and reinforces an antithetical notion of how a poet creates a place for himself in literary history. Both Augustine and Dante follow Virgil himself in evoking Dido as an apotropaic embodiment of influences condemned as threats to their vocations; Chaucer, in contrast, figures his poetic identity less in terms of abandonment and repudiation than in terms of intertextual dialogue. For him, the power of Dido's abandonment lies precisely in its generation of diverse interpretations. In both *The House of Fame* and *The Legend of Good Women*, he recalls it as an occasion for bringing various, often contradictory, influences and attitudes into collision.

Several critics have noticed how *The House of Fame* challenges Virgil's tributes to Aeneas as a hero by incorporating Ovid's alternative view of him as a "traytour."[30] This juxtaposition of Virgilian and Ovidian subtexts subverts the Neoplatonic defense of classical narratives as *integumenta* concealing transcendent wisdom. Chaucer presents them instead as potential perversions of a truth that can never be ascertained by ordinary epistemological means. His emphasis on truth's elusiveness discredits the *Aeneid*'s reception as an allegorical account of Everyman's spiritual enlightenment. From the skeptical perspective that he adopts, no text is capable of guiding its readers out of the confusions of phenomenal experience. His depiction of the dreamer's epistemological impasse presses beyond an indictment of classical texts on the grounds of their potential falsehood. By bringing him through a series of allegorical temples and houses, Chaucer preserves the form of the educational progress; but by exposing the futility of that progress, he undermines the basis for the canonization of ancient authors in medieval Christian culture.

Chaucer centers his challenge to the *Aeneid*'s Neoplatonic reception around the conspicuous revision of Aeneas's experiences at Juno's temple. Although scholars have acknowledged the Virgilian episode as a principal source for *The House of Fame*, they have generally not explored the heuristic force of Chaucer's imitation.[31] By casting the *Aeneid* itself as a beguiling ekphrasis, Chaucer rejects Virgil's authority as a moralist. The story that the dreamer finds engraved on a tablet in Venus's temple appears to be a faithful redaction of Virgil, beginning with a close translation of his opening lines. But the redaction's form renders its content suspect: as an ekphrasis located in the temple of a Roman goddess, it takes the place of Juno's murals. For Bernard Silvestris, the spectacle of Aeneas "feeding his spirit on false pictures" (*animum pictura pascit inani*, I.464, translation mine) allegorized the newborn soul's helpless submission to sensory experience. Chaucer revises Bernard's interpretation so that the topos becomes instead an indictment of the mind's dependence on textual mediation.[32] Through a reversed synecdoche, a substitution of the whole for a part, he taints Virgil's entire narrative with the opprobrium accorded Juno's pictures in the commentary tradition. The *Aeneid* becomes one more equivocal surface discredited in the quest for truth.

As in the *Aeneid*, the dreamer's discovery of the ekphrasis precipitates a hermeneutic crisis: Venus's tablet bewilders him with competing versions of Aeneas's career. Instead of merely transcribing Virgil's narrative, the tablet challenges its reliability. As scholars have long noted, it develops simultaneously the Virgilian view of Aeneas as a hero who reluctantly abandons Dido in obedience to the gods and the Ovidian view of him as a blackguard who betrays her and lies about a divine mission to gloss over his treachery.[33] At first, Chaucer follows Virgil in presenting him as an exemplar of both familial and patriotic devotion who carries his father from the ruins of Troy and settles his people in Latium. But the moment Aeneas meets Dido, Chaucer draws instead on the *Heroïdes* in castigating him for seducing and betraying her: "For he to hir a traytour was; / Wherfore she slow hirself, allas!" (267–68).[34] Like Ovid and the writers of vernacular romance, Chaucer blackens Aeneas's character by minimizing Dido's vindictiveness and by heightening the pathos of her complaint, by suggesting that she is carrying his unborn child, and by linking him to such other classical "traytours" as Paris, Jason, Hercules, and Theseus.

Chaucer's ekphrasis does not actually deceive the dreamer but confronts him with an unresolvable interpretive dilemma hinging on the question of whether or not Mercury actually appeared to Aeneas and ordered him to abandon Dido. At first, Chaucer seems to follow Ovid in dismissing the appearance as Aeneas's fabrication. By observing that men often invent false "causes" to repudiate their lovers after they "have caught that what [them] leste," he implies that Aeneas deserts her on spurious grounds (283, 282). But if Chaucer's stance toward the claim of divine intervention is skeptical, it is not entirely dismissive. When he finally mentions Mercury's descent, he attributes the story not to Aeneas but to "the book." The question of Aeneas's personal sincerity is suspended and ultimately subsumed in larger questions about the reliability of texts:

> But to excusen Eneas
> Fullyche of al his grete trespas,
> The book seyth Mercurie, sauns fayle,
> Bad hym goo into Itayle,

And leve Auffrikes regioun,
And Dido and hir faire toun.

(427–32)

Chaucer's attitude toward "the book" is characteristically ambiguous. The rhe-torical assurance of the phrase "sauns fayle" is undercut by the uncertainty of what it is supposed to guarantee. If the lines mean that the *Aeneid* introduces Mercury simply to cover up Aeneas's crimes, they indict Virgil as a co-conspirator with his hero. But if they mean that Chaucer himself wants to excuse Aeneas on the basis of Virgil's account, they can be read as a genuine concession to Virgilian authority.

In *The House of Fame,* false appearances do not mask a finally accessible truth; Fame's arbitrariness has so confounded truth and falsehood that they cannot be discriminated. Since one version of history is likely to be as false as another, neither Chaucer's dreamer nor his audience can determine whether Aeneas was a hero, a scoundrel, both, or neither. All anyone can do is weigh the competing claims of diverse authorities and experiences. In contrast to the Neoplatonic Aeneas, the dreamer never comes to certain knowledge; he may leave the ekphrastic temple, but he cannot escape the epistemological impasse that it represents. His departing plea that God save him "fro fantome and illusion" (493), which echoes Virgil's dismissal of Juno's murals as "empty pictures," is never answered. Neither his flight with the eagle nor his later exploration of the Houses of Fame and Rumor assures him of anything but his perpetual uncertainty.[35]

When Chaucer retells Dido's story again in *The Legend of Good Women,* Cupid's demand that he write a history documenting how men have mistreated women prevents him from balancing his sources' competing claims. His *exordium* suppresses contradictions between the *Aeneid* and the *Heroïdes* by suggesting that both Ovid and Virgil view Dido as a victim of Aeneas's treachery:

Glorye and honour, Virgil Mantoan,
Be to thy name! and I shal, as I can,
Folwe thy lanterne, as thow gost byforn,
How Eneas to Dido was forsworn.
In thyn Eneyde and Naso wol I take
The tenor, and the grete effectes make.

(924–29)

The subsequent account of Aeneas's adventures confirms the dreamer's tendency to distort any text that might justify Dido's abandonment. He consistently mis-reads Virgil in Ovidian or romance terms. In contrast to the narrator of *The House of Fame,* he underplays Aeneas's heroism in recounting the escape from

Troy and places even greater emphasis on Dido's complaint. He unequivocally rejects Aeneas's principal defense by attributing the story of Mercury's descent not to "the book" but to Aeneas's own words enhanced by "his false teres" (1301).

But as complete as this adoption of Ovidian biases seems to be, inconsistencies in the narrative remind us that Chaucer himself sees the classical past less monolithically. Much of the case against Aeneas, for instance, rests on the dreamer's description of how Dido was seduced during the storm:

> For there hath Eneas ykneled so,
> And told hire al his herte and al his wo,
> And swore so depe to hire to be trewe . . .
> And as a fals lovere so we can pleyne,
> That sely Dido rewede on his peyne,
> And tok hym for husbonde and become his wyf . . .
>
> (1232–34, 1236–38)

But the narrator's claim that this incident initiates "the deep affeccioun / Betwixe hem two" refutes his earlier description of how Dido fell in love with Aeneas when he first arrived (1229–30, 1155ff.).[36] If Dido was already passionately in love with him, he might still be blamed for deserting her, but not for tricking her into loving him in the first place.

The inconsistency arises from the persistent subtextual presence of the *Aeneid,* with its Apollonian account of how Cupid rather than Aeneas inflamed Dido with her fatal desire. Throughout the *Legend,* the dreamer notes that he has deleted several things from Virgil's account because they do not pertain to his central matter:

> But of his aventures in the se
> Nis nat to purpos for to speke of here,
> For it acordeth nat to my matere.
>
> (953–55)
> I coude folwe, word for word, Virgile,
> But it wolde lasten al to longe while.
>
> (1002–3)

As Copeland has argued, such instances of *abbreviatio* and *occupatio* "play up the comic reluctance of the narrator-persona to conform to the strictures imposed upon him" (198). Although he claims to dismiss certain things for their alleged irrelevance, their conspicuous absence becomes a backhanded reminder of testimony suppressed in obedience to Cupid.[37] The dreamer's most notable exclusion, his suppression of Virgil's tributes to Aeneas's *pietas* in surrendering private

47

desire to the dictates of fate, pertains as significantly as possible to his "matere."
His failure even to acknowledge the gods' decrees suggests that he condemns
Aeneas as yet another classical "traytour" on insufficiently considered evidence.

This oblique, subversive evocation of the *Aeneid* culminates when the
dreamer awkwardly mentions Venus's exchange of Cupid and Ascanius at Dido's
banquet:

> But natheles, oure autour telleth us,
> That Cupido, that is the god of love,
> At preyere of his moder hye above,
> Hadde the liknesse of the child ytake,
> This noble queen enamored to make
> On Eneas; but, as of that scripture,
> Be as be may, I take of it no cure.
>
> (1139–45)

Aeneas's adventures on the sea may not have been relevant to the dreamer's
"matere," but the question of Cupid's disguise most certainly is. It places the
ultimate blame for Dido's tragedy not on Aeneas but on Cupid, the same god
who has commissioned him to write a history attributing women's suffering to
treacherous men rather than meddling deities. In referring to Cupid's interven-
tion at all, Chaucer departs from his own example in the *House of Fame*. By
evoking divine agency here, he establishes a countertext undermining the drea-
mer's official condemnation of Aeneas as a "traytour" who first seduces Dido
and then abandons her.

For Chaucer, Dido's abandonment can never be an act of straightforward
heroism or unquestionable villainy; it marks instead an occasion for ongoing
debate and for narrative proliferation. Although he never again takes up her
case, his interest in bringing alternative perspectives to bear on a single subject
manifests itself throughout his later works. In *The Canterbury Tales,* the debate
over Aeneas's character may yield to debates over marriage or the relative merits
of experience and authority, but Chaucer remains an irrepressibly dialogic poet.
As I will argue in later chapters, his openness even in a single work to diverse
opinions, attitudes, styles, and genres raises a compelling alternative to the stig-
matization and exclusion that fashioned other writers' public identities.

The Renaissance Dido: Ariosto and Tasso

The association of a writer's authority with the language of particular texts
reached its climax in Renaissance humanism. By the beginning of the sixteenth
century, writers and critics had more rigidly defined notions of what constituted

48

Virgilian writing than their medieval predecessors. In 1509, for example, Gavin Douglas charged that Chaucer "greitlie Virgile offendit" by portraying Aeneas as a "traytour" to Dido.[38] For Douglas, a retelling of the *Aeneid* that suppressed its tributes to Aeneas had no claim to Virgilian authenticity. In this more textually centered atmosphere, using the *Aeneid* as a model for new epics became just as controversial an undertaking as recasting its story. By the middle of the century, dozens of critics had written treatises condemning the *Orlando Furioso* not for misrepresenting Virgilian characters but for violating Virgilian decorums.

Nevertheless, the shift from medieval to humanist methods of interpreting, retelling, and imitating classical texts was a gradual and uneven process. In actual practice, the variety that characterized medieval appropriations of the *Aeneid* persisted well into the Renaissance. Despite Douglas's attack on Chaucer, for instance, his own Scots translation of the *Aeneid* is filled with historical anachronisms; its prologues and glosses freely incorporate Christian and Neoplatonic interpretations of events like Aeneas's journey to the underworld.[39] The Prologue to Book IV draws on Fulgentius and Bernard in condemning Dido for her "brutall appetite" and "fuliche lust" (2:127). Douglas's contempt toward Dido is ultimately no more true to the letter of Virgil's text than is Chaucer's sympathy. But such hermeneutic inconsistency characterizes many writers throughout the period. It gave poets like Ariosto, Tasso, and Spenser considerable ground to develop original, flexible relationships to the classical past. By the end of the period, poetic precedents and critical defenses attributed exclusive Virgilian authority to a variety of alternative styles and structures.

Before examining the controversies raised by Ariosto and Tasso's imitations of the *Aeneid,* I want to review the diverse approaches to Virgil that were available to early modern writers. As D. C. Allen and Michael Murrin remind us, readers continued to allegorize Virgil's plot and characters throughout the sixteenth century.[40] Medieval copies of Fulgentius and Bernard were still available in Renaissance libraries. Fulgentius's *Exposition* was reprinted in 1589. Although the *Commentary* attributed to Bernard was never printed during the period, it influenced later interpretations of the *Aeneid* by Jodocus Badius Ascensius, Cristoforo Landino, Philip Melanchthon, and others whose annotations were frequently printed in columns surrounding Virgil's text. These Renaissance commentators joined their medieval predecessors in explicating Book IV as an exemplum about the dangers of concupiscence. For Badius, Book IV stands as a testimony that "no one is safe from the snares of Venus but those who know how to subdue the excess [excessive urges] of the flesh" (*cum nemo sit a Venereis laqueis tutus, nisi qui . . . carnis luxum domuerit*).[41] Melanchthon notes that Dido's tragedy "deftly illustrates love's violence" (*Vim enim amoris in persona Didonis graphice depingit*).[42] In a tract that uses the *Aeneid* to illustrate the virtues of fortitude, Girolamo Balbi explores the soul's vulnerability to two particular passions, desire and anger, which Aeneas encounters in the persons of Dido and Turnus.[43]

Other commentators expanded the range of interpretive possibilities without challenging the fundamental assumption that Dido's tragedy admonished its readers through negative example. Although most glossed it as a warning about men's vulnerability to passion, Maphaeus Vegius argued that Virgil "takes pains through Dido's characterization to warn even women by what rules they ought to run their lives either for the reward of praise or for fear of shame and the unhappiest possible death."[44] In the *Aeneid*'s most significant Neoplatonic commentary, Landino maintained that Dido represented the seductions of the active life.[45] According to Landino, Aeneas triumphed over sensuality earlier in his career when he decided to follow the *Venus coelestis,* who leads men to the highest good of contemplation, rather than the *Venus vulgaris,* who leads men like Paris to their destruction (120–27). But even after a man has committed himself to the contemplative life, he must resist the attractions of politics and civil magistracy that Dido embodies as the founder of Carthage.

More sympathetic views of Dido as a tragic victim also persisted into the Renaissance. In early vernacular poems like *L'Elegia di Madonna Fiammetta* and the *Filocolo,* Boccaccio portrays Dido as one who was betrayed in love.[46] In the *Amorosa visione,* he maintains that her sufferings would move the cruelest reader to tears.[47] Like writers of twelfth-century romance, Boccaccio resists the official justification for her abandonment by suppressing Mercury's descent. In 1552, Joachim Du Bellay published French translations of Virgil's Book IV and Dido's complaint from the *Heroïdes* in a single volume. The juxtaposition allowed the Ovidian view of Dido's character to modify the *Aeneid*'s harsher assessment. In *Le Livre de la Cité des Dames* (c. 1405), Christine de Pizan decries Aeneas as a scoundrel who not only abandoned Dido but absconded with her wealth and treasure. Like Boccaccio, Christine deletes Mercury's descent, Aeneas's imperial mission, and anything else that might dampen absolute sympathy with Dido.[48] Dramatists like Jodelle in France and Marlowe in England also treated Dido sympathetically, even if they did not explicitly condemn Aeneas as a "traytour." For them, Dido's tragedy was one not of simple erotic betrayal; rather it dramatized the irreconcilable conflict between private desires and public destinies.[49]

As Douglas's example suggests, humanism exposed the inadequate textual foundation for defenses of Dido as a victim of Aeneas's deceit. Virgil's Aeneas might have had his faults, but he was not a lothario. While humanism discredited the old Ovidian and romance defenses, however, it provided fresh terms for discussing Dido's tragedy by reviving a late classical distinction between the *Aeneid*'s passion-driven queen and the "historical" founder of Carthage who never even heard of Aeneas because they lived centuries apart. The latter, a widow devoted to her husband's memory, became an exemplar of chastity by killing herself to avoid being forced into a second marriage. As Craig Kallendorf has noted, Boccaccio abandoned his sympathetic, romance view of Dido when he fell under Petrarch's humanist influence. His later Neo-Latin writings repeatedly evoke the two-Dido thesis in contrasting her lust with her historical counterpart's virtue. Following Macrobius and Jerome, he argued that Virgil transformed the chaste Dido into a woman driven mad by desire to demonstrate "the reasons why we are carried away into wanton behavior by the passion of concupiscence" (*quibus ex causis ab appetitu concupiscibili in lasciviam rapiamur*).[50]

The distinction between the two Didos became a commonplace in fifteenth- and sixteenth-century discussions of the *Aeneid*. Lydgate introduced it to England in *The Fall of Princes* and Caxton included it alongside the story of Dido's affair with Aeneas in his 1490 translation of a French romance. Its popularity lay in its ability to resolve long-standing contradictions between sympathetic views of Dido as a tragic victim and critical views of her as a temptress. One could pity the virtuous widow without condemning Aeneas for abandoning his concupiscent hostess. The two-Dido thesis exonerated Virgil himself from suspicions of slander, since his didactic aims justified his departure from historical fact. As Boccaccio and other humanists argued, Virgil portrayed Dido as a woman enraged by love to bolster his readers' commitment to chastity.

By the beginning of the sixteenth century, poets and commentators availed themselves of more interpretations of Dido's tragedy than at any previous moment in literary history. But the ascendancy of the two-Dido thesis underscores the period's primary interest in Virgil as a didactic poet urging discipline, restraint, and obedience to higher powers. This emphasis figures strikingly in writers as diverse as Mazzoni, Scaliger, Salutati, Giraldi Cintio, Tasso, Sassetti, Minturno, Sidney, and Harington. Henry Parker's "The Bridle" attests to a pervasive association of Virgil with strict moral counsel throughout Renaissance England. Parker's Virgil exhorts readers to bridle their appetites for debauchery:

> Do as oure Virgill counseles and ye shall lyve in reste
> Tye up both wyne and Venus fast fetered with a chayne
> Lest that with their rewardes the mynde be not opprest
> Let wyne but quenche thy thurst so is that lycour best
> Let Venus serve to multiply our nature that doth excel
> But and ye passe these bondes then is the godnes ceast
> If that ye note this doctryne, doubtles ye shall do wel.[51]

Even writers who sympathized deeply with Dido hailed Aeneas's abandonment of her as an important lesson for Virgil's readers. Sidney, for instance, maintains that although "all passionate kindness" and "even the human consideration of virtuous gratefulness" urged Aeneas to stay in Carthage, his disregard of such considerations exemplified perfect obedience to "God's commandment."[52]

When Renaissance poets began writing dynastic epics, the question of whether or not they urged their readers to virtuous discipline was central to their canonization as vernacular Virgils. If a poem like the *Orlando Furioso,* the *Gerusalemme Liberata,* or *The Faerie Queene* aspired to Virgilian authority, it presumably had to teach the same lessons that commentators found in the *Aeneid.* This stress on didacticism as the hallmark of Virgilian writing added a fresh dimension to the way retellings of Dido's tragedy tested a poet's laureate potential. Since commentators from Bernard Silvestris to Boccaccio and Melanchthon had associated Mercury with eloquence and interpretation, his ability to free Aeneas from Dido's spell provided an image of literature's ability to liberate its readers from vice. By reinforcing this implicit defense of poetry in vernacular retellings of the episode, a writer confirmed his right to enter the Virgilian tradition.

Not every Renaissance imitation of the Dido episode, however, upholds the exalted view of literature that humanist commentators associated with it. The *Furioso* became the period's most controversial poem by flouting assumptions about human behavior on which Virgil's own reception as a didactic poet depended. In representing what Albert Ascoli has called "a crisis in humanistic education," Ariosto challenges Boccaccio's appeal to the two-Dido thesis as a justification for poetry's didactic distortions of historical facts.[53] Whereas Boccaccio argued that Virgil charged Dido with concupiscence to "demonstrate the reasons why we are carried away into wanton behavior" (Osgood, 68), Ariosto's San Giovanni implies that Virgil did it because her descendants failed to offer him palaces and great estates:

> Aeneas was not as devoted, nor Achilles as strong, nor Hector as ferocious as their reputations suggest. . . . What has brought them their sublime renown have been the writers honoured with gifts of palaces and great estates donated by these heroes' descendants. Augustus was not as august and beneficent as Virgil makes him out in clarion tones—but his good taste in poetry compensates for the evil of his proscriptions. . . . Listen on the other hand to what reputation Dido left behind, whose heart was so chaste: she was reputed a strumpet purely because Virgil was no friend of hers.

> > Non sì pietoso Enea, né forte Achille
> > fu, come è fama, né sì fiero Ettorre . . .
> > ma i donati palazzi e le gran ville

dai descendenti lor, gli ha fatto porre
in questi senza fin sublimi onori
da l'onorate man degli scrittori.

Non fu sì santo né benigno Augusto
come la tuba di Virgilio suona.
L'aver avuto in poesia buon gusto
la proscrizion iniqua gli perdona. . . .

Da l'altra parte odi che fama lascia
Elissa, ch'ebbe il cor tanto pudico;
che riputata viene una bagascia,
solo perché Maron non le fu amico.
(XXXV.25–26, 28)[54]

From Ariosto's perspective, Aeneas's abandonment of Dido offers a lesson not
in obedience and restraint but in the fiscal realities of patronage. Just as poets
conceal their patrons' vices, humanist commentators conceal their poets' venality
by disguising it as an altruistic concern for educating their readers. The difference
between the chaste and unchaste Didos reveals Virgil's umbrage over insufficient
payment rather than his desire to promote chastity. What Dido's tragedy really
warns us to avoid is not concupiscence but stinginess, especially toward writers.[55]

While the San Giovanni episode questions the motives underlying poetry's
didactic defense, Ruggiero's encounter with Alcina challenges its practicality.
Poetry can only enlighten its readers if they are capable of being enlightened; if
humanity is fundamentally ineducable, poetry cannot be expected to ennoble
the human character. The recurrent question of whether Ariosto's stance toward
Virgil is dismissive or recuperative arises from Ariosto's own ambivalence toward
the didactic thesis. The *Furioso* encodes his doubts about people's general ed-
ucability and about the specific didactic effectiveness of artistic pleasure. At his
most optimistic, he qualifies the rigid antithesis between passion and reason that
Virgil's commentators found in the *Aeneid* by imagining a love like Ruggiero's
for Bradamante that reconciles private desire and public commitment. Such a
revision suggests that the Virgilian model of heroism might better accommodate
human sexuality, yet it does not reject the possibility of heroism per se. As long
as eros is channelled into socially acceptable forms, it does not necessarily un-
dermine an individual's commitment to noble enterprise. At other times, how-
ever, Ariosto challenges even his own compromise between reason and passion.
His insistence that desire inevitably resists reason subverts any defense of art as
a force of moral edification. At his most pessimistic, Ariosto suggests that the

only thing poetry can do is to remind its readers of their inevitable subjection to instinct.

The basis for Ruggiero's involvement with Alcina is not simply the Dido episode in Virgil but its familiar interpretation in Neoplatonic commentary as a warning against concupiscence. Like Dido in Bernard's *Commentum,* Alcina embodies sensual indulgence. Just as Mercury commands Aeneas to abandon Dido's Carthage, Melissa urges Ruggiero to leave Alcina's decadent gardens and palaces. Bernard and Landino agreed that Aeneas's subsequent descent into the underworld remedied his truancy in Carthage. After renouncing the life of the senses, or, in Landino's terms, the *activa vita,* he embraces the mysteries of contemplation. Ariosto follows this reading of the *Aeneid* by opposing Ruggiero's education in Logistilla's realm to his debauchery in Alcina's. Such details as the Charon-like boatman who ferries him to Logistilla's island identify it as a type of Virgilian underworld. Ariosto patterns Logistilla herself on the sybil who enlightens Aeneas with Neoplatonic truth.

Both Bernard's *Commentum* and Landino's *Disputationes Camaldulenses* conclude abruptly after allegorizing Aeneas's education in the underworld. By truncating Virgil's narrative, they suggest that nothing significant could possibly follow the hero's initiation into the *vita contemplativa.* From their interpretive perspective, contemplating divine mysteries constitutes the highest good of human experience. Logistilla's boatman explicitly asserts the superiority of her Neoplatonic teachings to other pleasures:

> She will teach you more alluring preoccupations than music and dancing, perfumes, baths, and fine fare: rather, how your mind, better informed, can soar to the heights, loftier than the kite: and how the glory of the blessed can in part permeate the bodies of mortals.

> Ella t'insegnerà studii più grati,
> che suoni, danze, odori, bagni e cibi;
> ma come i pensier tuoi meglio formati
> poggin più ad alto che per l'aria i nibi,
> e come de la gloria de' beati
> nel mortal corpo parte si delibi.
>
> (X.47)

The boatman assures Ruggiero that "all other good dwindles to little value" (*ogn'altro ben ti par di poca stima*) in comparison with Logistilla's intellectual delights (X.46). Once Ruggiero has soared to the "more alluring" heights of contemplation, nothing could presumably tempt him back to mundane, transitory passions.

But the fiction in which Ariosto embeds the boatman's tributes suggests that Logistilla's visionary delights might not fully diminish other considerations. The boatman himself notes that the "glory of the blessed . . . can permeate the bodies of mortals" only "in part" (*parte*). As long as souls are incarnate in mortal bodies, transitory concerns cannot be entirely dispelled. This qualification hints that Ariosto evokes the Neoplatonic *Aeneid* only to challenge its most basic values. In contrast to Bernard's or Landino's Aeneas, Ruggiero never fully renounces either the active or the sensual life. He soon leaves Logistilla's realm to resume his former worldly occupations.

One of the *Furioso*'s most conspicuous imitations of a Virgilian subtext—Melissa's appearance to Ruggiero on Alcina's island—underscores Ariosto's departure from the Neoplatonists' *Aeneid*. When Melissa disguises herself as Atlante and castigates Ruggiero for neglecting his heroic career, her words recall Mercury's exhortations to Aeneas. But when she doffs her disguise so that she might "set all the facts" (*il tutto*, VII.67) of Bradamante's affections before him, Ariosto rejects the commentator's belief that sexual desire must be transcended in the pursuit of moral perfection. The spectacle of a female messenger pleading the hero's duty not just to his posterity but to the woman who loves him, moreover, overturns the gender hierarchy long attributed to poetry in the Virgilian tradition. Ariosto privileges neither men over women, reason over passion, nor objective knowledge over feeling. Melissa challenges Ruggiero not with naked moral fact but with a truth tempered by "warmth of feeling" (*in quanto il vero e l'affezion comporta*, VII.69). Ruggiero ultimately rejects Alcina not for Logistilla but for a Bradamante whose true sensual appeal distinguishes her both from Logistilla's disembodied beauty and from Alcina's illusory charms.

But the reconciliation of passion with reason suggested by Ruggiero's pursuit of Bradamante proves fragile and temporary. Only a few cantos after Melissa has shown Ruggiero his depravity and Logistilla has introduced him to the contemplative life, he tries to rape Angelica. His relapse into sensuality proves that erotic impulses can never be fully disciplined by rational persuasion. Throughout the poem, the spectacle of other Christian and pagan heroes forgetting their highest commitments in a moment's passion reinforces this impression. Their irrepressible sensuality undermines the basis not only of Virgil's didacticism but of Ariosto's own attempt to revitalize it by championing marriage as a socially constructive channel for desire. From the disillusioned perspective that Ariosto assumes in the Ruggiero-Angelica episode, the only story that can be written of humanity's moral education is one of repeated failures.

Ariosto reinforces his critique of the commentators' confidence in passion's submission to reason by rejecting the *Aeneid*'s comparatively linear plot. The stylistic correlative of libidinal resistance to containment is narrative resistance to allegorical coherence and closure. As Patricia Parker has observed, the crucial concept that links Ariosto's moral argument with his digressiveness is error, interpreted both in its ethical and structural senses.[56] Ruggiero's choice of Bradamante over Alcina suggests Ariosto's commitment to a fiction permeated with the light of Logistillan truth. But when Ruggiero relapses into lasciviousness, Ariosto renounces conventional didacticism for a poetry that continually subverts its moral premises. Dido's abandonment and Francesca's damnation allowed their creators to distance themselves from poetic influences stigmatized as incompatible with their epic vocations. If Ruggiero remained permanently faithful to Bradamante, the Alcina episode might be read as a similar defense against Boiardo and chivalric romance, which Ariosto consistently recalls as a poetry devoid of didactic value.[57] But Ariosto finally presents romance decentered from didactic intentions as a discourse that can neither be resisted nor fully accommodated to didactic allegory. Just as eros overpowers his hero's attempts to lead a good life, romance indeterminacy defeats his own efforts to write a poem teaching straightforward lessons in virtue.[58]

Because of the *Furioso*'s flagrant structural departures from the *Aeneid,* critics immediately debated whether or not it constituted a heroic poem in the Virgilian tradition.[59] From the moment the controversy began, Ariosto's detractors linked charges of indecency to complaints about his multiple plots, digressions, juxtapositions of grave and farcical actions, mixtures of high and low characters, and other violations of classical decorums. Intuiting his own construction of libidinal impulse as a trope for his narrator's inability to finish one story before dashing off on another, critics like Antonio Minturno and Filippo Sassetti lamented his deviations from Virgilian *pudor* and Virgilian formal discipline. Sassetti, who denied that the *Furioso*'s rambling narrative developed a consistent didactic allegory, complained that many of its passages aroused illicit desires.[60] Critics focused their moral objections on Ariosto's introduction of a hero who is driven mad by love at the center of an epic action. But they also decried the bawdry of specific episodes like Ricciardetto's encounter with Fiordispina and the infamous Host's tale, which even so staunch a champion of Ariosto as Harington failed to defend in the Preface to his 1591 translation.

But if the *Furioso* had its detractors, it also had its defenders, who argued that a poem could be written in the *Aeneid*'s heroic, didactic spirit without adopting every aspect of its style, characterization, and narrative structure. For Giovan Battista Giraldi Cintio, departure from the ancient models was part of an inevitable and necessary process of generic evolution. In his *Discorso intorno al comporre dei romanzi* (1554), he asserted that poets "ought not so to limit their freedom within the bounds set by those who wrote before them that they dare not set foot outside the tracks of others."[61] Virgil's own departures from Homer demonstrated that "good writers, treading where the ancients trod, can turn aside somewhat from the beaten path" (39). Giraldi justifies several of Ariosto's most frequently condemned deviations from Virgil on the grounds that they achieve "the variety that is the spice of delight." Like Sidney, Giraldi sees that delight as the first step toward effective moral instruction.

Whereas Giraldi justified the *Furioso*'s departures from its classical models, Ariosto's editors partially effaced them. As Javitch reminds us, Renaissance editions soon compensated for the poem's frustrating entrelacement by including marginal glosses indicating where Ariosto resumed an interrupted plot (91). They also included commentaries by Porcacchi, Toscanella, Fornari, Bononome, and others that were modelled on Virgilian commentaries and that treated the *Furioso* as a consistent moral allegory. Following Fulgentius's, Bernard's, Boccaccio's, and Badius's readings of the Dido episode, for instance, Bononome interprets Ruggiero's encounter with Alcina as an exemplum about lust. But after celebrating the Logistilla episode as Ruggiero's induction into the *vita contemplativa*, he never mentions Ruggiero's attempt to rape Angelica.[62] Even Toscanella and Porcacchi, who mention the assault in their glosses, simply note that it underscores the difficulty of resisting sensual temptation. They do not see it as a challenge to their earlier confidence in Ruggiero's conversion.[63] By underplaying such traces of Ariosto's skepticism, they canonize the *Furioso* in the same didactic terms that governed the *Aeneid*'s canonization as an exemplum about human struggles toward perfection.

Despite such efforts to assimilate the *Furioso* to the Virgilian tradition, controversy over its status as a heroic poem persisted throughout the sixteenth century. The most complex response to this debate came from Torquato Tasso. His multiple revisions of his own theoretical positions, as well as of his own heroic poem, reveal his uncertainty about the extent to which a work could deviate from the *Aeneid*'s structural model without surrendering Virgilian authority. He reassesses the compatibility of romance and epic decorums in every major work. At times, he portrays Ariosto as someone who wandered too far from classical precedent, but whose central poetic was not fundamentally opposed to it. At other times, he repudiates Ariosto as a dangerously misleading influence threatening his own Virgilian, as well as Christian, integrity.

Before examining how Tasso's ambivalence toward Ariosto and the *romanzi* figures in his transformation of Dido's abandonment, I want to consider its impact on theoretical works like the *Discorsi dell'arte poetica e del Poema Eroico* and the *Apologia . . . in difesa della sua "Gerusalemme Liberata."* In all his critical writings, Tasso objects to Ariosto's multiple plots, his lack of verisimilitude in representing marvels, and his tendency to privilege delight over moral instruction. But more often than not, Tasso qualifies the distinctions that he first emphatically draws so that they seem more like subtle differences in degree rather than obvious differences in kind. If he praises verisimilitude, he warns that too narrow a focus on particular truths inhibits a grasp of the universal. While he condemns multiple actions, he stresses the importance of variety in modern poetry written for an audience more jaded than Virgil's. If the aspiring poet simply had to avoid anything that resembled Ariosto and contrasted with Virgil, his task would be simple. But from Tasso's perspective, real artistic merit lies in disciplining Ariostan flamboyance with Virgilian moral and aesthetic rigor. Claiming that "it is indeed an easy and artless thing to get a great variety of incidents in many separate actions," Tasso equates the attainment of "an equal variety in one sole action" with an act of Virgilian heroism: *hoc opus, hic labor est.*[64]

Tasso continually questioned his own success in achieving the elusive balance between the marvelous and the implausible, the variety that is compatible with unity and the diversity that undermines it. As Margaret Ferguson has noted, a comparison between the *Furioso* and the *Liberata* hardly illustrates the distinctions that Tasso's early theoretical works draw between epic true to the Virgilian spirit and romance.[65] In actual poetic practice, the *Liberata* adopts some of Ariosto's most striking formal and thematic departures from the *Aeneid*. Tasso later regretted these accommodations to romance convention: he transformed the *Liberata* into the *Conquistata* by further suppressing Ariostan influence. What he originally conceived as instances of the marvelous struck him retrospectively as implausibilities. What first appeared as an acceptable juxtaposition of erotic and martial themes for the sake of "pleasing variety" was later rejected as deviation from Virgilian rigor.

Like his precursors, Tasso defines his relationship to alternative literary influences by means of a fiction of female abandonment. As in the *Furioso*, the sorceress who ensnares the hero embodies romance itself, conceived as a genre that titillates its audience without instructing it in virtue. But the *Conquistata*'s version of Armida's repudiation extensively revises the *Liberata*'s. What differentiates the two accounts is Tasso's increasing fear that romance might be utterly incompatible with epic in the Virgilian tradition. In the *Liberata*, Armida's eventual conversion to Christianity suggests the possible recuperation of Ariostan influence to reinforce a central moral allegory. In the *Conquistata*, however, Tasso's greater skepticism toward Ariosto demands Armida's repudiation as an irredeemable pagan.

The *Liberata*'s greater toleration of Ariostan influence depends on the belief that romance can be redeemed from moral and aesthetic error through Christian dogma. Previous critics have seen Tasso's departures from Ariosto as a function of his religious commitment.[66] I want to argue instead that Tasso's Christianity answers his primary poetic need to define himself as a poet truer to the Virgilian spirit than Ariosto was. Throughout the *Liberata,* his imitations of the *Furioso* suggest that he recognized its critique of Virgil's belief in human educability. He reaffirms that belief in the Armida episode by maintaining that individuals can overcome their baser desires through reason informed by grace. This confidence in turn allows him to recuperate certain features of Ariostan narrative as compatible with, rather than critical of, Virgilian closure and narrative coherence.

Tasso's revisionary stance toward both Virgil and Ariosto manifests itself most clearly in Ubaldo's exhortations when he discovers Rinaldo in Armida's gardens. The moment conspicuously revises both Mercury's descent to Carthage and Melissa's arrival at Alcina's pleasure palace. As we have seen, Melissa tempers her diatribe against Ruggiero with promises of Bradamante's love. Like Ariosto, Tasso agrees that castigation alone is insufficient to restore the hero to his quest. From his perspective, however, rebukes must be complemented with promises not of earthly love, as in the *Furioso,* but of divine forgiveness. After Ubaldo upbraids Rinaldo for his lapses and the wise man lectures him on self-discipline, the hermit Piero grants him pardon and absolution.

Melissa's promises failed to insure Ruggiero against future lapses into concupiscence, but Piero's ministry has a lasting impact. Divine grace shields Rinaldo against further temptation. From Tasso's perspective, Ariosto's skepticism toward human resolution is justified, but his contempt for Virgil's confidence in the possibility of moral reformation is not. Humanity's efforts to better itself might be limited by its fallen nature, but God can overcome those limitations and decisively liberate an individual from his or her bondage to the flesh. By evoking the Christian theology of grace, Tasso supplies the missing terms that allow him to preserve Virgil's fundamental narrative structure. Like Aeneas, but in striking contrast to Ruggiero, Rinaldo recovers from his single lapse into concupiscence never to fall again.

After a theology of grace provides Tasso an answer to Ariosto's skepticism, he can recast romance themes and motifs so that they support rather than compromise a Virgilian didactic vision. In the *Discorsi del Poema Eroico,* he declares love a suitable subject for epic and admits that Virgil's portrayals of erotic passion were unnecessarily restrained: "he might have said much more about the loves of Aeneas, of Iarbas, of Turnus and of Lavinia, but kept silent about these matters or barely suggested them" (Cavalchini and Samuel, 45). But Tasso's only precedent for a less "restrained" representation of love in a heroic poem was Ariosto's portrayal of desire continually deteriorating into lust. Once more, Tasso appeals to Christianity to overcome his poetic impasse and to help him imagine a love compatible with valor. The same grace that allows Rinaldo to surmount his concupiscence eventually transforms Armida's desire for him into a commitment to his God.

Armida's surprising conversion, which reconciles her with Rinaldo after he has fulfilled his quest, sanctions yet another feature of Ariostan romance, its notorious capriciousness.[67] In the *Furioso,* sudden transports of desire usually thwart characters' commitments and defer narrative resolution. But in Tasso, apparent capriciousness turns out to be Providential design. The sudden passion that prevents Armida from murdering the sleeping Rinaldo effectively reverses Ruggiero's attempt to rape Angelica after he rescues her from the Orc: Armida's desire guarantees rather than threatens his physical safety. While their subsequent affair interrupts his quest and sets the stage for her later despair, a second peripeteia reveals the Providential scheme that transforms even their respective falls into a single *felix culpa*. Just before Armida reenacts Dido's suicide, the "veil of paganism" (*del paganesmo . . . il velo*) drops from her eyes and frees her to marry the hero (XX.135).[68]

By sanctioning Rinaldo's marriage to the same woman he previously abandoned, Tasso departs dramatically from epic precedent. His hero leaves his Dido only for a time. Once she herself abandons the paganism incompatible with his spiritual commitments, he reclaims her. As Fichter has suggested, Tasso's thematic interest in conversion reinforces his formal concern with converting romance conventions into themes and motifs suitable for Christian purposes. But the conversion of a woman who echoes Dido's speeches throughout the poem also accommodates romance to epic in the Virgilian tradition. Ultimately, it creates a place within that tradition for the narrative and discursive practices through which Ariosto called its fundamental values into question.

Shortly after the *Liberata* appeared, critics like Gonzaga and Speroni assailed it for moral and stylistic indecorums similar to those that Tasso himself attacked in Ariosto. From their perspective, the poem neither redeemed nor converted romance conventions inherently unsuitable to epic's didactic ends; it simply perpetuated them.[69] With the publication of *La Gerusalemme Conquistata* in 1593, Tasso himself joined the attack on his earlier poem by revising it more in favor of history and allegory than of fiction.[70] He also suppressed all the *Liberata*'s love interest with the exception of the Rinaldo-Armida plot. Although he left the first stages of their involvement intact, he excised its happy ending so that Armida, last seen in chains, rejoins Dido and Alcina in the ranks of women rejected once and for all by their heroic lovers. That particular cancellation emblematizes his earlier, more congenial rapport with Ariosto. In the *Conquistata,* Armida no longer stands for an alternative mode that can be redeemed as the basis of Christian epic. She embodies instead a seductive literary tradition that must be repudiated for Tasso to fulfill his vocation.

Late sixteenth-century controversies over the relative merits of Ariosto and Tasso attest to the flexibility still inherent in Virgil's cultural reception when Spenser began his career. His conspicuous allusion to the *rota Virgilii* in *The Faerie Queene*'s opening lines proclaims his vocation to write poetry in the Virgilian tradition. But it also suggests his willingness to redefine contemporary understandings of Virgil's legacy. His poem will not merely adopt the *Aeneid*'s themes, plots, character types, structural devices, motifs, images, topoi, and rhetorical configurations. His first stanza alone raises the amorous themes that Virgil himself stigmatized as distractions from martial and imperial interests:

> Lo I the man, whose Muse whilome did maske,
>   As time her taught in lowly Shepheards weeds,
>   Am now enforst a far vnfitter taske,
>   For trumpets sterne to chaunge mine Oaten reeds,
>   And sing of Knights and Ladies gentle deeds;
>   Whose prayses hauing slept in silence long,
>   Me, all too meane, the sacred Muse areeds
>   To blazon broad emongst her learned throng:
> Fierce warres and faithfull loues shall moralize my song.
>   (*FQ* I.Proem.1)

As critics have often noted, the first four lines paraphrase the statement of the *rota* that introduced the *Aeneid* in Renaissance editions. But the fifth line conspicuously echoes the *Furioso*'s opening parody of Virgil (*Le donne, i cavallier, l'arme, gli amori, / le cortesie, l'audaci imprese io canto,* I.1) to suggest that Spenser will adapt Virgil along Ariostan lines.[71]

Scholars have often attributed such juxtapositions to Spenser's syncretic disregard of incompatibilities among his sources. But they actually reveal a keen appreciation of intertextual conflict. If the First Proem's references to love adapt Virgilian forms to Ariostan themes, the qualification that those loves will be "faithfull" accommodates Ariosto to Virgil. With one word, Spenser counters Ariosto's skepticism regarding permanent reformation and commitment.

This particular balance between epic and romance conventions does not necessarily characterize all of Spenser's poetry. Book I itself, for instance, takes a more critical stance toward Ariostan influence by associating it with the sorceress Duessa. Book II similarly discredits Tasso by linking him to Acrasia. Only with Book III does *The Faerie Queene* begin to embrace romance under the terms of its opening Proem. Like Tasso, Spenser continually redefines his understanding of what counts as poetry in the Virgilian tradition. Perhaps his work can best be understood as a quest for Virgilian authority in a culture that debated where such authority might lie.

Paulo maiora canamus:
Epic Anticipations and Alternatives
in *The Shepheardes Calender*

A s Richard Helgerson and David
Lee Miller have argued, Spenser's revival of the Virgilian career created a place
for serious, public poetry in a literary system dominated by amateurs.[1] Through-
out *The Shepheardes Calender,* his hints about abandoning pastoral for an epic
rivalling the *Aeneid* equated his own poetic accomplishment with England's
increased cultural sophistication. By presenting Elizabeth as a second Augustus
presiding over an accomplished court, he claimed an exclusive right to serve as
her first laureate. But this Virgilian self-fashioning involves more than adopting
Virgil's signature genres. Dante, Petrarch, Ariosto, and Tasso had established a
precedent by which aspiring poets achieved their laureate identities through
heuristic imitations of Virgil's poetry. Like his continental predecessors, Spenser
had to bridge the cultural gap between Augustan Rome and his own society by
accommodating ancient poetic forms to new social and political conditions.

Alternative views of what constituted Virgilian authority that emerged during
the Middle Ages and Renaissance potentially abetted this process. The more
broadly Virgilian writing was conceived, the easier it was to reconcile contra-
dictions between ancient and contemporary cultural values. Virgil's portrayal of
Dido as an impediment to Aeneas's quest, for instance, reinforced Augustan bias

against female magistracy. But recollections of her tragedy might compromise an Elizabethan poet's attempt to write a conspicuously Virgilian epic in honor of his female sovereign. Bradamante's heroism or the newly recovered legend of an alternative Dido's exemplary chastity might help him resolve tensions between Virgil's antifeminism and the cult of the Virgin Queen.

Yet as we saw in the last chapter, humanists increasingly equated a work's Virgilian authority with its fidelity to Virgil's textual models. Poetry based on a more flexible understanding of Virgilian writing was open to charges that it was not really Virgilian in any meaningful sense. Humanism thus reinforced the ancient concept of epic as a genre that stigmatizes and excludes other kinds of writing. Taken to an extreme by critics like Bembo, Vida, and Scaliger, this position precluded designating anything as true to the Virgilian spirit but rigidly academic poems like the *Christiad,* whose themes, structures, rhetorical config-urations, and even vocabulary were copied faithfully from the *Aeneid.*[2]

In terms of style and form, works like the *Christiad* resembled the *Aeneid* more closely than either the *Furioso* or the *Liberata.* But they were less free to negotiate contradictions between ancient and modern culture. The court poet who aspired to a Virgilian identity was caught between the poles of inclusion and exclusion, divergence and continuity. If "Virgilian" could only refer to writing that had immediate precedent in the *Aeneid,* no one could truly follow Virgil's career in a society based on different social, political, and intellectual premises. But if it could refer to anything a boastful poet happened to call "Virgilian," it became a meaningless category that could designate amateurish entertainments as well as works of actual laureate stature.

Several scholars have addressed *The Shepheardes Calender*'s presentation of so-cial, political, religious, literary, and aesthetic conflicts in what, as Lynn Johnson has observed, "can seem an unfocused picture or an irresolute dialogue."[3] Ac-cording to Patrick Cullen, the *Calender* foregrounds contradictions between two divergent models of pastoral, the Arcadian tradition creating "a world in which man's instincts and desire for *otium* can be satisfied" and the Mantuanesque tradition creating "a largely predatory world from which only religion and eter-nity promise relief."[4] Harry Berger reads the poem as a confrontation between recreative and plaintive attitudes: its speakers are torn between expectations of a paradisal state and bitterness over having lost one.[5] Richard Halpern grounds the *Calender*'s ambivalences in the clash between "narrative knowledge," which depends on and reinforces customary social bonds, and "scientific knowledge," which sets itself apart from social determinants.[6]

While I share these critics' understanding of the *Calender* as a self-divided poem, I want to examine the particular ambivalences marking it as a product of Renaissance debates over the nature of Virgilian writing. Its tentativeness and fragmentation reveal Spenser's uncertainty about the extent to which he could revise Virgil's *Opera* without surrendering Virgilian authority. The *Calender* ostensibly imitates the *Eclogues,* but its recurrent concern with generic inclusiveness engages contemporary debates about the heroic poem that resurface in *The Faerie Queene.*

Like his predecessors in the Virgilian tradition, Spenser figures his relationship to modes and genres that might compromise his laureateship through fictions of erotic infatuation. After examining how "October" problematizes generic continuity, I will discuss Colin's obsession with Rosalind as a revision of the Dido episode. Rosalind's devastating impact on Colin's career casts Petrarchanism as the greatest threat to Spenser's own Virgilian ambitions. But if the plaintive eclogues discredit Petrarchanism as a deviation from the didactic and epideictic ideals commonly attributed to Virgil, "Aprill" and "November" recuperate it as a basis of Elizabethan compliment. As I will argue, the dual interpretive legacies both of Dido and of the disguised Venus develop a more positive view of Italianate love complaint. My final section examines how Spenser's distinction between the Romish and English Tityruses recalls Chaucer both as a mentor and as a potential threat to his Virgilian identity.

"October": Redefining the Virgilian Career

"October"'s unresolved debate between Piers and Cuddie centers around the possibility of reliving Virgil's career under changed historical circumstances.[7] Piers's willingness to adapt Virgilian genres to cultures other than ancient Rome's underlies his confidence that contemporary poets can revive the laureate office. Cuddie's pessimism arises from his more restrictive sense of the Virgilian enterprise as the product of a particular society at a particular point in history. If Cuddie's more sophisticated appreciation of anachronism makes him the better humanist, his sense of alienation from the classical past discourages him from writing publicly significant verse. But Piers's optimism also has its drawbacks. At times, his belief in a fundamental cultural continuity enabling poets to reenact their precursors' careers reveals a naive disregard for the discontinuities that Cuddie laments. The genres that Piers invites Cuddie to adopt depart so much from classical precedent that readers like Gavin Douglas or the later Tasso would probably deny their Virgilian status.

In the woodcut that accompanies the "October" eclogue in the 1579 volume, Piers's laurel crown and position before a classical temple identify him as the spokesman for an enduring Virgilian tradition.[8] He offers Cuddie the oaten reeds, symbolizing the initial stage of the progression from pastoral to epic. His gesture promises at first an unproblematic continuity between Virgil and the contemporary aspiring poet. But instead of accepting the offer, Cuddie points backward toward the temple, and to the antique culture that it represents, as the only situation where he might achieve a laureate career. From the illustration alone, it seems that the impasse lies solely in Cuddie's trepidation. But as the eclogue unfolds, Spenser reveals his own doubts about cultural continuity by pitting Cuddie's embittered practicality against Piers's stubborn optimism in ways that undercut both characters' pronouncements.

The shepherds' opening exchange over poetic reward exposes the weaknesses of their respective theoretical positions. Whereas Cuddie complains that he can no longer write because his "poor Muse" has got "little good . . . and much lesse gayne" (10), Piers insists that poetry's reward lies in rehabilitative powers that transcend mere fiscal considerations:

> O what an honor is it, to restraine
> The lust of lawlesse youth with good aduice:
> Or pricke them forth with pleasaunce of thy vaine,
> Whereto thou list their trayned willes entice.
>
> Soone as thou gynst to sette thy notes in frame,
> O how the rurall routes to thee doe cleaue:
> Seemeth thou dost their soule of sence bereaue,
> All as the shepheard, that did fetch his dame
> From *Plutoes* balefull bowre withouten leaue:
> His musicks might the hellish hound did tame.
>
> (21–30)

In contrast to this celebration of poetry's edifying potential, Cuddie's complaints about insufficient patronage seem self-seeking and mean-spirited. Piers's argument is initially more persuasive because his emphasis on public service suggests his own philanthropy. He strengthens his case further by appealing to the familiar topos of the poet as universal legislator. Echoing innumerable humanist defenses of poetry, he casts himself as the defender of time-honored truths against upstart doubts and discontents.

But if Cuddie's reductive view of poetry as a poor way to make a living sets off Piers's more exalted opinions, that idealism is undercut by Piers's inept command of his evidence. Although Renaissance writers often alluded to Orpheus's songs as a testimony to poetry's didactic effectiveness, Piers inadvertently recalls two moments in Orpheus's career when his gifts failed him. Orpheus not only lost his "dame" immediately after he fetched her "from *Plutoes* balefull bowre" but was himself later murdered by a "rurall route." The myth's conclusion, which Piers either ignores or never knew, adds a new dimension to Cuddie's complaint that the praise poets achieve in allegedly tempering the passions "is smoke, that sheddeth in the skye" (35). His metaphor conspicuously echoes Virgil's description of Eurydice's disappearance "like a vapor dissolving into thin air" (*ceu fumus in auras / commixtus tenuis*) in Book IV of the *Georgics* (IV.499–500, trans. mine). Cuddie evokes a specific Virgilian passage to subvert Piers's championship of poetry's power to "restraine / The luste of lawlesse youth with good aduice." Orpheus's failure to restrain himself from looking back too soon at his beloved Eurydice, as well as his later failure to charm the Bacchantes that murder him, suggest that poetry and "good aduice" cannot always discipline the passions.[9]

The first section of "October" questions assumptions about human educability that underlie Virgil's Renaissance canonization as a didactic poet. Its second section challenges the belief that his ancient genres can be adapted to present cultural circumstances. As editors and critics have often noted, Piers's exhortation that Cuddie abandon "the base and viler clowne" and sing instead "of bloody Mars, of wars, of giusts" alludes to the *Aeneid's* opening lines as they appeared in Renaissance editions (37–39). But if Piers wants Cuddie to follow Virgil's career, he does not insist on his unwavering fidelity to Virgilian textual precedents. The epic that he imagines Cuddie writing freely accommodates the genre to an *imperium* centered on Elizabeth rather than on Augustus:

> There may thy Muse display her fluttryng wing,
> And stretch her selfe at large from East to West:
> Whither thou list in fayre *Elisa* rest,
> Or if thee please in bigger notes to sing,
> Aduaunce the worthy whome shee loueth best,
> That first the white beare to the stake did bring.
>
> And when the stubborne stroke of stronger stounds,
> Has somewhat slackt the tenor of thy string:
> Of loue and lustihead tho mayst thou sing,
> And carrol lowde, and leade the Myllers rownde,
> All were *Elisa* one of thilke same ring.
> So mought our *Cuddies* name to Heauen sownde.

> (43–54)

Given Virgil's emphasis on martial valor, Elizabeth's gender might discourage poets from trying to write an epic in her honor. Nevertheless, Piers overcomes this obstacle by evoking Leicester, the "worthy" whose family crest showed a bear chained to a stump. When Cuddie wants to blazon martial deeds, Leicester will serve as an appropriate subject. Elisa can preside over a different phase of epic, or perhaps over a different genre lacking a clear Virgilian precedent.

Although some critics have hailed Piers as a spokesman for Spenser himself, his language repeatedly undermines his authority. William Kennedy has observed that the "string of facile rhymes" in which Piers couches his allusion to the Virgilian progression oversimplifies the transition from pastoral to epic.[10] His glibness also minimizes the difficulties of writing Virgilian poetry under contemporary social conditions. Leicester's introduction posits at best a slippery compromise to the problem of situating the queen in a genre tainted by long-standing antifeminist association. Elisa, as Piers describes her, still has less to do with "doubted Knights, whose woundlesse armour rusts, / And helmes vnbruzed wexen dayly browne" than with such recreative matters as rounds and carols (41–42). Finally, by 1579, the left-flank Protestant dream of a union between Leicester and the queen was no longer tenable: Leicester had married Lettice Knolles earlier in the year and Elizabeth herself was contemplating marriage to the French duke of Alençon.[11]

Piers also skirts questions about eroticism in heroic narratives that figured prominently in continental debates over the *romanzi*. His proposal that one might sing "Of loue and lustihead" after "the stubborne stroke of stronger stounds, / Has somewhat slackt the tenor of thy string" is ambiguous. He could mean that epic ought to address erotic subjects alongside descriptions of battles. But he could also mean that love ought to be relegated to less exalted genres with which a poet might amuse himself after writing a truly heroic poem. Songs "of loue and lustihead" suggest the sonnets and complaints written by the amateurs whom Spenser scorns throughout the *Calender*. Piers's ambiguity seems to follow from Spenser's own uncertainties about the proper relationship between his poetry of moral instruction and the amateurs' songs of private dalliance. The career Piers describes could look either backward toward Ariosto, whose *Furioso* transformed love poetry into a more public idiom, or forward to Daniel and Drayton, whose epics exclude the erotic matter of their sonnets.

Cuddie's response explicitly raises the issues that Piers evades:

> Indeede the Romish *Tityrus,* I heare,
> Through his *Mecoenas* left his Oaten reede,
> Whereon he earst had taught his flocks to feede,
> And laboured lands to yield the timely eare,
> And eft did sing of warres and deadly drede,
> So as the Heauens did quake his verse to here.

> But ah *Mecoenas* is yclad in claye,
> And great *Augustus* long ygoe is dead:
> And all the worthies liggen wrapt in leade,
> That matter made for Poets on to play.
>
> (55–64)

Cuddie demystifies Piers's idealistic conception of poetry by pointing to fiscal considerations that Piers overlooks. Drawing once more on his better knowledge of classical texts and cultures, he reminds us that Virgil did not abandon pastoral out of disgust with "the base and viler clowne." He only undertook his more patriotic works after Maecenas offered him patronage to write them. Until a latter-day Maecenas commissions and finances the epic that Piers imagines, Cuddie will never be able to write it.[12]

This economic concern raises broader questions of cultural divergence, such as the problem of reviving Virgil's heroic style after the *imperium* that inspired it has long since vanished. Cuddie's allusion to the Virgilian progression in lines 55–60 follows the *Aeneid*'s opening lines more closely than Piers's liberal paraphrase in lines 37–54. As an implicit correction of Piers's infidelity to Virgil's text, Cuddie's version challenges the Virgilian paradigm's accommodation to a female sovereign and songs "of loue and lustihead." From Cuddie's more conservative perspective, epic remains an essentially masculine genre devoted to martial themes of "warres and deadly drede." He cannot turn from pastoral to epic because he lacks not only a Maecenas but also an Augustus to occupy the center of his imperial vision. His persistent pessimism is a tacit complaint that Elizabeth and Leicester are poor substitutes for their ancient counterparts, and Piers does not refute him when he laments poetry's Astraea-like flight to heaven (79–84). As Louis Montrose has suggested, "an implicit concurrence seems now to exist between the interlocutors" that "Spenser's queen and his patron . . . are unfit subjects for an uncompromising and uncompromised poetry of praise."[13]

In the eclogue's final section, the debate about the Virgilian career yields to a seemingly unrelated debate about love's impact on noble enterprise. But as we have seen, the *Aeneid* was often treated by commentators as a warning against excessive passion. Throughout the *Calender,* the question of love's compatibility with noble enterprise serves as a metonymy for the question of epic's freedom to depart from the *Aeneid*'s thematic and stylistic precedents without surrendering claims to Virgilian authority. As the debate unfolds, Piers once again aligns himself with a more broadly defined concept of heroic poetry by praising Colin's love for Rosalind as inherently ennobling:

> . . . for loue does teach him climbe so hie,
> And lyftes him vp out of the loathsome myre:
> Such immortall mirrhor, as he doth admire,
> Would rayse ones mynd aboue the starry skie.
>
> (91–94)

But like his earlier allusion to Orpheus, his appeal to Colin's example inadvertently undermines his argument: throughout the *Calender,* Colin's infatuation hinders rather than promotes his career. From Cuddie's perspective, which the rest of the poem confirms, Colin's experiences prove that "lordly loue is such a Tyranne fell: / That where he rules, all power he doth expell" (98–99). Piers's Neoplatonic rhapsodies are an ineffectual mask for destructive desires. Instead of inspiring epic tributes to Elisa, "lordly loue" leads Colin to dissipate his talents in Petrarchan complaints.

"October"'s final impasse reveals Piers's failure to integrate his new themes and subjects with criteria established by generic purists as central to the Virgilian mode. The paradox of Spenser's Virgilian self-fashioning is that its success depends not on his ability to write poetry that looks like Virgil's but on his power to write poetry that makes Virgil's look like his own. This achievement demands sensitivity not only to Virgil's texts but to the interpretive and imitative traditions through which they were received. Bernard and Landino had canonized a Neoplatonic approach to the *Aeneid,* but Piers's Neoplatonic catchphrases hardly endow songs "of loue and lustihead" with epic *gravitas.* They resemble too closely the idioms that many contemporary poets and critics would judge incompatible with truly heroic art.

Since Piers's image of Elisa dancing in a ring recurs in "Aprill" and in Book VI of *The Faerie Queene,* critics have often equated his views with Spenser's. Spenser's own successful transition from pastoral to epic indicates that he too believed the ancient genres could be accommodated to contemporary cultural circumstances. But too close an identification of Piers with Spenser minimizes "October"'s dialectic complexities: Cuddie's more conservative aesthetic belongs just as much to Spenser's cultural inheritance as Piers's more flexible sense of epic decorum. Later in *The Faerie Queene,* Spenser himself will adopt more comprehensive definitions of the Virgilian that challenge the oppositions between earnestness and play, epic and romance, public and private discourse, incitements to desire and exhortations to restraint that dominated discussions of heroic poetry during the Renaissance. But throughout most of *The Shepheardes Calender,* he joins Augustine, Dante, and Tasso in defining Virgilian writing primarily against other modes.

Colin's Plight and the Carthage of Petrarchanism

The *Calender*'s frame story of Colin's love for Rosalind treats Petrarchanism as the greatest temptation a poet must overcome before he can follow Virgil in writing publicly significant poetry.[14] The movement was a seductive one for young poets because its conventions had been thoroughly established. Writers like Sir Thomas Wyatt and Henry Howard, Earl of Surrey had domesticated it for an English, Protestant audience through the same kind of heuristic imitations that writers of Renaissance epic used to define their relationship to Virgil. Nevertheless, Spenser presents revising Petrarch as an immeasurably easier task. As pervasive an influence as Petrarch had throughout European culture, his poetry did not have Virgil's canonical weight. Since he was esteemed as the founder of a movement rather than as the supreme practitioner of an exalted genre, his paradigms could be varied without risking major controversy. The composition of love complaints and sonnets was a leisurely undertaking compared to the labor of self-definition underlying Piers and Cuddie's disagreements in "October."

But if Petrarchan lyrics posed neither the risks nor the difficulties of adapting Virgilian genres for an English audience, they were unsuited to the public offices of praise and moral instruction. John Freccero and Giuseppe Mazzotta have characterized Petrarchanism as a fundamentally self-referential mode in which the lover projects rather than discovers the object of his enslaving passion.[15] Such solipsism and claustrophobia are incompatible with epic themes requiring the poet to look beyond his own situation and to celebrate his country's historical destiny. In distancing himself from Petrarchan influences, Spenser introduces Colin as a poet whose Virgilian aspirations are thwarted by a passion patterned on Petrarchan conventions of frustrated, egocentric longing. Throughout the *Calender,* two Virgilian subtexts, the First Eclogue and the Dido episode, underscore Colin's failures. Unlike Tityrus, his journey to the city leads him to write about private anguish rather than imperial glories. Unlike Aeneas, he never overcomes the desires that threaten his career.

Before turning to Spenser's revisions of the First Eclogue in "Januarye" and "June," I want to consider Virgil's presentation of the relationship between private desire and public commitment in the eclogue itself. In contrast to the *Aeneid*'s antithesis between *amor* and *patria,* Tityrus's experiences present Octavian's authority as the force that underwrites his privilege to sit in the shade and sing forever of his love for Amaryllis. According to Tityrus's account, she was indirectly responsible for his entrance into Octavian's service. He could never save enough money to go to Rome and purchase his freedom until he left his former mistress, Galatea, and became involved with a presumably less demanding woman.[16] Although Amaryllis's lament when he first goes to Rome anticipates Dido's, her abandonment is only temporary. Imperial patronage allows Tityrus to return to her after he meets the young god (*deus*) Octavian. In the *Aeneid,* patriotic devotion causes Aeneas to desert the woman he loves. In the First Eclogue, by contrast, patriotic devotion arises out of Tityrus's gratitude for the patronage preventing him from ever again having to leave his mistress.

By honoring Octavian for his generosity, Tityrus becomes a type of the imperial poet. His expressions of gratitude constitute an important aspect of his public labor of praise; the seemingly private focus of his love songs is qualified by their role as testimonies to Octavian's munificence. Just as his love for Amaryllis is compatible with his devotion to Octavian, his songs to her reinforce the hecatombs he offers his patron "twelve times a year" (*quotannis / bis senos cui nostra dies altaria fumant,* 42–43).[17] In honoring Amaryllis, Tityrus looks beyond his own pastoral contentment to celebrate the "young god" who makes it possible. Recognizing the public, imperial dimension of the couple's relationship, Servius treated it as an allegory of Virgil's commitment to Rome and to the imperial court.

During the Renaissance, commentators like Badius Ascensius began to see Tityrus's trip to Rome more cynically as a self-serving betrayal of his rural origins.[18] At the same time, poets like Mantuan recast it as an adventure that ends disastrously for the rustic who abandons the countryside's security for the city's opportunities. In Mantuan's Fifth Eclogue, a shepherd named Candidus leaves the Po valley in hopes of making a fortune in Rome but discovers instead flagrant papal corruption. This darkening of the First Eclogue's reception culminates when Spenser transforms the meeting that initiates Tityrus's poetic career into the encounter that derails Colin's.[19]

As a revision of the First Eclogue, Spenser's "Januarye" underscores the distinction between Petrarchan solipsism and Tityrus's poise between public and private interests. Colin's vocational crisis occurs when he decides "the neighbour towne to see" (50); the colosseum and aqueduct in the woodcut accompanying the eclogue identify that town as Rome and cast Colin as a second Tityrus.[20] But the aloof stranger who alters Colin's destiny turns out to be the elusive, disdainful mistress of Petrarchan convention rather than a benevolent monarch. The journey that began as a reenactment of Tityrus's leads instead to the sonneteer's chance encounter with a woman who distracts him from all public concerns. In structural terms, Rosalind combines the roles of Amaryllis and Octavian, the shepherd's mistress and the subject of his most extravagant praise. But she lacks Amaryllis's capacity to return the speaker's affections and Octavian's general benevolence. Erotic impasse leads to artistic stagnation. Tityrus's encounter with "the young god," which Servius glossed as Virgil's reception into Octavian's patronage, initiated his career as an imperial poet. Colin's encounter with Rosalind, however, silences his former tributes to Elisa. As his complaint unfolds, it reduces the hyperboles with which Tityrus praised Octavian into the stock complaints of sonneteers. Nothing remains of the hecatombs that Tityrus offered "twice six days each year" to celebrate his entrance into Octavian's service but the "thousand . . . / And eke tenne thousand sithes" with which Colin "blesse[s]" the hour that he met Rosalind (49, 51).

The more Colin's career deviates from Tityrus's, the more it resembles that of such thwarted pastoral lovers as Corydon and Gallus. But Spenser's principal strategy in underscoring Colin's collapse is to associate him with Meliboeus, the other speaker in the First Eclogue, who is banished from his farm by the same young god who patronizes Tityrus. Although Colin's meeting with Rosalind is modeled on Tityrus's with Octavian, her effect on him is closer to Octavian's on Meliboeus. Colin's failure to fulfill his destiny as an epic poet constitutes a kind of vocational exile. The "barrein" landscape in which he envisions himself recalls the hardships that Tityrus, secure in his own property, will never experience:

> . . . your lands will then remain
> Yours and enough for you, although bare rock
> And slimy marsh reeds overspread the fields.
> Strange forage won't invade your heavy ewes,
> Nor foul diseases from a neighbor's flock.

> . . . ergo tua rura manebunt
> et tibi magna satis, quamuis lapis omnia nudus
> limosoque palus obducat pascua iunco:
> non insueta grauis temptabunt pabula fetas,
> nec mala uicini pecoris contagia laedent.
>
> (46–50)

Colin's neglected sheep are just as miserable as those literally banished and forced to feed on strange fodder:

> Thou feeble flocke, whose fleece is rough and rent,
> Whose knees are weake through fast and euill fare:
> Mayst witnesse well by thy ill gouernement,
> Thy maysters mind is ouercome with care.
>
> (43–46)

At the First Eclogue's conclusion, Meliboeus contrasts Tityrus's privilege to pipe forever on his "rustic reed" with his own dejection by announcing that he will never sing again. Spenser recalls this despondency at the end of "Januarye," when Colin breaks his oaten pipe and vows that "pype and Muse, shall sore the while abye" (71). The passage completes Colin's metamorphosis from a type of Tityrus, of Virgil himself in his pastoral youth, into a figure of artistic failure.

The crucial difference between Meliboeus's exile and Colin's is not simply that one is real and the other metaphorical. Unlike Meliboeus's sufferings, which result from political and historical developments beyond his control, Colin's despair is self-generated and self-imposed. In the First Eclogue, one external event, Octavian's reward of confiscated land to the veterans of Philippi, imposes two separate relationships to nature on Tityrus and Meliboeus. While the lucky ones get to enjoy the "soft pastoral" of the *locus amoenus,* the unfortunate ones experience the "hard pastoral" of exile to barren hills and famished herds.[21] In *The Shepheardes Calender,* one internal phenomenon, Colin's obsessive love for Rosalind, so distorts his perception of the natural world that he transforms any setting, regardless of how pleasant, into a forbidding landscape of exile. At first, his emphasis on the bleakness of his surroundings might seem appropriate to the season: "Thou barrein ground, whome winters wrath hath wasted, / Art made a myrrhour, to behold my plight" (19–20). But the stanza introducing his complaint explicitly states that it occurs "when Winters wastful spight was almost spent, / All in a sunneshine day" (2–3). Colin's use of the passive voice in maintaining that the ground is "made a myrrhour" to his plight begs a crucial question of agency. It is not nature that transforms the landscape into an image of his anguish but his own imagination blinding him to the promise of spring.

Seeing everything as a reflection of his own suffering, Colin displays a Petrarchan solipsism inimical to Virgilian ideals of public service. The more precisely a lover analyzes and bemoans his feelings, the less capable he becomes of treating imperial themes or exhorting his audience with "good aduice." As the *Calender* unfolds, Spenser presents Colin not only as a shepherd incapable of managing his flocks but as a once-aspiring laureate sidetracked into mind-deadening interiority. Throughout the poem, characters like Piers, Cuddie, Hobbinol, and Thenot lament the unfulfilled promise of his early poetry. Works like the "Aprill" ode to Elisa reveal a talent for poetry of national significance now squandered on a haughty mistress.

If Mantuanesque inversions of the First Eclogue provide a pattern for Colin's fall into Petrarchanism, Aeneas's truancy in Carthage underlies its persistent influence on Colin's verse. Although "June" primarily imitates the First Eclogue, with Colin playing the banished Meliboeus to Hobbinol's Tityrus, their dialogue transcends its pastoral origins by placing Colin's career in an epic perspective. Describing himself as an exile whom "cruell fate, / And angry Gods pursue from

coste to coste" ("June," 14–15), Colin echoes Virgil's opening description of
Aeneas as one whose

> fate
> had made him fugitive; he was the first
> to journey from the coasts of Troy as far
> as Italy and the Lavinian shores.
> Across the lands and waters he was battered
> beneath the violence of High Ones . . .
> until he brought a city into being
> and carried in his gods to Latium;
> from this have come the Latin race, the lords
> of Alba, and the ramparts of high Rome.

> . . . Troiae qui primus ab oris
> Italiam fato profugus Lauiniaque uenit
> litora, multum ille et terris iactatus et alto
> ui superum . . .
> . . . dum conderet urbem
> inferretque deos Latio; genus unde Latinum
> Albanique patres atque altae moenia Romae.
>   (I.1–7 [M:1–6, 9–12])

The allusion serves as a startling reminder of the vernacular *Aeneid* that Colin
fails to write. Anglicizing the dynastic epic would constitute an aesthetic feat
comparable to Aeneas's translation of Trojan culture to the Lavinian shore. But
just as Colin fell short of Tityrus's career by finding a Petrarchan mistress instead
of an imperial patron, he falls short of Aeneas's by reducing his prototype's
heroic mission to a metaphor for private, erotic discontent.

Spenser underscores Colin's vocational failure by bringing Petrarchan and
epic vocabularies into collision. The echo of the *Aeneid*'s opening lines dimin-
ishes the heroic scope of Aeneas's voyage "as far as . . . the Lavinian shores" to
the storm-tossed travels of the Petrarchan sonneteer. Whereas Virgil emphasized
the imperial goal of Aeneas's quest, "the ramparts of high Rome," Colin focuses
only on the journey's personal costs. His sense of fate is the trivialized one of
a Petrarchan sonneteer, the star-crossed desire of Sidney's "O fate, O fault,
O curse," rather than the driving force of history. He readily substitutes the
continued errancy of finding "nowhere . . . to shroude [his] lucklesse pate"
for Aeneas's achievement in founding a city and an empire (16). Throughout

the passage, the clash between Colin's words and their Virgilian source exposes the solipsistic vanity of his passion.

As an overview of the *Aeneid*'s central political itinerary, the Virgilian invocation to which Colin alludes never mentions Aeneas's involvement with Dido. But by judging Colin's career as a failed reenactment of Aeneas's, Spenser establishes the Dido episode as an implicit prototype for his disastrous infatuation with Rosalind. Since Aeneas's fault lies in consummated rather than unrequited desire, the parallel between Aeneas's relationship with Dido and Colin's with Rosalind is not exact. Nevertheless, if a private love affair constitutes dereliction of duty for an Augustan hero, complaints about private, erotic alienation count as vocational negligence for a poet destined to higher themes. In the same way that Aeneas accepted Carthage as a convenient substitute for his destined home in Latium, Colin's Petrarchanism spares him the labor of creating a place for laureate poetry in a resistant literary system. For both Colin and Aeneas, the supreme danger of erotic enthrallment is lost opportunities for cultural transmission, failures to create a home for the old gods—or for the old heroic genres—in a New Troy.

Virgilian Recuperations: "Aprill" and "November"

Colin's infatuation with Rosalind reinforces "October"'s characterization of love as a "Tyranne fell" and, by metonymy, his implication that songs of "loue and lustihead" have no place in laureate poetry. But if the *Calender*'s frame tale presents Petrarchanism as a Dido distracting poets from their public vocations, "Aprill"'s ode to Elisa and "November"'s elegy for Dido recuperate it as a medium potentially compatible with the Virgilian tradition. In creating these two self-contained poems, Spenser alludes explicitly to two female characters from the *Aeneid*, Venus and Dido. Since Neo-Latin commentators treated each figure sometimes as an agent of virtue and sometimes as an embodiment of concupiscence, their antithetical reception histories provided Spenser with a framework for exploring alternative views about the relationship between epic and erotic verse.

By using Aeneas's apostrophes to his mother, *O quam te memorem virgo?* and *O dea certe*, as "Aprill"'s emblems, Spenser associates Elizabeth's epiphany as "Elisa, Queene of Shepheardes" (34), with Venus's appearance as a Diana-like huntress. During the centuries that intervened between the two texts, the spectacle of the goddess of love posing as a goddess of chastity generated conflicting interpretations.[22] While some commentators focused on Aeneas's encounter with her as a temptation to fleshly desire, others upheld it as a precious but elusive glimpse of transcendental beauty. In the *Seniles,* Petrarch treats the episode as an allegory about sensual deception:

> In the midst of the wood appears Venus. She is lust, which is hotter and keener around midlife, and assumes a maidenly semblance and garb to deceive the unknowing.

> Venus obuia, syluae medio, ipsa est uoluptas, circa tempus uitae medium, feruentior atque acrior, os habitumque uirgineum gerit, ut illudat insciis.[23]

Badius Ascensius also describes Venus as a schemer seducing the imprudent by her pleasant appearance and discourse (*vt non solum specie: sed etiam sermone imprudentes traduceret,* 176, verso). In the *Disputationes Camaldulenses,* however, Landino provides an alternative, Neoplatonic interpretation of her as the *Venus coelestis* leading Aeneas from sensuality to heavenly contemplation (120–27). From Landino's perspective, she opposes the dangerously alluring *Venus naturalis* who leads Paris to disaster.

By printing Badius Ascensius's and Landino's commentaries together in the margins of Virgil's poem, sixteenth-century editions of Virgil's *Opera* offered readers a choice between the goddess's favorable and unfavorable treatments. The same choice was available to poets imitating the scene in their aspirations to Virgilian authority. At first, Spenser seems to center his tribute to Elizabeth completely around the passage's Neoplatonic reading. In contrast to Petrarch's Venus, whose chastity is only a pretense "for the purpose of deceiving the unwary," Elisa really is a virgin. Like the *Venus coelestis,* she derives from "heauenly race" and may not be tainted by "mortall blemishe" (53, 54). Spenser insists on her chastity throughout the ode by reminding us that she is a virgin who appears only in the company of other virgins. He specifically evokes the Muses as the "*Virgins,* that on *Parnasse* dwell" (41, emphasis mine). When he invites the shepherds' daughters to join them in honoring Elisa, he wards off any whose impurity might offend her: "Let none come there, but that *Virgins* bene, / to adorne her grace" (129–30, emphasis mine).

If Elisa's heavenly birth associates her with the *Venus coelestis,* the speaker's anxiety about affronts to her chastity evokes the *Venus naturalis* as a compelling alternative influence. From Spenser's perspective on his subtext's antithetical interpretations, the Venus scorned as the embodiment of carnal pleasures occasions the other Venus's virtue. In an analogous way, "Aprill"'s evocations of a world charged with erotic energy sets off Elisa's numinous virginity. Spenser places the ode in this particular eclogue precisely to establish a dialectical relationship between her purity and the sexual awakening conventionally associated with the month. Later in the *Mutabilitie Cantos,* he depicts April as a month "full of lustyhed, / And wanton as a Kid" (VII.33). The Elisa ode also evokes an April potentially full of "lustyhed" from its opening invocation of the "dayntye Nymphs" bathing their breasts to its climactic image of Elisa crowned with "Sops in wine / worne of Paramoures," "loued Lillies," and "the fayre flowre Delice" (138–44). But here in *The Shepheardes Calender,* Elisa's chastity holds the month's generational energies in check. The nymphs' brooks are "blessed," and the floral coronation subsumes fertility rite in imperial compliment.

Throughout the ode, Elisa's authority over vernal, erotic impulses becomes a trope for Spenser's ability as the English Maro to discipline poetic influences that might violate celebratory decorums. As readers have often noted, Spenser bases the ode on such potentially dissonant modes and discourses as Ovidian myth, Marian epideictic, Petrarchan compliment, and folk ritual. Any of these could supply a subversive countertext undermining the poem's ostensible compliments to Elizabeth. The Petrarchan lady's elusiveness could degenerate into *hauteur* and bawdy gods might unsettle tributes to a "mayden Queene" (57). But Spenser revises his sources so that they reinforce rather than compromise his patriotic enterprise. He preserves just enough of a particular myth or figure's original significance to reveal the distance between it and his own chastened rhetoric.

Whether E. K.'s notes were written by Harvey, Kirke, Spenser himself, or someone else, they often set off the ode's purity by supplying the erotic narratives that Spenser expurgates.[24] According to E. K., Chloris was "a Nymph, . . . of whome is sayd, that Zephyrus the Westerne wind being in loue with her, and coueting her to wyfe, gaue her for a dowrie, the chiefedome and soueraigntye of al flowres and greene herbes, growing on earth" ("Glosse" on l. 122). But when Spenser introduces her in the ode, he mentions neither her "marriage," itself a bowdlerization of what Ovid and later mythographers presented as a rape, nor her eventual metamorphosis into Flora: "Chloris, that is the chiefest Nymph of al, / Of Oliue braunches beares a Coronall" (122–23). Of all the "flowres and greene herbes growing on earth" that were associated emblematically with Flora as a fertility goddess, Chloris brings only olive branches signifying peace. Although E. K. notes that "the word Nymphe in Greeke signifieth . . . a Spouse or Bryde," nothing in the ode suggests that either Chloris or the nymphs of which she "is the chiefest" will one day marry ("Glosse" on l. 50). By excluding references to eventual marriages or offspring, Spenser endows the nymphs with the same aura of perpetual virginity that surrounds the "mayden Queene" herself.

A similar bowdlerization of classical myth occurs when Spenser proclaims Elisa the daughter of Pan and Syrinx. As E. K. reminds us, Pan was another would-be rapist and Syrinx a victim spared only by her metamorphosis into reeds ("Glosse" on l. 50). Spenser suppresses that account of unbridled desire and threatened chastity by presenting them as a proud and joyful royal couple. All that remains of the original story are their names and the sacred aura of a chastity that Spenser transfers from Syrinx to her daughter:

> Of fayre *Elisa* be your siluer song,
>> that blessed wight:
> The flowre of Virgins, may shee florish long,
>> In princely plight.
> For shee is *Syrinx* daughter without spotte,
> Which *Pan* the shepheards God of her begot:
>> So sprong her grace
>> Of heauenly race,
> No mortall blemishe may her blotte.
>
> (46–54)

By tracing Elisa's genealogy from "heauenly race," Spenser protects her not only from the spots and mortal blemishes of sexual generation but also from the embarrassments of dynastic history. Pan and Syrinx's happy marriage suppresses not only an Ovidian rape but Anne Boleyn's execution for incest and adultery. By means of these revisions, Elizabeth, once denounced by Catholics and Henry VIII as a bastard, acquires a mythic status analogous to the Virgin Mary's.

Throughout the ode, Spenser curbs the sexual associations of particular images and allusions by reinscribing them in imperial rather than in erotic fields of reference. I have already described how he exchanges Flora's prolific foliage for olive branches suggesting a peaceful realm. In *The Faerie Queene,* Duessa's and Malecasta's costumes remind us that scarlet robes and ermines can emblematize lasciviousness. When Elisa appears "Yclad in Scarlot like a mayden Queene, / And Ermines white," however, they indicate only her royalty (57–58). The mingling of red and white in the lady's face is a Petrarchan commonplace, but as E. K. suggests, the "Redde rose medled with the White yfere" in Elisa's cheeks commemorates a stable Tudor succession founded on the union of York and Lancaster ("Glosse" on l. 68). In general, the penultimate stanza's floral catalogue marks the ode's closest approach to unmasked erotic celebration. But even its "coronations" (138) reinforce the general drift from erotic to political epideictic. Sixteenth-century writers called the flowers both "carnations" and "coronations," and the spellings reflected two distinct etymologies. While "carnation" derives from *carnis* to emphasize the flower's flesh-like color, "coronation" refers to its shape, "dented or toothed aboue . . . like to a littell crownet."[25] When Spenser describes Britomart's blush as "pure yuory / Into a cleare Carnation suddeine dyde" (*FQ* III.iii.20), the etymon *carnis* heightens her skin's figurative association with the flower's color. In "Aprill," he avoids fleshly suggestions to emphasize instead Elisa's sovereignty.

Perhaps what "Aprill" most redeems for the sake of imperial compliment is the Petrarchan lady's elusiveness. Like Rosalind, Elisa stands silent at the center of her admirers' devout, adoring gaze. But her silence indicates dignity rather than haughtiness or disdain, and nothing in the poem hints that she ought to grace her subjects with anything more than an opportunity to contemplate her virtues. The devotion she inspires contrasts with Colin's destructive, solipsistic passion, both in its communal character and in its compatibility with imperial commitment. The elusive lady has become the First Eclogue's young god, or the *parvus puer* of the Fourth, an obvious subtext for this fourth eclogue in Spenser's cycle.

The spectacle of Elisa crowned with flowers and surrounded by nymphs and shepherdesses strikingly accommodates Virgilian forms to post-Augustan influences. But it does not endorse all the revisionary implications of Piers's "October" vision of her carolling loud and dancing in the "Myllers rownde." "Aprill" admits an *imperium* centered in a female sovereign, but it does not extend Virgilian sanction to songs "of loue and lustihead." By casting Elisa as an avatar of the *Venus coelestis* untainted by "mortall blemishe," it still presents eros as a threat to virtue. Piers's Elisa may be paired with the "worthy whome shee loueth best," but no men appear in the company of Colin's "mayden Queene." Her resolute chastity distinguishes her from both the deceptions of the *Venus naturalis* and the rustic merriment of her "October" counterpart.

Later in *The Faerie Queene,* Spenser will revise the Virgilian paradigm in more radical ways that challenge Virgil's reception as an antierotic moralist. But in the 1579 *Shepheardes Calender,* he portrays only a positive relationship between members of the opposite sex in the elegiac context of "November"'s lament for Dido. Since McLane first noted that Elissa was the alternate, Punic name for Virgil's heroine, critics have tried to account for "Aprill"'s relationship to "November" in terms of her tragedy.[26] McLane himself and later new historicists have argued that Dido is a mask for Elizabeth herself, metaphorically dead to committed Protestants because of her marriage negotiations with the Catholic Alençon. But as Cullen maintains, a subtext critical of Elizabeth would have to run perversely counter to the ode's overtly celebratory stance toward Dido (92n). Bono suggests that Spenser based his Dido less on Virgil's heroine than on her chaste historical counterpart. More recently, Donald Cheney has suggested that Spenser evokes the memory of both Didos in figuring the queen as both "passionate woman and royal virago."[27]

Spenser's evocation of the *Venus coelestis* as an alternative to the *Venus naturalis* supports Bono's and Cheney's arguments by confirming Spenser's interest in recuperative interpretations of Virgil's female characters. He introduces Dido in "November" not to subvert his earlier tributes to Elizabeth but to suggest another way of representing relationships between the sexes in Virgilian poetry. Whereas "Aprill" admitted restraint alone as the proper response to Venerean impulse, "November" hints at an experience of mutual affection without destructive consequences. While this Dido is certainly not a temptress, she is also not an austere "mayden Queene" shown only among her fellow virgins. Her gifts of "coloured chaplets" and "knotted rushrings" (115–16) to a shepherd named Lobbin, identified by E. K. as her "louer and deere frende," do not necessarily imply marriage or betrothal ("Glosse" on l. 113). But they do suggest something more intimate than a patron's relationship to her retainer.

Spenser distinguishes Dido's open and affectionate nature from Elisa's aloofness by reversing the "Aprill" ode's deployment of pastoral conventions.[28] The mourners decking her hearse recall the revelers crowning Elisa with flowers in "Aprill," but men as well as women pay tribute to Dido:

Shepheards, that by your flocks on Kentish downes abyde,
Waile ye this wofull waste of natures warke:
Waile we the wight, whose presence was our pryde.

(63–65)

Spenser replaces the restraint and prohibition of "Let none come there, but that Virgins bene" with nostalgia for Dido's courtesy toward the opposite sex:

She while she was, (that was, a woful word to sayne)
For beauties prayse and plesaunce had no pere:
So well she couth the shepherds entertayne,
With cakes and cracknells and such country chere.
Ne would she scorne the simple shepheards swaine,
    For she would cal hem often heame
    And giue hem curds and clouted Creame.
        O heauie herse,
Als *Colin cloute* she would not once disdayne.
        O carefull verse.

(93–102)

When Colin transferred Hobbinol's presents to the scornful Rosalind, the pastoral gift exchange revealed his unrequited love's destructive impact on his community. Dido's graciousness in reciprocating his favors corrects Rosalind's Petrarchan hauteur. Her gifts to him and his fellow shepherds also revise the gift exchange in "Aprill." Elisa, who retains a considerable degree of Petrarchan elusiveness, receives presents but does not give any in return. This shift in gift-giving renders Dido a warmer, more humane figure than the mythical daughter of Pan and Syrinx, who is more a Muse than a woman of "earthlie mould" (158). Above all, Dido's love for Lobbin indicates an openness to natural generation from which Elisa's unswerving chastity precludes her.

But if Dido's relationship with Lobbin grants her the warmth that Elisa lacks, it also deprives her of Elisa's invulnerability to time as an icon of unswerving virginity. Dido dwells not in an eternal springtime but in a world of seasonal transition continually raising the specter of death. Elisa's garlands become the "faded flowres" decking Dido's hearse (109), and "November"'s nymphs, unlike their "Aprill" counterparts, must exchange their "greene bayes" and "Oliue braunches" for "balefull boughes of Cypres" (144–46). As in the Gardens of Adonis, time emerges as the troubler of those who frankly know their paramours:

> Ay me that dreerie death should strike so mortall stroke,
> That can vndoe Dame natures kindly course:
> The faded lockes fall from the loftie oke,
> The flouds do gaspe, for dryed is theyr sourse.
>
> (123–26)

Later in Book III of *The Faerie Queene,* Spenser appeals to an eternity achieved through successive generations as a compensation for individual mortality. But here in *The Shepheardes Calender,* the consciousness of death limits his depiction of love as a socially constructive force. Dido's death may not result from unrestrained passion, but it does suggest a tragic principle inherent in natural generation.

At this point in his career, Spenser offers Christian redemption as that tragedy's sole compensation. Divine love, unlike its mortal counterpart, succeeds in resisting mutability. Once Dido is "vnbodied of the burdenous corpse" binding her to generative nature (166), she acquires something of Elisa's static, iconic quality:

> There liues shee with the blessed Gods in blisse,
> There drincks she *Nectar* with *Ambrosia* mixt,
> And ioyes enioyes, that mortall men doe misse.
>
> (194–96)

The spectacle of Dido reigning as "a goddess now emong the saintes" is not simply a syncretic fusion of classical and Christian images (175). Dido's triumph expands the Virgilian paradigm to encompass the love not only between men and women but also between an eternal Creator and His mutable creation. In conspicuous contrast to Virgil's Dido, who mourns forever in the *lugentes campi,*

Spenser's Dido enters the Elysian fields enjoyed in the *Aeneid* only by male heroes. Her simultaneous entrance into a Christian heaven distinguishes her further from the chaste Dido of history, whom Boccaccio reluctantly consigned to hell for dying before Christ's dispensation.

Medieval commentators often allegorized Virgil's Fourth and Fifth Eclogues as a kind of sacred diptych: whereas the Fourth foretold Christ's birth, the Fifth, a lament for the shepherd Daphnis, prophesied Christ's later crucifixion. Renaissance commentators like Badius Ascensius and Valerianus downplayed these Christological readings. But they continued to pair the eclogues as historical allegories respectively about the birth of Pollio's son or Augustus's nephew Marcellus and about the death of Julius Caesar.[29] This conventional association of the two eclogues underlies the prosodic, imagistic, and thematic similarities linking "Aprill," a recollection of Eclogue IV, to "November," a recollection of Eclogue V. But if the model for their complementary relationship lies in the *Bucolics,* their dominant intertextual concern is with the *Aeneid*'s stigmatization of desire.

Tributes to Tityrus: Situating Chaucer in the Virgilian Tradition

By referring to Chaucer throughout the *Calender* as Tityrus (the shepherd believed by Renaissance readers to be a pastoral mask for Virgil himself), Spenser implies the cultural compatibility of his primary English and classical precursors. Even though Chaucer and Virgil lived centuries apart and wrote in different genres, both provided models for a writer hoping to revive public, didactic poetry. Colin's recollection of Tityrus in "June" as "the soueraigne head / Of shepheards all, that bene with loue ytake" (83–84) reminds us that Renaissance editions of Chaucer's works included love complaints like "La belle Dame sans Mercy," "The Complaint of the Black Knight," and "The Complaint Unto Pity." But unlike Colin, Chaucer could "slake / The flames, which loue within his heart had bredd" ("June," 85–86). His poetry never stagnated into the claustrophobic Petrarchanism that impedes Colin's career. In general, the *Calender* honors the English Tityrus primarily as a moralist. Even Colin's recollection of his "mery tales" keeping the other shepherds awake so that their sheep might safely feed ("June," 88–89) privileges an art that is both *dulce et utile.*

In praising Chaucer as the English Tityrus, Spenser joins a long tradition of writers who equated his cultural authority with Virgil's.[30] Lydgate and William Caxton recalled Chaucer as an English laureate on the order of "Virgile in Rome toun" and as a "noble and grete philosopher."[31] Hoccleve upheld him as a moralist, philosopher, and embellisher of the language who followed "the step-

pës of virgile in poesie."[32] At the beginning of the sixteenth century, Stephen
Hawes hailed his power to kindle our hearts

> . . . with the fyry leames
> Of morall vertue / as is probable
> In all his bokes / so swete and prouffytable.[33]

As the century passed, the addition to collections of Chaucer's works of satires
like the Plowman's Tale and "Jack Upland" heightened his reputation as a
moralist and even as a proto-Protestant. In *Toxophilus*, Roger Ascham praised
the Parson's and the Pardoner's Tales for exposing the evils of gambling, drink-
ing, swearing, lying, wastefulness, and blasphemy.[34]

But by the time Spenser composed *The Shepheardes Calender*, an alternative
view of Chaucer as a teller of bawdy tales and an inventor of vain entertainments
arose that challenged his earlier reception as a moralist in the Virgilian vein. We
have already seen how Gavin Douglas condemned the sympathetic treatments
of Dido in *The House of Fame* and *The Legend of Good Women* for compromising
the *Aeneid*'s fundamental antieroticism. Edmund Becke, Hugh Latimer, and
Thomas Cranmer focused on *The Canterbury Tales* in particular as enticements
to vanity. In the Preface to his 1549 edition of the Bible, Becke complained
that magistrates and nobles would abandon "all blasphemyes, swearing, carding,
dysing" if they spent as much time reading the Gospel as they did reading
"Cronicles & Canterbury tales."[35] Becke saw Chaucer as someone who en-
couraged the same vices Ascham argued he suppressed. In 1591, John Harington
indicted Chaucer for "flat scurrilitie . . . not onely in his millers tale, but in the
good wife of Bathes tale, & many more."[36] Concern about the fabliaux' inde-
cency seems to have mounted so much after Harington's attack that Francis
Beaumont defended Chaucer against charges of "inciuilitie" in a letter prefacing
Speght's 1598 edition of Chaucer's works.[37]

Spenser's tributes to the "English Tityrus" might suggest that he had never
heard these critiques or that he simply rejected them and aligned himself instead
with Chaucer's champions. In general, proponents of the sage and serious Chau-
cer never mentioned the bawdy narratives that provoked Harington's attack and
probably led Becke, Cranmer, and Latimer to dismiss *The Canterbury Tales* as
morally unsound. John Burrow sets Spenser squarely in the company of those
who ignored the bawdy tales by arguing that he was primarily interested in
Chaucer as a writer of complaints, romances, and beast fables.[38] The more Spen-
ser ignored works like the Miller's or Merchant's Tales, the more easily he could
honor Chaucer as an English laureate in the didactic, Virgilian spirit.

Although Spenser's overt praise for Tityrus suggests straightforward reverence for Chaucer as a moralist, his actual appropriations of Chaucer's poetry develop a more ambivalent intertextual relationship. I want to argue that the fabliaux figure more significantly in the *Calender* than critics like Burrow have acknowledged. Spenser recognizes their incorporation of antithetical moral and aesthetic perspectives as a challenge to Chaucer's canonization as an English Virgil.[39] His response to that challenge is perhaps even more ambivalent than his stance toward Petrarchanism. At times, he seems to present the more ludic Chaucer as an influence to be renounced or contained through heuristic imitations. But at other times, he toys with expanding the Virgilian paradigm itself to embrace the alternative voices and moral positions characteristic of fabliaux. The dialogic structure of an eclogue like "Februarie," with its ultimately suspended debate over the respective claims of youth and age, anticipates his later conception of epic as an exchange between diverse, equally autonomous influences.

I want to focus my discussion of Chaucer's place in the *Calender*'s exploration of Virgilian possibilities on "Februarie" and "March." These sequential eclogues bring the fabliaux' championship of youthful desire into conflict with the advocacy of restraint found in the *Aeneid* by medieval and Renaissance readers.[40] As we saw in the last chapter, commentators from Fulgentius and Bernard to Badius glossed Book IV of the *Aeneid* as a warning specifically against adolescent concupiscence. Taken out of context, Tityrus's tale of the oak and the briar, a testament against youthful impertinence, seems to align Chaucer with Virgil as an antierotic moralist. But Spenser contains the fable in a pastoral dialogue that dismisses its contempt for youth as a manifestation of its elderly teller's bitterness. "Februarie" itself recuperates a fabliau-like interplay between competing ethical perspectives. Yet this openness to the more ludic side of Chaucer's canon is short-lived: as an inversion of Sir Thopas's comic tribute to sexual awakening, "March" counters "Februarie" by suggesting the end of youthful delight in misery.

When Thenot proposes telling a "tale of truth / . . . cond of *Tityrus*," Cuddie's enthusiasm suggests that their common respect for Chaucer might settle their quarrel over the respective merits of youth and age ("Februarie," 91–92). They can agree on one point: both respect Chaucer's ability to temper traditional wisdom with diversion and caprice. While Cuddie respects whatever the "good old man bespake," Thenot concedes that Tityrus told "many meete tales of youth . . . / And some of loue" (97, 98–99). The fable that Thenot attributes to Chaucer, however, dismantles this construction of him as a genial figure pleasing both young and old. Like Book IV of the *Aeneid* in the eyes of Bernard Silvestris and the commentators, the tale of the oak and briar exposes "the dangerous nature of young manhood." By transforming the youth-age conflict into an issue of social hierarchy, of the briar's ambitious irreverence for the oak's authority, the narrator suppresses sympathy for the representative of youth, the "spitefull brere" (147). When the briar finally dies because it lacks the oak's protective shelter, Thenot's case against youthful impertinence is complete: "Such was thend of this Ambitious brere / For scorning Eld" (237–38).

The fable's situation at the eclogue's climax might lend it rhetorical authority as the final word in the shepherds' quarrel. But Spenser undercuts that effect by presenting it less as an unbiased third-party's pronouncement than as a further example of Thenot's bitterness. Earlier in the eclogue, Thenot's misappropriation of a passage from *The House of Fame* suggests that his envy skews his Chaucerian recollections:

> So loytring liue you little heardgroomes,
> Keeping your beastes in the budded broomes:
> And when the shining sunne laugheth once,
> You deemen, the Spring is come attonce.
> Tho gynne you, fond flyes, the cold to scorne,
> And crowing in pypes made of greene corne,
> You thinken to be Lords of the yeare.
> (35–41)

In Chaucer, the pipes made of green corn figure among dozens of other instruments played by minstrels before the House of Fame:

> Tho saugh I stonden hem behynde . . .
> That craftely begunne to pipe,
> Bothe in doucet and in rede,
> That ben at festes with the brede;
> And many flowte and liltyng horn,
> And pipes made of grene corn,
> As han thise lytel herde-gromes
> That kepen bestis in the bromes.
> (1214, 1220–26)

Although Chaucer implicitly indicts poets as the ministers of Fame's arbitrary judgments, "thise lytel herde-gromes" are present only in a simile. While Fame's minstrels have adopted the shepherds' instruments, the shepherds themselves belong to a pastoral world untainted by the corruptions of her court.[41] Nothing in this passage or in the rest of *The House of Fame* suggests that they are Thenot's irresponsible "heardgroomes," leading their flocks into the early spring sunshine only to be "with cold . . . annoied" (48).

By attributing the view of Chaucer as an antierotic moralist to a speaker who conspicuously distorts Chaucerian subtexts, Spenser discredits its hermeneutic authority. Another Chaucer exists, to whom readers like Thenot are blind. This alternative Chaucer is interested less in enforcing particular codes of behavior than in exploring alternative ethical perspectives. He is preeminently the Chaucer of the fabliaux, who qualifies the Christian idealization of marriage by evoking the ancient, comic championship of youth over age. His "meete tales" of youth and love never condemn characters like Nicholas and Alisoun for *concupiscentia*. Nor does he ever suggest that desire's social disruptiveness is any worse than the frustrations of an inappropriate marriage. Precisely because this Chaucer resists final ethical pronouncements, he defied Reformation readers who equated conventional moralizing with poetic authority. They either condemned him for "scurrilitie" or replaced him with his alter ego, "the noble and great philosopher" admired as a successor of Virgil by Hoccleve and Lydgate.

If Thenot's tale suppresses Chaucer's more ludic aspects, "Februarie"'s overarching dialogic structure restores them. Spenser creates a situation in which antithetical canons of judgment collide. If Thenot has social hierarchy and proverbial wisdom on his side, Cuddie has spontaneity and a more sensitive appreciation of nature on his. Throughout the eclogue, Thenot's remarks trail off in pat sentences: "For Youngth is a bubble blown vp with breath, / Whose witt is weakenesse, whose wage is death" (87–88). By contrast, Cuddie generates fresh arguments out of his immediate experience. He challenges Thenot not by quoting proverbs but by finding a negative image of his decrepitude in his weary flock: "Seemeth thy flocke thy counsell can, / So lustlesse bene they, so weake so wan" (77–78). Thenot, in his desiccation and bitterness, clearly recalls the *vieillard* of the darker fabliaux. Both Berger and Johnson have identified the Reeve, who "list not pley for age," as one of his principal precedents (Reeve's Prologue, 3867).[42] Cuddie's origins, on the other hand, lie in witty clerks like Nicholas, John, and Aleyn, who assert natural instinct over restrictive social conventions by cuckolding the doting *vieillard*.

Instead of siding with one shepherd against the other, Spenser explores the strengths and limitations of their respective points of view. Just when Thenot seems about to have the final word, Cuddie interrupts him and undercuts his authority one last time:

> Such was thend of this Ambitious brere,
> For scorning Eld—
> ### CVDDIE
> Now I pray thee shepheard, tel it not forth:
> Here is a long tale, and little worth.
> So longe haue I listened to thy speche,

That graffed to the ground is my breche:
My hartblood is welnigh frorne I feel.

(237–43)

"Februarie" ends three lines later, and the "March" eclogue that follows is shorter and less overtly moralizing. For at least a time, Spenser privileges the ludic over the didactic Chaucer. He underscores this turn against the "noble and great philosopher" by modeling Cuddie's interruption on the Host's tirade against Chaucer the Pilgrim's Tale of Sir Thopas. At that point in *The Canterbury Tales,* Chaucer the Poet seems to reject his own playfulness for overt didacticism:

> Heere the Hoost stynteth Chaucer of his Tale of Thopas
> "Namoore of this, for Goddess dignitee,"
> Quod oure Hooste, "for thou makest me
> So wery of thy verray lewednesse
> That, also wisly God my soule blesse,
> Myne eres aken of thy drasty speche."
>
> (919–23)

When the Host requests something "in prose somwhat, at the leeste, / In which ther be som murthe or som doctryne," Chaucer the Pilgrim satisfies him with the dully sententious Tale of Melibee (934–35). By reversing this transition from jest to earnestness, Spenser undercuts Thenot's emphasis on a moralizing Chaucer. The prolix tale "cond of *Tityrus*" yields to the recreative "March," written in almost the same stanza form as Sir Thopas. With its jokes about sporting in delight with Lettice, "March" seems to evoke its Chaucerian subtext as a lighthearted tribute to adolescent desire.

The more playful Chaucer recalled by this transition resists facile equation with Virgil. But just when an alternative view of the English "Tityrus" might challenge the "Romish" one's authority, Spenser himself retreats once again into a more judgmental, moralizing attitude toward his subject. Beneath its surface levity, "March" restores the frame tale's depiction of love as a dangerous, socially disruptive force. Although it takes the form of a pastoral debate, it does not present its speakers' positions in truly dialectical fashion: Thomalin, the shepherd who has experienced love's treachery firsthand, is noticeably wiser than his opponent. Willye's desire to waken "little Loue" and "learne with Lettice to wexe light" (22, 20) appears more as adolescent naiveté than as a viable alternative to Thomalin's disillusionment.

As Thomalin and Willye recount their encounters with Cupid, Spenser resists a more dialogic reception of Chaucer by incorporating Chaucerian subtexts to heighten the eclogue's warnings about erotic dangers. Both "March"'s tail-rhyme stanzas and its thematic concern with awakening sexual desire link it to Sir Thopas. Its "Argvment" underscores Thomalin's descent from the mock hero who falls in love with the elfin queen:

> . . . in the person of Thomalin is meant some secrete freend, who scorned Loue and his knights so long, till at length him selfe was entangled, and vnwares wounded with the dart of some beautifull regard.

Sir Thopas also rejected many an offer of love because "he was chaast and no lechour" until he too suddenly fell "in love-longynge" (745, 772). The Host interrupts Chaucer's tale just before his hero returns to battle the giant Sir Olifaunt, the imposing supernatural figure who stands between him and the object of his desire. But before "March" opens, Thomalin has already fought a comparable battle with Cupid and received a wound that "ranckleth more and more" (100). In this revision of Sir Thopas's quest, love itself becomes the hero's primary mythic opponent.

In a sense, Spenser presents Thomalin's history as a completion of Chaucer's unfinished tale. The subtext's interruption appears retrospectively as a failure to depict the disillusionment that follows a romantic attachment's enthusiastic first stages. "March" implies that Sir Thopas, like any other lover, would eventually experience the disastrous end of all erotic pursuits. Fulfilling his quest would only occasion further misery. The elfin queen might scorn his advances outright, or entertain them for a time only to betray him later, but she would not bring him lasting happiness. By imposing this dark conclusion on an apparently light-hearted mock romance, Spenser transforms Chaucerian play into an antieroticism fully consonant with the message that commentators found in Book IV of the *Aeneid*. As Thomalin's emblem reminds us, love's "Honye is much, but the Gaule is more."

Thomalin's account is only one of "March"'s admonitions about love's treachery. When Willye recounts his father's story of netting Cupid in the family pear tree, his inexperience blinds him to its darker implications. But as Thomas Cain has suggested, the incident recalls two archetypal stories of adultery, Vulcan's entrapment of Venus and Mars, and January's discovery of May and Squire Damian in a pear tree.[43] In a final turn against fabliau convention, Spenser evokes the Chaucerian example that most challenges the genre's comic amorality. Unlike the other fabliaux, the Merchant's Tale never lets us forget that the lovers' triumph over age violates the trust and sanctity of marriage. By subtly alluding to the tale in this particular eclogue, Spenser leaves us wondering whether Willye's "stepdame eke as whott as fyre" (41) is another fabliau heroine bent on betraying his father. "March" joins Sir Thopas in a long tradition of stories about adolescent desire, but it promises only two possible fates awaiting the boy who feels love's first stirrings. He may pine away with unrequited desire or he may win his beloved only to reenact the farce of January's marriage to May.

Throughout *The Shepheardes Calender*, shifting conceptions of Virgilian authority are a function of shifting constructions of Chaucer as a principal mediational influence. The more Spenser sides with Neo-Latin commentators in honoring Virgil as a moralist, the more he embraces Hoccleve and Lydgate's view of Chaucer as a "great and noble philosopher." While this recollection of both Virgil and Chaucer as moral teachers ultimately dominates the *Calender*, Spenser occasionally starts to redefine the education achieved by poetry endowed with their cultural authority. The dialogism of a work like "Februarie" teaches its readers not so much how to behave as how to appreciate diverse ethical perspectives. Although Spenser does not fully develop this revision of the Virgilian paradigm in *The Shepheardes Calender*, he will return to it in *The Faerie Queene*.

From *Roma Aeterna*
to the New Hierusalem:
The Virgilian Origins of Book I
of *The Faerie Queene*

While the Bible gave Spenser a virtuous woman wandering in the wilderness, a harlot clad in scarlet riding a seven-headed beast, and an apocalyptic encounter with Satan in the guise of a dragon, medieval and Renaissance interpretations of the *Aeneid* as an account of the hero's moral education provided the basis for Redcrosse's spiritual biography.[1] Like the *Aeneid*, Book I opens in medias res when a storm drives the hero off course and forces him to take shelter in a harbor that conceals an even greater threat to his heroic mission. Scholars have long recognized the Polydorus episode as the origin of Redcrosse's encounter with Fradubio, and the Dido episode as a primary source for his fornication with Duessa. Duessa's descent to Aesculapius's den parodies Aeneas's visit to Anchises in the underworld; as we shall see later in this chapter, Redcrosse's instruction on the Mount of Contemplation corrects the same Virgilian episode, which was repeatedly allegorized as Aeneas's initiation into the *vita contemplativa*. Finally, Maphaeus Vegius's account of Aeneas and Lavinia's marriage in a Thirteenth Book usually appended to Renaissance editions of the *Aeneid* underlies Redcrosse and Una's betrothal in canto XII.

But if Spenser drew on the thousand-year-old Christian allegorization of

Aeneas's adventures as an account of humanity's struggle against temptation, he also recognized inconsistencies between the commentators' emphasis on natural fortitude and the centrality of grace in Reformation thought. By explaining away Virgil's pagan gods as tropes of human psychology, interpreters from Fulgentius to Petrarch and Boccaccio presented Aeneas's achievements as a testimony more to his innate virtues than to a providential order. Natural attributes play an unambiguously positive role in all the commentaries as the powers that redeem us from our bondage to the flesh. In glossing Mercury's admonitions to Aeneas, Fulgentius notes that "it is by the urging of the intellect that youth quits the straits of passion" (127). Gavin Douglas's marginal comments attribute Aeneas's reformation to reason: "Wyse men are oft times parturbet with affectionis of mind, neuertheles they giue place to reson at the last" (2:192).

For Protestants believing in justification by faith alone, however, the commentators' emphasis on reason, labor, and merited reward was intolerably bound up with Pelagianism and works righteousness. Calvin and Luther often embellish their writings with quotations from the *Aeneid* and praise classical authors for moral insight within the limited order of nature.[2] But the Reformers simultaneously lament "heathen" blindness to the means of humanity's final deliverance from sin. Even so ardent a champion of humanistic studies as Melanchthon condemns Aeneas's religious rites as pagan abominations.[3] Lawrence Humphrey charges that ancient poetry distracted its readers from "weyghtie studyes tendiyng to encrease of godlynes, dignytie, or true and sounde commodity."[4] Throughout his Protestant courtesy book, Humphrey upholds Christ, rather than any classical hero, as the pattern of true nobility.

In accommodating Virgilian conventions to the ideological conditions of Elizabeth's court, Spenser had to reconcile them with Protestant skepticism toward humanity's ability to overcome the effects of original sin without divine assistance. He shared the commentators' concern with bridging classical and Christian cultures. But their interpretation of events like Mercury's descent did not emphasize grace enough to satisfy a poet hoping to endow a Protestant sovereign with the aura of the Augustan past. Although the precise character of Spenser's understanding of grace remains a point of controversy, even the most moderate Protestants of his day believed, with Richard Hooker, that "the naturall powers and faculties . . . of mans mind are through our native corruption soe weakened and of themselves soe averse from God, that without the influence of his speciall grace, they bring forth nothing in his sight acceptable, noe nott the blossoms or least budds *that tende to the fruit of eternall life.*"[5]

Scholars have often noted that Book I transforms conventional heroism to reinforce Protestant beliefs about humanity's dependence on grace in overcoming original sin. Most recently, John King has argued that Book I's syncretism accommodates such genres as hagiography, romance, pastoral, georgic, and tragedy to Reformation ideology.[6] In this chapter, I trace how Spenser creates an identity for himself as a Protestant in the Virgilian tradition specifically by revising episodes, motifs, and characterizations from the *Aeneid* to dispel their potential for Pelagian interpretation. The Reformers' critique of reason and the will challenged fundamental assumptions about human educability underlying the Renaissance canonization of epic as the didactic form par excellence. In transforming the *Aeneid* of medieval and Renaissance commentary into the *Aeneid* of the Reformation, Spenser ultimately revised its reception as a vehicle of moral instruction. With its emphasis on supernatural rather than natural agency, Book I stands less as a courtesy book urging its readers to perfect their own characters than as a testimony to faith alone as the grounds of their salvation.

Paul Alpers has argued that moments like Satyrane's admiration of Una's "wisedome heauenly rare" temper the book's darker, Calvinistic tendencies by stressing humanity's accomplishments in a state of unredeemed nature (I.vi.31).[7] But such passages typically fall outside Redcrosse's quest for salvation. In structuring his hero's adventures on Aeneas's career interpreted as an allegory of moral development, Spenser consistently departs from his Catholic precursors by emphasizing imputed merit. Redcrosse's perfection of character results not from his natural resistance to temptation but from God's willingness to forgive him for his failures and to strengthen him with grace. Just before Redcrosse encounters the dragon, Spenser foregrounds this Protestant recuperation of epic convention by transforming Virgil's opening lines:

> Faire Goddesse lay that furious fit aside,
>> Till I of warres and bloudy *Mars* do sing,
>> And Briton fields with Sarazin bloud bedyde,
>> Twixt that great faery Queene and Paynim king,
>> That with their horrour heauen and earth did ring,
>> A worke of labour long, and endlesse prayse:
>> But now a while let downe that haughtie string,
>> And to my tunes thy second tenor rayse,
> That I this man of God his godly armes may blaze.
>
> (xi.7)

Distinguishing Redcrosse's Christian heroism from Aeneas's martial valor, Spenser sets his epic apart from Virgil's. For at least the time being, he qualifies his classical model by singing not "arms and the man" but the "godly armes" of a "man of God." The alexandrine's double insistence on God challenges the conventional characterization of a hero as someone whose valiant accomplishments attest to his inherent strength. Everything that Redcrosse accomplishes is by virtue of his status as a "man of God."

Spenser explicitly constructs his turn from martial to Protestant heroism as a deferral rather than as a rejection of the *Aeneid*'s values. After he returns to the more temporal theme of Gloriana's wars, he promises to resume the "furious fit" he now asks the Muse to lay aside. The epic high style, which serves here as a metonymy for the *Aeneid*'s confidence in human agency, is appropriate for celebrating worldly accomplishments. As we shall see in the next chapter, Spenser readopts it in championing Guyon's powers of resistance and perseverance under temperance's more secular aegis. But since the struggle against diabolical powers rests in God's hands, it requires a humbler aesthetic glorifying God more than the human vehicles through whom He manifests His will.

Here as elsewhere in Book I, the question of poetic decorum is inseparable from Reformation polemic. Beneath Spenser's assertion that different conventions govern portrayals of spiritual heroism lies the Protestant tenet that human reason and volition, though valid enough in temporal affairs, have no role in matters of the spirit. Like "the furious fit," the haughtiness of the string that Spenser asks the Muse to "let downe" refers primarily to epic's conventional stylistic elevation. But the suggestion of arrogance raises a critique of epic's conventional values when applied to the struggle for salvation. From Book I's Protestant perspective on literary history, the championship of the natural man that typifies classical epic constitutes spiritual pride, the sin of attributing to human agency results that can only be achieved through grace.

In defending epic as the highest form of didactic poetry, commentators like Giraldi Cintio, Tasso, and Sidney maintained that heroes like Aeneas and Achilles inspired readers to emulate their virtues. But this familiar humanist argument assumes that people can perfect their nature through perseverance and self-discipline.[8] Since Redcrosse cannot overcome his spiritual foes by his own power, his story challenges epic's reception as a didactic genre. His adventures testify more to God's forgiveness than to human initiative. Although Spenser implicitly urges his readers to add faith unto their force, he insists that their faith is a divine gift rather than something that can be achieved through voluntary effort. Instead of inspiring them to do anything meriting their salvation, he encourages a passivity akin to Redcrosse's by reminding them that their destiny rests not in their hands but in God's promises to His elect.

The rest of this chapter examines how Spenser identifies himself as an English Protestant in the Virgilian tradition by transforming the Dido episode into Redcrosse's misadventures with Duessa. On one level, Duessa's repudiation suggests Spenser's abandonment of the Papist commitment to free will that dominated previous interpretations of epic heroism. As a personification of the Roman Church, Duessa embodies a Pelagian contempt toward grace. Her close association with Orgoglio links Redcrosse's involvement with her to his overconfidence in his own powers. As scholars like John Shroeder and Isabel MacCaffrey have noted, Spenser underscores this fatal trust in natural virtue when Redcrosse discards the Ephesian armor of God just before he sleeps with Duessa and succumbs to Orgoglio.[9]

But if Spenser denounces the Pelagianism inherent in the *Aeneid*'s canonization as a didactic epic, he also rejects Ariosto's view that nothing can liberate humanity from carnal bondage. As we have seen, the Alcina episode challenged the interpretation of Dido's abandonment as a testimony to reason's power over passion by suggesting that reason's ascendancy is only temporary: Ruggiero tries to rape Angelica only a few cantos after leaving Alcina's island. To an extent, the commentaries by Pigna, Fornari, Toscanella, Porcacchi, Bononome, and others neutralized Ariosto's critique by attributing to the *Furioso* the same didactic program that allegorists found in the *Aeneid*. But charges that the *Furioso* was indecent persisted in Italy through the end of the sixteenth century. While there are no records of a comparable debate over its status in England, the defensiveness of Harington's 1591 Preface suggests that its morality had often been challenged.[10] Although a Protestant readership may not have recognized it as such, the persistent concupiscence of characters like Ruggiero offered a critique of human dignity and volition similar in some ways to the Reformers'. Ariosto shared their sense that irresistible carnal impulses continually thwart humanity's natural efforts to improve itself. But their confidence in grace's power to rectify this corruption ultimately distinguishes their position from the irredeemable skepticism underlying Ariosto's comic surfaces.

Although we can never determine the precise way in which Spenser read a work as polyvalent and ambivalent as the *Furioso*, we can recover his use of it as a foil to his own revision of Virgil. As Alpers has argued, Spenser appreciates textures and surfaces of Ariosto's poetry that do not figure in its Renaissance allegorizations.[11] If Spenser's reading was not wholly mediated through the commentaries that reconciled the *Furioso* with the moralized *Aeneid*, he might well have recognized how it subverted Virgil's portrayal of Aeneas as a character capable of rectifying his errors. Spenser no more shares such confidence in human reason and volition than Ariosto, but his juxtapositions of Virgilian and Ariostan subtexts throughout *The Faerie Queene* treat the *Furioso* as a work that trivializes the *Aeneid*'s moral earnestness without offering a viable alternative to its ethical vision.

Almost paradoxically, the same theology of grace that discredits the lessons found in the moralized *Aeneid* provided Spenser both an answer to Ariosto and a means of recuperating Virgil's basic narrative structure. While he joins Ariosto in rejecting the commentators' belief in humanity's ability to overcome its faults in a state of nature, he maintains that lasting reformation is possible in a state of grace. In contrast to Ariosto's Ruggiero, who assaults Angelica only a few cantos after repenting his affair with Alcina, Redcrosse escapes from Duessa never again to lapse into concupiscence. Although he is empowered by grace rather than by merely natural virtues, his career is conspicuously closer to Aeneas's, as it was intepreted by Neo-Latin commentators, than that of any Ariostan hero. Like Aeneas, Redcrosse perseveres in his quest and is rewarded with marriage to a princess and a kingdom charged with eschatological significance.

In modeling Redcrosse's career on Aeneas's, Spenser continually recasts Virgilian passages that Ariosto had parodied in the *Furioso*. The next sections of this chapter examine Spenser's transformations of two episodes, Aeneas's encounters with Polydorus and Mercury, that demonstrate the Virgilian hero's ability to heed monitory examples and divine decrees. In each case, Spenser situates himself between the Pelagianism of Virgil's text as interpreted in the commentary tradition and the cynicism characterizing Ariosto's revisions of it. Redcrosse's inability even to understand the warnings that he receives about Duessa attests to a darker sense of humanity's carnal bondage than Aeneas's immediate obedience to Polydorus and Mercury. At the same time, however, his final rescue from Duessa's influence by Arthur and Una promises a more permanent liberation than does Ruggiero's escape from Alcina.

Polydorus Revisited

The Fradubio episode brings a Virgilian subtext, Aeneas's encounter with Polydorus, into dialogue with its Ariostan parody, Ruggiero's conversation with the arborified Astolfo. By appealing to Protestant doctrine, Spenser eventually "overgoes" features of both texts that might subvert his accommodation of Virgilian forms to Elizabethan cultural conditions.[12] The Polydorus episode attests to Aeneas's characteristic ability to correct his errors and profit from monitory examples: the moment the murdered prince warns him about the dangers of lingering in Thrace, Aeneas leads his Trojans away to safety. Ariosto challenges Virgil's confidence in human educability by replacing Polydorus's admonitions with Astolfo's complaints about the futility of trying to protect Alcina's future victims against her charms: "I have gladly given you warning, not that I imagine it will be of any use to you" (*Io te n'ho dato volentieri aviso; / non ch'io mi creda che debbia giovarte, OF* VI.53). Astolfo's skepticism is confirmed by Ruggiero's struggle to convince himself of the unreliability of Astolfo's counsel as soon as he lays eyes on Alcina: "Everything he had been told about her he dismissed as false" (*e tutto quel ch'udito avea di lei, / stima esser falso*, VII.17). Preferring to believe that Astolfo's metamorphosis punishes his ingratitude to his hostess, Ruggiero willfully cooperates with her deceptions by reinterpreting Astolfo's account of her malice as slander. Here and throughout the *Furioso,* Ariosto suggests that reason's inevitable surrender to concupiscence undermines even the most committed resolutions to resist temptation. In the presence of sufficient enticement, Ruggiero's reason virtually panders to concupiscence.

Throughout Redcrosse's conversation with a speaking tree, Spenser too challenges Virgil's confidence in human initiative. But he also rejects Ariosto's unrelenting skepticism. His darker tone aligns him more conspicuously with Virgil than Ariosto and suggests his desire to reestablish a place in epic for certain conviction. Although he follows Ariosto in presenting Fradubio's metamorphosis as a consequence of his carnal involvement with a sorceress, he excludes the comic touches that distinguished Ariosto from Virgil. When Aeneas first tries to pluck a branch from Polydorus, dripping gore and a low groan signal the onset of a supernatural experience. Ariosto undercuts the solemnity of the Virgilian scene by replacing these omens with Astolfo's complaints about the fidgety horse that Ruggiero tethers to his branches. Spenser reestablishes Virgilian decorums by restoring "gory bloud" and "a piteous yelling voyce" as signs that the hero has violated a sacred place (I.ii.30, 31). Whereas Ruggiero jumped back in his astonishment and apologized to the tree, Redcrosse, like Aeneas, is paralyzed with horror:

> My body shudders, cold. My blood
> is frozen now with terror.

> mihi frigidus horror
> membra quatit gelidusque coit formidine sanguis.
> (*Aen.* III.29–30 [M:39–40])

> Astond he stood, and vp his haire did houe,
> And with that suddein horror could no member moue.
> (*FQ* I.ii.31)

As in the *Aeneid,* the spectacle temporarily turns the hero himself into a kind of inanimate object by freezing his blood and leaving him stone-like ("astond") with terror.

The introduction of a second human-tree, Fraelissa, distinguishes the episode structurally from both its Virgilian and Ariostan models. Since Fradubio betrayed Fraelissa for Duessa, however, her appearance reinvests the episode with the pathos of victimized innocence that dominated Aeneas's encounter with Polydorus. Like Virgil's Polydorus—a young prince murdered for his gold—but unlike Ariosto's Astolfo, Fraelissa does nothing to merit her fate. It stands as a testimony solely to Duessa's malevolence. Alcina's wicked deeds result from a perverse sexual appetite that she herself cannot control. Duessa's deeds, by contrast, arise from a fundamental hostility toward humanity. Although her cold-blooded treachery is more reminiscent of the Thracian king than Alcina, her malice surpasses even his in its quintessentially diabolical nature.

Spenser revives Virgil's darker tonalities primarily to challenge Ariosto's analysis of human motivation. If Ariosto rejects the possibility of heroes like Aeneas, who can clearly perceive and follow the course of virtue, he also qualifies his villains' malevolence. Alcina is a victim of forces she can neither understand nor control. Ariosto presents her not as a murderess but as a nymphomaniac who disposes of each lover in succession as soon as she tires of him. Since her particular infatuation with Ruggiero results from a spell that Atlante casts on her, she is not fully in conscious control of her actions. Nor is Atlante himself acting malevolently: he orchestrates the affair between Alcina and Ruggiero, his foster son, to forestall a prophecy of Ruggiero's death. Ariosto ultimately rejects the dichotomies that Virgil establishes between the Thracian king's treachery and Aeneas's valor to create a world in which the actions of everyone reflect a madness inherent in the human condition.[13] Absolute praise and condemnation yield to the bemused pity typifying the *sorriso* detected by critics like Croce throughout Ariosto's poetry.[14]

From Spenser's perspective on literary history, Ariosto's sardonic humor betrays a superficial apprehension of evil. By embracing the Protestant categories of election and reprobation, he restores the absolute moral distinctions dissolved by Ariosto's evocations of universal madness. For Spenser, the sorceress is never fully unmasked until her malice is judged according to the inexorable canons of Christian allegory. Behind Alcina lies the well-intentioned magic of Atlante, but behind Duessa and Archimago lurks the "Prince of darknesse and dead night" whom Archimago invokes in casting his spells (I.i.37). If the *Furioso* grounds humanity's viciousness in its uncontrollable passions, Book I of *The Faerie Queene* grounds it in the corruptions of original sin that make people vulnerable to Satanic deceptions. Spenser dismisses Ariosto's tendency to explain evil in terms of human psychology as a blindness to its overarching theological and metaphysical determinants.

A Protestant emphasis on the intellectual impairment that results from original sin underlies Spenser's principal departure from both the *Aeneid* and the *Furioso*. Whereas Aeneas and Astolfo are warned in advance of the dangers awaiting them, Redcrosse only hears about Duessa after he has already met her and succumbed to her enchantments. He plucks Fradubio's branch in the first place to make a garland for her, and she is present throughout the episode. If Ruggiero's predicament exemplified passion's capacity to subvert reason and a resolved will, Redcrosse's inability even to perceive that he is being warned suggests reason's fundamental unreliability in questions of salvation. As William Nelson has observed, Fradubio's account of Fraelissa's repudiation strikingly recalls Redcrosse's previous treatment of Una.[15] But Redcrosse's failure to recognize such parallels testifies to a blindness so impervious to natural enlightenment that it can only be relieved by grace.

Yet the possibility of such grace in the "liuing well" that will restore Fradubio and Fraelissa "to former kynd" reestablishes the confidence in human perfectibility that Ariosto rejected (ii.43). As a revision of its Italian subtext, the Fradubio episode suggests that Ariosto failed to discern not only the cause of humanity's carnal bondage but also its sole means of escape. Beneath the *Furioso*'s comic surface, Spenser sees only a despairing vision of our subjection to drives and impulses that can never be bridled. He shares Ariosto's view that the commentators from Fulgentius through Boccaccio were mistaken in championing natural perseverance as the means to perfect the hero's character. Nevertheless, he maintains that it can be brought to perfection through Christ's imputed merits. If Ariosto transformed the Polydorus episode into a statement about humanity's ineducability, Spenser recasts it as a parable about humanity's dependence on grace.

From Mercury to Orgoglio, Arthur, and Despaire

Spenser continues to define himself against both Ariosto and the Virgilian commentary tradition by revising the primary topos, the hero's abandonment of the woman jeopardizing his quest, through which epic poets distinguished themselves from suspect influences. In representing the supernatural intervention that frees Redcrosse from Duessa's enchantments, he once more plays Ariostan against Virgilian effects to construct his own Protestant version of Mercury's command that Aeneas abandon Dido. Like Polydorus's warning about the dangers of Thrace, Mercury's admonition leaves Aeneas stunned:

> The vision stunned Aeneas, struck him dumb;
> his terror held his hair erect; his voice
> held fast within his jaws.

> At uero Aeneas aspectu obmutuit amens,
> arrectaeque horrore comae et uox faucibus haesit.
>
> (IV.279–80 [M:373–75])

But as we have seen, he quickly regains his composure and abandons Dido in what commentators allegorized as a triumph of *ingenium* or *eloquentia* over *libido*. Mercury, a personification of eloquence empowered by reason, liberates the soul from passion. In the *Furioso*, Ariosto diminishes reason's authority over desire by supplementing Melissa's Mercury-like rebukes with promises of Bradamante's love. At the same time, he reduces the shock of her confrontation with the offending hero. If Melissa proves less austere than Mercury in offering Ruggiero consolation, Ruggiero appears less traumatized than Aeneas in encountering a supernatural messenger. Although he is ashamed, his hair is not standing on end and he is not frozen with terror.

For Spenser, the choice between Virgil's and Ariosto's accounts of the intervention becomes a choice between the inexorable voice of reason demanding the suppression of passion and the more indulgent voice of "truth [tempered] with warmth of feeling" (*in quanto il vero e l'affezion comporta*, OF VII.69). In critiquing the ethical alternatives posed by his precursors, he rewrites Mercury's descent at least three times. Orgoglio and Despair provide demonic parodies of the topos that undermine the commentators' prescription of eloquence as a remedy for sensual bondage.[16] Between their appearances, Arthur and Una's redemption of Redcrosse from Orgoglio's dungeon corrects Mercury's intervention by countering carnal impulses not with reasonable persuasion but with forgiveness and sanctification.

The moment that Redcrosse reaches the nadir of sensual abandonment, subtextual pressures make us expect a messenger like Mercury or Melissa to interrupt his dalliance. "Pourd out in loosnesse on the grassy grownd, / Both carelesse of his health, and of his fame," Redcrosse is as oblivious to his reputation as Aeneas and Ruggiero were when Mercury and Melissa discover them dressed in "the delicious softness" of their mistresses' apparel. Like them, he has succumbed fully to "sloth and sensuality" (*FQ* I.vii.7; *OF* VII.53). But instead of a messenger to rehabilitate him either through rebukes or consolations, Redcrosse encounters Orgoglio, an outward manifestation of his own interior corruption. While preserving the trauma of the Virgilian subtext, Spenser suppresses its morally recuperative effects. The horror that first leaves Aeneas stunned and silent when Mercury encounters him spurs him on to Latium immediately afterwards. Redcrosse's enervation, which stems as much from the poisons of Duessa's well as from his panic before Orgoglio, persists when he is thrown into a dungeon where "all his vitall powres / Decayd, and all his flesh shronk vp like withered flowres" (viii.41).

Scholars have paid considerable attention to Orgoglio's relationship to the Titans through his maternal descent from Gea, the Earth.[17] But they have overlooked how his paternal descent from "blustring *Aeolus*" raises a critique of

Virgil and of his cultural reception as a champion of reason's ability to contain
passion (vii.9). Some Renaissance mythographers and commentators implicitly
linked Aeolus to Mercury by treating him as another embodiment of reason
controlling the storms of anger and desire.[18] But when Spenser introduces Aeolus
as Orgoglio's father, he recalls him more as the destructive agent who figures
in Fulgentius's and Bernard's earlier treatments of the storm episode as an alle-
gory of birth. Deriving his name from *eonolus*, the destruction of the spirit,
Bernard sees him as the birth process itself that oppresses the divine spirit with
"the heaviness . . . and . . . passions of the flesh" (7). This Aeolus, rather than
the agent of rational restraint honored by Balbi, fathers Orgoglio as an embod-
iment of carnal bondage:

> The greatest Earth his vncouth mother was,
> And blustring *Aeolus* his boasted sire,
> Who with his breath, which through the world doth pas,
> Her hollow womb did secretly inspire
> And fild her hidden caues with stormie yre,
> That she conceiu'd.
> (I.vii.9)

While Virgil's description of Aeolia as a vast womb "pregnant with the raging
south winds" (*feta furentibus Austris*, I.51, translation mine) underlies the myth
of Orgoglio's conception, Spenser presents the chaos of a terrestrial womb filled
with stormy winds as something that Aeolus causes rather than governs. Like
Fulgentius and Bernard, Spenser associates Aeolus with passion itself rather than
with the reason and prudence that overcome it.

Redcrosse's encounter with Orgoglio recasts neither Mercury's descent nor
the Aeolus episode according to their commonplace interpretation as allegories
about reason's power to free humanity from carnal bondage. Yet another re-
vision of Mercury's descent, the Despaire episode, advances this critique by
suggesting that reasonable persuasion can lead only to a conviction of sinfulness
but not to salvation. In Virgil, Aeneas's sudden decision to abandon Dido dem-
onstrates his absolute obedience to the gods. But the allegorization of Mercury's
admonitions either as *ingenium*, sheer force of mind, or as the reproof of some
outspoken or trustworthy friend suggests that Aeneas's change of heart results
from a sudden realization of his sinfulness. This interpretation culminates in *La
Gerusalemme Liberata*, when Ubaldo liberates Rinaldo from Armida by showing
him a mirror that reveals his effeminate degradation (XVI.30). Behind both
Tasso's fiction and the didactic readings of the *Aeneid* lies the assumption that
once the hero recognizes his faults, he can correct them through a free exercise
of his will.

Spenserians have often glossed the conflict between Despaire's indictment of Redcrosse's sins and Una's emphasis on atonement through grace as a conflict between the Old and New Covenants.[19] But that theological debate also establishes *The Faerie Queene* as a Protestant epic opposing the Pelagian confidence in human educability that underlies the *Aeneid*'s Renaissance canonization. Like Mercury, Despaire primarily instills in the hero a conviction of his failures. Even as Mercury upbraided Aeneas for his involvement with Dido, Despaire condemns Redcrosse for his fornication with Duessa:

> Is not enough, that to this Ladie milde
> Thou falsed hast thy faith with periurie,
> And sold thy selfe to serue *Duessa* vilde,
> With whom in all abuse thou hast thy selfe defilde?
>
> (ix.46)

Like Orgoglio, Despaire leaves Redcrosse quaking and fainting in a fit of terror that recalls Aeneas's astonishment on hearing the gods' decrees. Although he effectively reveals Redcrosse's corruption, he offers him no means to overcome it. Instead of restoring Redcrosse to his quest, Despaire's appropriation of Mercury's rhetorical strategies drives him toward suicide.

Within the literary history that Spenser constructs, Despaire's descent from Mercury suggests that eloquent reminders of one's depravity lead only to desperation in questions of human salvation. As varied and compelling as Despaire's syllogisms might seem, they lead to one inexorable conclusion:

> Is not his law, Let euery sinner die:
> Die shall all flesh? what then must needs be donne,
> Is it not better to doe willinglie,
> Then linger, till the glasse be all out ronne?
> Death is the end of woes: die soone, O faeries sonne.
>
> (ix.47)

As Hooker argues in *The Laws of Ecclesiastical Polity,* "the light of nature is never able to finde out any way of obtayning the reward of blisse, but by performing exactly the duties and workes of righteousnes." Since no one is capable of such an exact performance, reason fosters only the despairing conviction that "all flesh is guilty of that for which God hath threatened eternally to punish."[20] By showing how Redcrosse's conviction of his sinfulness leads to despondency rather than to renewed perseverance in his quest, Spenser suggests that the ethical vision of his predecessors in the Virgilian tradition was tragically limited. Their overconfidence in nature blinded them to humanity's only true comfort.

Spenser overcomes that blindness by presenting Una and Arthur, the characters who finally help Redcrosse resume his quest, as agents of grace and forgiveness rather than of eloquence informed by natural reason. When Arthur rescues Redcrosse from Orgoglio's dungeon, he deliberately refrains from discussing what has happened: "The things, that grieuous were to do, or beare, / Them to renew, I wote, breeds no delight" (viii.44). Arthur's litotes suggests a delicacy and tact that conspicuously distinguishes him from Mercury. Throughout the episode, he avoids upbraidings that would breed only self-loathing and despair.

Una departs even more from Mercury's precedent by transferring the blame for Redcrosse's failures onto an "euill starre" that

> On you hath fround, and pourd his influence bad,
> That of your selfe ye thus berobbed arre,
> And this misseeming hew your manly looks doth marre.
>
> (viii.42)

Since Una usually speaks in Christian terms of "faith" and "mercy," her remarks about astral influence seem out of character. But we cannot dismiss them as mere courtesy toward the suffering knight. The passage's dense allusiveness suggests Spenser's struggle to define himself as a Protestant poet against the "influence bad" of his continental precursors. Mercury accuses Aeneas of neglecting the "labor of praise" (*laude laborem*, IV.273, translation mine), Melissa charges Ruggiero with forgetting the promise of his destiny (*OF* VII.58), and Ubaldo upbraids Rinaldo for the lethargy that "has so lulled [his] manhood" (*qual letargo ha sì sopita / la tua virtute*, GL XVI.33). Una's observations that Redcrosse's "manly looks" have been marred by an "euill starre" suggests that Spenser's epic precursors have misrepresented human errancy by overlooking its supernatural cause. In the light of nature, evil seems a matter of distorted faculty psychology, of reason's subversion by passion. Through the illumination of grace, however, it becomes a question of diabolical forces contending for the human spirit. From faith's higher perspective, the accusations lodged against Redcrosse's predecessors seem misplaced. The individual sinner needs pardon and encouragement rather than castigation.

Spenser departs from his precursors both in attributing Redcrosse's truancy to forces beyond his own psychology and in attributing his recovery to grace rather than to self-mastery. In this Christian *Aeneid,* "heauenly mercies" rather than divine castigations restore the hero to his quest (ix.53). Ariosto anticipated Spenser's mitigation of Mercury's severity; as we have seen, Melissa not only rebuked Ruggiero but encouraged him with promises of Bradamante's love. But Spenser overgoes Ariosto's revision, first by rejecting Mercury's rebukes altogether and then by transcendentalizing the love that frees the hero from carnal bondage. From the perspective of Spenserian Holinesse, the human "affection" with which Ariosto tempers reason is no more effective against diabolical temptations than is reason alone. If "blisse may not abide" in any "state of mortall man," the insufficiency of Bradamante's love to contain Ruggiero's sensuality would come as no surprise to Spenser (viii.44). Beneath Ariosto's laughter, he recognized the same despair that he heard in the Virgilian commentators' emphasis on natural *ingenium* and *eloquentia*.

The Redemption of Epic Form

In the remainder of this chapter, I want to examine how Book I's formal peculiarities reinforce Spenser's stance against Ariosto's skepticism toward human educability. As we have seen, Ariosto's digressiveness serves as a structural correlative for abandoning the commentators' view that passion might be resisted through rational discipline. Just as erotic arousal continually subverts Ruggiero's quest, the impulse to digress continually frustrates the Ariostan narrator's efforts to complete his story. In Book I of *The Faerie Queene,* Spenser constructs romance digression as a threat to his vocation as a Protestant laureate by associating it with Redcrosse's deviation from his quest. As Patricia Parker has argued, the book explores the relationship between "error" as an assessment of moral action and as a description of narrative structure.[21] The moment Redcrosse abandons Una for Duessa, Spenser abandons the unified plot that critics like Minturno and Pellegrino proclaimed essential to poetry in the Virgilian tradition.[22] Just when the hero falls under Duessa's spell, Spenser seems to fall increasingly under Ariostan influence. The story of Redcrosse's mission to rescue Una's parents from the dragon fragments into multiple, interlaced accounts of his adventures with Duessa and Lucifera and of her encounters with the lion, Corceca and Abessa, Sansloy, and the Satyrs.

But as soon as grace redeems Redcrosse from the consequences of his affair with Duessa, Spenser returns to a more unified plot conspicuously modeled on the *Aeneid*. The hero's final escape from Duessa mirrors Spenser's own escape from Ariostan influence. Although the Alcina episode figures prominently as a subtext throughout the book's central cantos, the last three have little in common with the *Furioso*. What Spenser embraces instead is the Christian allegorization of Aeneas's career after his departure from Carthage. Ruggiero's adventures on Logistilla's island partially inform Redcrosse's experiences at the House of Holinesse, but Spenser's primary model is Ariosto's own source, Aeneas's descent into the underworld to hear Anchises's prophecy. Ruggiero soon forgets what Logistilla taught him and relapses into concupiscence, but the knowledge that Redcrosse receives from Contemplation, like that which Aeneas learns in the underworld, inspires him to complete his quest.

As Hamilton has remarked, Spenser parodies Aeneas's descent as a quest for arcane knowledge when Duessa descends to Aesculapius with the wounded Sansjoy.[23] But since Redcrosse himself never visits an underworld per se, critics have overlooked how the House of Holinesse provides the true type of the same classical topos parodied earlier. Both episodes derive from the same Virgilian source that Bernard, Landino, and others glossed as the hero's initiation into the contemplative life. When Duessa and Night take on the Sibyl's role in leading Sansjoy down "the yawning gulfe of deepe *Auernus* hole," they see only the horrors that Virgil describes (v.31). Never entering the Elysian fields, they seek physical healing for their charge rather than spiritual wisdom. But the moment Redcrosse approaches the House of Holinesse, the narrative draws closer to the Virgilian episode interpreted as an education in divine truth.

Throughout the episode, Spenser models details of Redcrosse's experiences on Aeneas's in the underworld. Caelia's surprise at seeing an armed knight entering the House recalls Charon's at seeing a living hero among the departed shades:

> Whoever you may be who make your way,
> so armed, down to our waters, tell me now
> why you have come. . . .
> > no living bodies
> can take their passage in the ship of Styx.

> quisquis es, armatus qui nostra ad flumina tendis,
> fare age, quid uenias iam istinc . . .
> corpora uiua nefas Stygia uectare carina.
> [*Aen.* VI.388–89, 391 [M:512–14, 515–16])

> Strange thing it is an errant knight to seek
> > Here in this place, or any other wight,
> > That hither turnes his steps.
> > > (*FQ* I.x.10)

Guided by the Sibyl, Aeneas expresses remorse to Dido for the consequences of abandoning her and later hears the scourgings and groans of the damned. Guided by Una, Fidelia, and Mercie, Redcrosse grieves "with remembrance of his wicked wayes" and suffers "the paines of hell" (x.21, 32). Una hears "his ruefull shriekes" from the dungeons of penance (x.28). Redcrosse no more enters the Elysian fields than does Duessa or Sansjoy, but he sees their Christian equivalent from afar when his reenactment of Aeneas's descent culminates in his ascent of the Mount of Contemplation.[24]

As in his revisions of Polydorus's and Mercury's admonitions, Spenser recasts the *catabasis* to reconcile Virgilian convention with Protestantism. Redcrosse's education, unlike Aeneas's Neoplatonic one in Bernard's and Landino's commentaries, conforms to the Reformation's emphasis on faith in the Gospels.[25] Redcrosse learns about neither cosmology nor the exalted powers of human intellection. Figures like Mercie and Fidelia tutor him instead in things "that weaker wit of man could neuer reach," such as divine miracles and forgiveness for his former sins (x.19). His experiences particularly revise the terms in which Renaissance critics upheld epic as a medium of moral instruction. Instead of learning how to resist carnal inclinations, Redcrosse learns that grace alone can overcome them:

> What man is he, that boasts of fleshly might,
>   And vaine assurance of mortality,
>   Which all so soone, as it doth come to fight,
>   Against spirituall foes, yeelds by and by,
>   Or from the field most cowardly doth fly?
>   Ne let the man ascribe it to his skill,
>   That thorough grace hath gained victory.
>   If any strength we haue, it is to ill,
> But all the good is Gods, both power and eke will.
>
> (x.1)

According to the House of Holinesse's reformed theology, not only the military heroism celebrated in the *Aeneid* itself but the moral heroism found in it by commentators from Fulgentius to Boccaccio, Vegius, and Badius suggests the sinful Pride that Redcrosse encounters in so many forms. Spenser offers his own Protestant *Aeneid* less as a courtesy book instructing its readers how to resist the "spiritual foes" than as an exhortation that they too must learn to trust in God's mercy.

As the House of Holinesse episode's climax, Redcrosse's encounter with Contemplation parallels and revises Aeneas's conversation with Anchises at the end of Book VI. More than anything else in the *Aeneid*, Anchises's sermon on cosmology defied commentators' attempts to assimilate Virgil's paganism to Christianity. In *The City of God*, Augustine rejects Anchises's implication that the sufferings of the wicked after death are purgatorial.[26] Its conspicuously Pythagorean elements refuted promises of individual, heavenly transcendence. Describing Anchises's vision of recycled souls as "sour blackberries" thrown in the midst of "sweet apples," Fulgentius wonders why Virgil "put out the torch of

[his] luminous wisdom" in writing the passage (133). Virgil's spirit apologizes for "so foolish a line of defense" by reminding Fulgentius that pre-Christian knowledge is limited: "I would not be a pagan if I did not leaven so many Stoic truths with a pinch of Epicurean foolishness" (132, 133).[27] Gavin Douglas remarks in a gloss that Aeneas and the Sibyl meet "godly and lerned pristis prophetes and gud religious men" when they enter Elysium (3:54). But shortly afterwards, Douglas dismisses Anchises's doctrines as "Pithagoras vane opinion of the transformacion of saulis in new bodies" (3:58). In the standard Tudor translation of the *Aeneid,* Phaer and Twyne gloss them similarly as "pagans opinions."[28] According to Sir John Harington, "no passage of ye booke vyrgill doth swarve more from the rewls of trew fayth then in this, bearing in hand that sowls are put into new bodyes, after theyr fyrst bodyes have been ded and buryed many yeers." Harington devotes an entire section of his commentary on Book VI to refuting Virgil's views on the soul's "transycion."[29]

In casting himself as a Protestant Virgil, Spenser rejects Anchises's Pythagoreanism entirely by transforming the vision of souls about to be reborn into the world into Redcrosse's vision of saints entering the New Jerusalem. When Aeneas asks about the people crowding the Lethe's banks, Anchises identifies them as spirits purified after their death by water, wind, and fire (VI.740–43). As an analogue to Catholic speculation about purgatory, this aspect of Virgil's cosmology rests particularly uneasily beside Reformation teaching. In glossing the passage, Harington observed that "the Pagans opinion of Purgatory . . . hath so great affynity with the popysh that they seem to have spronge one of an other" (3). The Twyne-Phaer translation identified the passage as a description of "the painims purgatory" (Gloss to VI.778). Melanchthon skirted around the embarrassing issue by suggesting that Achises's three purgations allude to different ways of disposing of corpses rather than to divergent eschatological conditions.[30] When Redcrosse echoes Aeneas's inquiry by asking about the "vnknowen nation . . . empeopled" in the New Hierusalem (x.56), Contemplation's emphasis on the sinner's immediate and imputed justification counters Anchises's portrayal of the soul's purgation as a recurrent process:

> Faire knight (quoth he) *Hierusalem* that is,
>   The new *Hierusalem,* that God has built
>   For those to dwell in, that are chosen his,
>   His chosen people purg'd from sinfull guilt,
>   With pretious bloud, which cruelly was spilt
>   On cursed tree . . .
>   (I.x.57)

Once more, Spenser stresses humanity's dependence on grace rather than on its own actions and experiences. The saints living in the New Hierusalem do not have to undergo the tortures endured by their Virgilian counterparts to be cleansed of their sins: Christ suffered their torments for them when he died at Calvary. His one perfect and eternal sacrifice replaces the cycles of individual purgation central to Anchises's understanding of the cosmos.

Substituting a Protestant for a pagan eschatology overcomes the pathos of loss and alienation that pervades Aeneas's descent to the underworld. Although Anchises remarks that a few fortunate souls can finally enter Elysium (*pauci laeta arua tenemus*), their reduction to pure sparks of ether (*purumque . . . aetherium*) suggests the extinction of individual personality (VI.744, 746–47). While Aeneas sees the spirits who will someday govern the Roman state that he will establish, they belong to a future that he will never personally experience. By contrast, Contemplation assures Redcrosse that he will one day join the saints whom he beholds in the New Hierusalem. As the Augustan myth of empire yields to the Christian myth of individual salvation, the hero's education ends with his discovery of his personal origin and destiny rather than with a revelation of national history.

When Aeneas sees that the newly cleansed souls are eager to resume a corporal existence, he cannot fathom their "wild longing for the light of earth" (*quae lucis miseris tam dira cupido?* VI.721 [M:952]). His contempt for the world recurs in Redcrosse's desire either to remain with Contemplation or to enter heaven immediately: "O let me not (quoth he) then turne againe / Backe to the world, whose ioyes so fruitlesse are" (I.x.63). But like the souls of future Romans and like Aeneas himself, Redcrosse must fulfill his historical obligations. His descent from the Mount of Contemplation marks a dramatic departure from the Neoplatonic commentary tradition and a reaffirmation of Virgil's original narrative structure. Privileging the *vita contemplativa* as the highest good of human existence, both Bernard's commentary and Landino's *Disputationes Camaldulenses* end abruptly after glossing Book VI. Spenser's continuation of Redcrosse's story beyond the House of Holinesse suggests that true contemplation, the meditation on Christ's promise to redeem His elect, reinvigorates commitment to the *vita activa*, interpreted in a Protestant sense as sanctification in this life.[31]

Once more, Spenser redeems Virgil's narrative from the Catholic hermeneutic traditions governing its reception on the continent. For him as for Virgil, the *catabasis* stands not as an end in itself but as a step toward a higher goal that Redcrosse achieves in his apocalyptic encounter with the dragon and in his subsequent betrothal to Una. Neither withdrawing from the world in a Neoplatonic rapture nor relapsing like Ruggiero into concupiscence, Redcrosse emerges as a truer Aeneas in his unwavering commitment to duty.

For modern readers, his career's final stages look even less Virgilian than his visit to the House of Holinesse. But here too, Spenser interweaves biblical and Virgilian typologies in ways that become apparent when *The Faerie Queene* is read against the background of Renaissance commentary and of Vegius's frequently reprinted Thirteenth Book.[32] Like Book XII of the *Aeneid*, canto xi of the Legend of Holinesse concludes when the hero vanquishes his epic antagonist. As long as we read the *Aeneid* outside an allegorical hermeneutic, the pathos of Turnus's defeat seems to contrast with the jubilation accompanying the dragon's death at Redcrosse's hand. But the same medieval and Renaissance commentators who glossed Dido's abandonment as a triumph over lust allegorized Turnus's death as a triumph over rage and other vices. By identifying Turnus as Satan, Vegius read the episode in allegorical terms identical with those governing *The Faerie Queene*:

> Aeneas . . . sails this great and wide sea of earthly life. . . . Then, before he attains to the promised rest in Latium, he meets his enemy, Turnus, that is, the devil.

> Tum nauigat hoc mare mundi magnum et spaciosum . . . Tum priusque, promissam latio quietem assequatur turnum id est dyabolum infestum habet.[33]

The eschatological significance of Redcrosse's battle with the dragon as Christ's ultimate confrontation with Satan is only a step beyond the moral allegory found by commentators in the *Aeneid*'s last book.

In both Spenser's Legend of Holinesse and the thirteen-book Renaissance *Aeneid*, the hero's struggle culminates in a marriage that rewards his valor. Vegius's Book XIII splits into two parts, the first treating Turnus's funeral and the second Aeneas's wedding. Canto xii of the Legend of Holinesse divides similarly, with stanzas 1–12 focusing on the wonder raised by the dragon's carcass and 13–24 on the betrothal festivities. Details throughout the canto reinforce this structural parallel to develop Redcrosse's eventual marriage as a reenactment of Aeneas's. The joy brought to Adam's subjects by the dragon's death contrasts with the starkness of Turnus's defeat in Virgil. But in Vegius, Turnus's death delights the Trojans and eventually even Latinus's war-weary people. Honoring Aeneas's valor and celebrating his union with Lavinia, Trojans and Latins dance to the sound of the harp; Adam's "ioyous people" similarly strew the streets with their garments and bring Redcrosse to the palace "with shaumes, and trompets, and with Clarions sweet" (xii.13).

Vegius's transformation of Turnus's death from tragedy into an apocalyptic triumph of good over evil culminates when the counselor Drances describes him as a scourge inflicted on the Latins:

> But rather more encenst, wilde fires from flaming iawes did spue,
> And frantickly himself, and vs, to causelesse warres he drue . . .
> Thee all the Italians wish aboue the golden starres to reign.
> Thee great in war, and great thy force in heauenly armes to streine
> They do extoll . . .
>
> . . . and do reioyce
> For Turnus slaine by thy right hand, with loud triumphing voyce.
>   (P-T XIII.363–64, 371–73, 377–78)

>   quin acrius ignem
> Spumabat ferus ore vomens, bellumque ciebat.
> [Te] omnes Itali super aurea mittunt
> Sidera, et ingentem bello, et caelestibus armis
> Extollunt, et vera canunt praeconia voces.
>   . . . Turnumque sub armis
> Exsultant cecidisse tuis.[34]
> (350–51, 359–61, 365–66)

Spenser adopts Vegius's striking metaphorical transformation of Turnus into a dragon spewing "wilde fires from flaming iawes" and bringing misery to a nation. In both poems, men and women of all ages praise the hero as their liberator and embrace him as their lord (xii.6). Their championship of him as their new ruler hints that their current king, who has shown himself incapable of conquering his enemy, is too old to rule. Just as Vegius refers to Latinus's "tired age" with the regularity of an epithet, Spenser depicts Adam, "that aged Sire, the Lord of all that land" coming to view the dragon's body with "feeble speed" (P-T XIII.452; FQ I.xii.3). Yet both writers treat the old king as respectfully and sympathetically as possible. By freely selecting the heroes as their sons-in-law and future heirs, Latinus and Adam neutralize any potential crisis in confidence and guarantee a peaceful succession.

In offering his daughter's hand, each king hails the upcoming marriage as a compensation for past miseries:

> But now come on most noble *Troian* lord, since all the spring
> Of strife is gone, and cause of fact so vile and sinfull thing,
> Accept thy wife, and marriage erst promised of yore.
> Some realmes I haue, and towne with walles full strong surrounded store.
>   (P-T XIII.448–51)

Nunc age, magne Phrygum ductor, quando omnis origo
Seditionis abest, et tanti criminis auctor,
Connubiis succede, et promissis hymenaeis.
Sunt mihi regna, iacent ereptis oppida muris.

(434–37)

Then said the royall Pere in sober wise;
    Deare Sonne, great beene the euils, which ye bore
    From first to last in your late enterprise
    . . .

    But since now safe ye seised haue the shore,
    And well arriued are, (high God be blest)
Let vs deuize of ease and euerlasting rest.

    By dew desert of noble cheualree,
Both daughter and eke kingdome, lo I yield to thee.

(*FQ* I.xii.17, 20)

The displaced Roman customs joining Redcrosse and Una with "sacred rites and vowes for euer to abyde" (xii.36) stem in part from the wedding in Vegius:

Then were the Princes both in wedlock band eternall knit,
And *Hymen* songes were sung, with prayses great for Princes fit.
Then shoutinges shrill, and muttrings loude of men mount vp to skies
Of such as wish them well, whose voice the court through ringing flies.

(P-T XIII.491–94)

    Tum vero aeterno iunguntur foedera nexu
    Connubi, multaque canunt cum laude hymenaeum:
    Dehinc plausus fremitusque altum super aera mittunt,
    Et laetam vocem per regia tecta volutant.

(474–77)

The anachronistic sacramentalism of Vegius's reference to wedlock's "band eternall" paves the way for Spenser's Christianization of such rites as sprinklings with wine and water and the lighting of Hymen's "bushy Teade" (xii.37). In Vegius, Lavinia and Aeneas's frugal wedding banquet contrasts with the lavish supper in Carthage: no troops of servants wait upon the tables and the guests eat only until their "hunger slaked was with meates" (*compressa fames,* 509). Redcrosse and Una's "bare and plaine" supper contrasts similarly with the orgiastic feasts at Lucifera's hall, where "excessiue *Gluttonie*" serves as steward (xii.14; iv.43). After an exchange of gifts between father-in-law and hero, Aeneas and Redcrosse both recount their respective adventures. According to Vegius, Aeneas tells "sometime of *Troyan* chaunces hard to treat, and *Greekish* bandes" (*Nunc duros Troiae casus, gentesque Pelasgas,* XIII.511, P-T 533), the same stories he tells Dido in Books II and III of the *Aeneid* proper. Redcrosse does not talk about Greeks and Trojans. But by echoing the *Aeneid*'s opening invocation, Spenser's reference to "the too importune fate, / That heapd on him so many wrathfull wreakes" identifies him as a second Aeneas suffering many hardships in fulfilling his destiny (xii.16).

In his own Christian allegorization of the *Aeneid,* Vegius glosses Aeneas's marriage as his heavenly reward for persevering against evil. Spenser follows Vegius in presenting Redcrosse's betrothal as a reward for victory over evil, but he departs from his Catholic precursor by grounding that victory in imputed rather than in natural powers of perseverance. In accordance with the Protestant view of salvation, Redcrosse's "reward" results from God's free election rather than from his own intrinsic merit. As Hume and King have remarked, he defeats the dragon not through his own strength but through infusions of grace represented by the Well and the Tree of Life that appear just when his own powers fail.[35] Throughout the episode, his armor remains that of the Ephesian soldier whose shield is faith and whose sword is the Word of God.

Spenser's reclamation of Virgil's narrative from a Pelagian hermeneutic culminates in Redcrosse's increasing identification with Christ as an apocalyptic agent. Whereas Augustine, Vegius, and others anticipated Spenser's transformation of Aeneas's marriage into an allegory of personal salvation, Spenser alone links it to the Marriage of the Lamb. This intersection of biblical and Virgilian typologies surpasses even Augustine and Dante in transcendentalizing the *Aeneid*'s political vision. Redcrosse's betrothal adumbrates the time when all things, even empire itself, will cease. Up to this point, Redcrosse has appeared primarily as a representative member of the Elect: Christ's active presence within him empowers his resistance to temptation. But to the extent that the dragon's death suggests Satan's defeat as prophesied in the Book of Revelation, Redcrosse stands allegorically as Christ Himself, who vanquishes evil once and for all at the end of time. Christ's establishment of His millennial kingdom becomes the one great epic action. It subsumes not only earthly dynasties but all instances of individual salvation. Since He is the sole protagonist of these events, their narration completes Spenser's transformation of Virgilian epic into a form wholly committed to divine rather than human enterprise.

As Redcrosse's gradual identification with Christ leads him beyond Duessa's powers, the Bible's subtextual presence increasingly distinguishes Book I from Italian romance. Although Spenser posits a quest ending in the transition from time to eternity, his apocalyptic vision of history restores Virgil's narrative linearity. But the moment his redeemed version of Aeneas's career approaches its apocalyptic culmination, Duessa reappears. Although Adam refutes her charges against Redcrosse, Spenser returns to the *romanzi*'s characteristic narrative suspension by deferring Redcrosse's marriage.

Fichter has argued that "epic is built to evoke man's struggle to orient himself in time" (4). Although Renaissance commentators never describe the genre in such terms, their emphasis on its didactic function links it to inherently temporal conceptions of spiritual and moral development. Passages like Redcrosse's contemplation of the New Jerusalem or his betrothal to Una approach a devotional mode that Spenser may have felt was unsuited to the genre's metaphysical horizons. Since epic heroes define themselves by resisting their antagonists, they virtually cease to exist as heroes the moment they overcome their final enemy. On one level, the tranquility of the Contemplation episode and the jubilation of Redcrosse's betrothal threaten his heroic identity as much as do Duessa's charms.

Duessa's reappearance returns the poem not just to romance error but also to the fallen historical order where epic action conventionally unfolds. The evocation preceding Redcrosse's fight with the dragon promises to set down the genre's "haughtie string" only for "a while." If humanity can accomplish nothing against its spiritual foes, it can achieve limited success in its struggles against the natural vices confronted by Spenser's other knights. But if the shift from an eternal to a temporal perspective revalorizes human agency, it exposes other changes in historical circumstances that challenge the *Aeneid*'s adaptability to Elizabethan culture as much as Book I's Protestantism.

⟨ F I V E ⟩

Tempering the Two Didos:

Romance and Allegorical Epic in Book II

W hen Virgil established his poetic in-
dependence from Homer by championing a hero who embodied Roman virtues
against female characters associated with Hellenic excess and duplicity, he re-
inforced Augustus's systematic devaluation of women's political and social status.
But when Spenser set out to establish himself as Virgil's English successor, he
faced a political situation diametrically opposed to imperial Rome's. Whereas
the female ruler who figures most prominently in the *Aeneid*'s field of historical
allusion is Cleopatra, the one standing behind *The Faerie Queene* is Elizabeth I,
the poem's principal patron.¹ Like other Elizabethan poets, painters, and apol-
ogists, Spenser needed to bolster confidence in female magistracy when diverse
cultural forces were coalescing to erode it.²

The Reformation's literal interpretation of Pauline scripture advocated wom-
en's silence rather than their participation in public life. At the same time, a
developing market economy confined women increasingly to the private sphere.
In order to counter such developments, Spenser could transform Virgilian epic
into a medium of Elizabethan compliment only if he first dispelled the genre's
conventional antifeminism. Above all, he had to modify the recurrent association

of powerful women like Dido, Alcina, and Armida with literary influences antithetical to poetry in the laureate tradition.

Book II of *The Faerie Queene* might seem at first to reinforce rather than reform epic's antifeminist tendencies. Spenser persists in defining his single hero and comparatively linear plot against the *romanzi*'s narrative proliferation. As in Book I, he figures his own penchant for digression through his hero's vulnerability to feminine allure. More than any previous work, Book II reveals an obsessive intertexual concern with Dido's abandonment. In Book I, Dido drops out of the story the moment Redcrosse escapes Duessa; as we have seen, the final cantos recast Aeneas's triumphant progress from Carthage to Latium. But from Amavia's suicide to Guyon's final encounter with Acrasia, Book II is organized around multiple rewritings of the Dido episode. Spenser no longer presents the alluring woman who seduces men from virtue as an obstacle to be overcome before the hero can fulfill his quest. Resisting her becomes the end of the quest itself. As Guyon's principal antagonist, Acrasia plays both Dido and Turnus to his Aeneas. From the perspective of Spenserian temperance, overcoming the *luxuria* that medieval and Renaissance commentators associated with Carthage subsumes even the conquest of Latium in moral significance.

But if Spenser evokes feminine allure more than ever as a figure for Italian romance, he also evokes feminine chastity, particularly the Virgin Queen's, to restore the confidence in human educability that romance subverts. In Book I, the Protestant doctrine of sanctification through grace provided the grounds for believing that human beings might finally overcome their baser instincts. Elizabeth's exemplary virginity provides an analogous answer to Ariostan doubts in Book II. This chapter examines how Spenser draws on divergent aspects of Dido's medieval and Renaissance reception in transforming her not only into figures of Italianate voluptuousness like Phaedria and Acrasia but also into such surrogates of the Virgin Queen as Alma and Medina. Concupiscent Didos languishing in their enchanted gardens continue to recall the *romanzi* as a poetry of dangerously seductive surfaces. But the temperate Didos governing their starkly allegorical castles suggest a literature whose end is moral instruction. Dido's dual legacy ultimately allows Spenser to align the queen's chastity with his own poetic restraint vis-à-vis Ariosto and Tasso.

Belphoebe: Ariostan Allure Tempered by Virgilian Restraint

Before tracing Book II's complex revisions of Dido's tragedy, I want to examine Belphoebe's dual origins in the *Aeneid* and in the *Furioso*. Her characterization achieves a balance between Ariostan and Virgilian effects that typifies Spenser's project of tempering Italian influences with Virgilian restraint. Since

Guyon's foes are recalcitrant natural impulses rather than diabolical enchant-ments, Book II endorses the Virgilian commentators' belief that humanity might learn to resist temptation.[3] Spenser distances himself from Ariostan skepticism by presenting Belphoebe as an exemplar of chaste resistance to concupiscence. In an audacious turn from literary precedent, he models this surrogate of the Virgin Queen herself on the seductress Alcina and the Venus associated by some commentators with sensual pleasure. By conspicuously chastening her poetic antecedents, he presents himself as a champion of aesthetic restraint who imposes a didactic agenda on prior erotic representations.[4]

As scholars have often noted, Spenser's ten-stanza description of Belphoebe's appearances before Trompart and Braggadocchio imitates Ariosto's *blazon* de-scribing Ruggiero's first glimpse of Alcina.[5] But Spenser endows Belphoebe with an Alcinan voluptuousness specifically as a foil to her Virgilian *pudor*. The more al-luring she appears, the greater proves her chastity in holding intemperate desires in check. Whereas Alcina's beauty is a mere show calculated to inflame its beholders with lust, Belphoebe's manifests an interior virtue that restrains whatever carnal impulses her appearance might arouse. When Ariosto imagines *Amor* flitting around Alcina's eyes as if he would "let fly his full quiver and openly steal away all hearts" (*e ch'indi tutta la faretra scarchi, / e che visibilmente i cori involi, OF* VII.12), he foreshadows Ruggiero's failure to resist her charms. Spenser similarly imagines many Graces "working belgards" beneath "the shadow of [Belphoebe's] euen browes" (II.iii.25). But by stressing her "dredd Maiestie, and awfull ire," which prevent "the blinded god" from kindling in her eyes "his lustfull fire," he antici-pates her later rejection of Braggadocchio's advances (*FQ* II.iii.23).

Similar revisions of Ariosto's Petrarchan tropes evoke Belphoebe's alluring beauty primarily to set off her chastity against Alcina's concupiscence.[6] Spenser's greatest departure from Ariosto, his elaborate account of her costume, underscores her role as an icon of desirability disciplined by modesty and self-control. Whereas Ariosto never mentions Alcina's clothing, Spenser tempers Belphoebe's enticing "silken Camus lylly whight" with images of physical restraint. Her cordovan straps and "golden aygulets" seem more suited to Amazonian armor than to a nymph's diaphanous gown (iii.26). Spenser no sooner borrows Alcina's *due pome acerbe* in depicting Belphoebe's breasts, "which like young fruit in May / Now little gan to swell," than he conceals them under a golden baldric recalling Penthesilea's in Ju-no's murals (*OF* VII.14; *FQ* II.iii.29). By evoking the Virgilian heroine's militant chastity, Spenser disciplines the Ariostan one's voluptuousness.

This shift from Ariostan sensuality toward Virgilian continence culminates in the flowing hair, bow, and quiver that link Belphoebe ostensibly with the Vir-gilian Venus, interpreted by Neoplatonists as the Venus Urania leading humanity from carnal bondage to contemplation.[7] But as we have seen, that particular interpretation competed throughout the Renaissance with a darker interpretation of the disguised Venus as a dissembler whose appearance and discourse deceive her unwary interlocutors (*vt non solum specie: sed etiam sermone imprudentes traduceret*).[8] If Landino treated the episode as an instance of divinity manifesting itself to human consciousness, Petrarch and Badius read it as an account of chicanery. For them, Venus's resemblance to Diana and her virginal nymphs is utterly inauthentic. The corruption festering beneath her disguise is just as repulsive to rational minds as the deformities that Ruggiero beholds once he discovers Alcina's true nature. In remarking that "the mere sight of [Venus] would no doubt make [one] flee in horror" if one could see her for what she really is, Petrarch anticipates Fornari and other commentators on Alcina.[9] Within the exegetical tradition, Venus and Alcina both embody deceptive, carnal pleasures luring men to their doom.

Since the disguised Venus was as likely to be associated with illicit desire as with chaste restraint, Spenser transforms his Virgilian as well as his Ariostan subtext to honor Elizabeth's virginity. Although Belphoebe wears Venus's costume, she shows no traces of Venus's deceptiveness when her conversation with Trompart and Braggadocchio reenacts Venus's with Aeneas and Achates. Unlike Venus, Belphoebe really is a huntress. When she asks Trompart if he has seen the bleeding hind she has wounded, her question is not a ruse. Whereas the attributes that cause Aeneas to mistake Venus for "Apollo's sister" or one of her nymphs are feigned, Belphoebe is truly related to Diana. Later in Book III, Spenser reveals that Diana, rather than the potentially treacherous Venus, adopted Belphoebe as a foster daughter when the two contrary goddesses found her with her sister Amoret.

Instead of canceling Venus's duplicity altogether, however, Spenser transfers it onto the male characters, Trompart and Braggadocchio. This displacement preserves the Virgilian confrontation between a sincere interlocutor and a dissembler. When Braggadocchio introduces himself as one "Endeuouring [his] dreadded name to raise / Aboue the Moone" (II.iii. 38), he echoes Aeneas's introduction of himself as one whose fame is known *super aethera* (I.379). But Braggadocchio is no more a hero on Aeneas's order than the Virgilian Venus is a Tyrian huntress or a goddess of chastity. Since his origins as a horse thief and braggart lie more conspicuously in the *Furioso* than in the *Aeneid,* the passage's humor arises from his falsification of poetic history.[10] Hardly an Aeneas, Braggadocchio is at best a failed Mandricardo, a lustful braggart incapable of even the dubious courage shown by his Ariostan precursors. By transferring Venus's dissimulation to him, Spenser reverses the gender lines of the original Virgilian encounter between the deceptive goddess and the sincere hero. Belphoebe emerges as a champion of Elizabethan virtue in opposition to masculine, Italianate duplicity.[11]

Spenser's revisions of both his classical and his Italian precursors culminate when Belphoebe's interplay of erotic attractiveness and sexual restraint so arouses Braggadocchio that he tries to embrace her. Her retreat into the forest recalls both Venus's sudden departure from Aeneas and Angelica's magical escape from Ruggiero, a conspicuous parody of the original Virgilian passage. Spenser first challenges Ariosto by reasserting humanity's ability to discipline its wayward passions. He then transforms Virgil by casting the vanishing woman, rather than the man she eludes, as the exemplar of virtue. In the passage that mediates between Virgil and Spenser, Ariosto characteristically overturns the *Aeneid*'s ethical dichotomies. As we saw in the first chapter, Aeneas's exasperation over his mother's disguise indicts the Homeric pantheon's typical chicanery in dealing with humans:

> Why do you mock your son—so often and
> so cruelly—with these lying apparitions?
> Why can't I ever join you, hand in hand,
> to hear, to answer you with honest words?

> quid natum totiens, crudelis tu quoque, falsis
> ludis imaginibus? cur dextrae iungere dextram
> non datur ac ueras audire et reddere uoces?
> (I.407–9 [M:581–84])

Ruggiero echoes Aeneas's plaintive words when he pleads for Angelica to abandon her tricks and to reveal herself to him: "Hide not your lovely face from me. I know, heartless one, that you hear me but will not answer" (*sol che 'l bel viso tuo non mi nascondi. / Io so, crudel, che m'odi, e non rispondi,* XI.8). But the preposterousness of the narrative situation undercuts this passing recollection of Virgilian pathos. Ruggiero is a frustrated rapist rather than a champion of faithfulness and sincerity: his sudden arousal has caused Angelica's equally sudden disappearance in the first place.

But if Ariosto anticipates Spenser in casting the abandoned male rather than the departing female as the offending party, he does not uphold Angelica as a model of chastity. While Ruggiero's shocking failure to contain his desire distinguishes him from Aeneas, Angelica's magical escape retains something of Venus's penchant for disguise. From Ariosto's sophisticated, ironic perspective, neither character is wholly admirable nor wholly culpable. What might appear to be a confrontation between vice and virtue actually resolves into a conflict between a sexual aggressiveness over which Ruggiero has no control and Angelica's equally instinctive self-protectiveness. Even in fleeing Ruggiero, Angelica is not an exemplar of chastity. Her misogynistic portrayal throughout the *Furioso* as a coquette devising subterfuges to keep each lover "in hope for so long as she had need of him" (*alcuna finzïone, alcuno inganno / di tenerlo in speranza ordisce e trama; / tanto ch'a quel bisogno se ne serva*, I.51) grounds her behavior more in coy, Petrarchan disdain than in embattled honor.

In revising the episode, Spenser rejects what retrospectively appears as Ariosto's failure of moral clarity. Ariosto overtly sympathizes with Ruggiero by arguing that the austere Xenocrates himself would have yielded to lechery in the same situation (*con la qual non saria stato quel crudo / Zenocrate di lui più continente*, XI.3). Spenser follows Ariosto in depicting Braggadocchio as someone overpowered by the beauty he beholds:

> But that the foolish man, fild with delight
> Of her sweet words, that all his sence dismaid,
> And with her wondrous beautie rauisht quight,
> Gan burne in filthy lust, and leaping light,
> Thought in his bastard armes her to embrace.
>
> (iii.42)

Passive verbs throughout the passage almost present Braggadocchio himself as a victim "rauisht quight" by impulses beyond his control. But in contrast to Ariosto, Spenser does not excuse Braggadocchio from responsibility for his actions or uphold his experience as evidence that "wondrous beautie" cannot be resisted. Ruggiero's lapse suggested that everyone, even the most stalwart hero, might yield to carnality. As a critique of Ariostan lenity, Braggadocchio's lapse suggests that a sensual hero like Ruggiero is really no hero at all but a lecher dressed in "bastard armes." By transforming Ruggiero into Braggadocchio, Spenser exposes Ariosto's belief that certain temptations can overpower the strongest moral commitments as a preposterous defense of "filthy lust."

Along with countering Ariosto's indulgence toward Ruggiero with explicit condemnation of Braggadocchio, Spenser transforms the chaste but manipulative Angelica into the wholly laudable Belphoebe. The moment she departs, Braggadocchio echoes Ruggiero's complaints about Angelica's discourtesy and ingratitude (*di quello atto / ingrato e discortese*, XI.7):

> What foule blot
> Is this to knight, that Ladie should againe
> Depart to woods vntoucht, and leaue so proud disdaine?
>
> (iii.43)

But if Angelica's previous behavior toward Rinaldo and others lends a perverse credibility to Ruggiero's charges, Braggadocchio's are conspicuously absurd. Threatening her attacker with "her Iauelin bright" (iii.42) before she retreats, Belphoebe retains nothing of subterfuge or coquetry but appears instead as a daimonized agent of chastity. Her directness and unqualified virtue restore the ethical polarities that Ariosto had blurred in rejecting Virgilian precedent. Like Aeneas, Belphoebe provides a pattern of honorable behavior for others to follow. As proof that unswerving commitment to noble action remains possible even in a fallen world, her chastity counters the skepticism that first led Ariosto to question the didactic terms of the *Aeneid*'s Renaissance canonization.

In rejecting the idea that carnal tendencies inevitably defeat virtuous intentions, Spenser renounces the ethical basis of Ariosto's digressiveness. In general, Book II's comparatively linear plot stands as the structural correlative of a renewed confidence in reason's resistance to erotic impulse. But as a particularly conspicuous digression from Guyon's quest, the Belphoebe episode might seem to align Spenser temporarily with the *romanzi*'s *entrelacement*. But what appears as digression on the narrative level reinforces on an allegorical level the book's central didactic thesis.[12] As we have seen, the canto's most strikingly irrelevant passage, the eleven-stanza portrait, provides an extended emblematic lesson on the virtues of restraint. Even as reason governs passion, allegory governs the divagations of Italian romance in a poem that earns its place in the Virgilian tradition by providing a delight whose end is moral instruction.

Misera ante diem: Dido, Amavia, and the Canons of Epic Judgment

Perhaps without any conscious knowledge of how the Venus episode revises its Odyssean subtexts, Spenser defines himself against Ariosto through the same kind of intertextual configurations that Virgil used in defining himself against Homer. But in constructing a compliment to Elizabeth, he reverses the Virgilian episode's gender dynamics so that the Venus-Diana figure, rather than the male who encounters her, exemplifies the epic's didactic ideals. At one point, he gestures toward a similar recuperation of Dido. As editors have often noted, the simile comparing Belphoebe to Diana "by the sandie shore / Of swift *Eurotas*, or on *Cynthus* greene" (iii.31) is based on the one that describes Dido when Aeneas first sees her directing the work of her future kingdom. The graciousness and regality Dido shows before she is undone by Cupid's wound provided Spenser a prototype of the chaste magistracy for which he honors Elizabeth.

The remainder of this chapter examines how he evokes the yet unfallen Dido so that she will no longer stand solely as an example of corrupt female rule, a queen undone by concupiscence and irascibility.

Aspects of Dido's characterization both in the *Aeneid* and in later commentaries and poetic imitations underlie every major female figure in Book II. Whereas Spenser recuperates the disguised Venus by displacing her duplicity onto Trompart and Braggadocchio, he creates temperate Didos like Medina and Alma by displacing the intemperance that commentators found in Virgil's Dido onto enchantresses like Phaedria and Acrasia. Since their origins lie more immediately in Italian romance, Spenser diminishes Virgil's own responsibility in establishing an antifeminist poetic. In constructing parallel dichotomies between virgins and temptresses, moralized epic and romance fantasy, Spenser draws on the commonplace distinction between Virgil's concupiscent queen and her legendary prototype, the widow who killed herself to avoid dishonoring her husband's memory. If Acrasia derives from the former, Alma arises from the latter transformed into a virgin in honor of the queen.

Yet if the female figures dominating Book II's allegory perpetuate the distinction between the chaste and the lascivious Didos, the opening episode recalls her more as an object of pity than of either praise or censure. Amavia's status both as a mother and as the narrator of her own sufferings recalls the sympathetic Didos portrayed by Ovid, Chaucer, and writers of medieval romances. But Spenser incorporates these later features to enhance a pathos and melancholy ambivalence that he discovered primarily in the *Aeneid* itself. As we have seen, Virgil presented Dido not as a criminal but as the victim of tragic forces beyond her understanding and control. Allegorists like Fulgentius and Bernard abandoned this tragic emphasis in transforming her story into an exemplum about unbridled passion. Spenser restores it in portraying Amavia's desertion by Mordant and her later victimization by Acrasia. Tempering ethical pronouncement with tragic insight, he establishes the boundaries between the transcendent perspective of Book I and Book II's greater concern with human action unfolding in time.

Since the eighteenth century, scholars have noted that the Amavia episode is filled with Virgilian echoes linking Guyon's intervention in Amavia's death agony to Anna's attempt to save Dido after she stabs herself.[13] Just as Dido struggles three times to raise herself and falls back three times on her couch, Guyon tries three times to raise Amavia:

> Three times she tried
> to raise herself and strained, propped on her elbow;
> and three times she fell back upon the couch.

ter sese attollens cubitoque adnixa leuauit,
ter reuoluta toro est . . .
(*Aen.* IV.690–91 [M:950–52])

The gentle knight her soone with carefull paine
Vplifted light, and softly did vphold:
Thrise he her reard, and thrise she sunke againe.
(*FQ* II.i.46)

Dido seeks heaven's light only to sigh when she has found it (*Aen.* IV.692).
After raising her eyes to the light reflected by Guyon's shining armor, Amavia
too sinks back in despair "as hating life and light" (*FQ* II.ii.45). The phrase "as
hating life and light" itself echoes Dido's reference to "the hated light," *inuisam
. . . lucem,* of existence that she extinguishes after Aeneas departs (IV.631 [M:
871]).

These imitations of Dido's last moments anticipate a climactic revision of
Virgil's pronouncements on her guilt. Guyon and the Palmer's discussion about
the propriety of burying a woman who has taken her own life recalls Proser-
pina's hesitation to release Dido's soul by cutting the lock sacred to the Stygian
gods:

For as she died
a death that was not merited or fated,
but miserable and before her time
and spurred by sudden frenzy, Proserpina
had not yet cut a gold lock from her crown,
not yet assigned her life to Stygian Orcus.

nam quia nec fato merita nec morte peribat,
sed misera ante diem subitoque accensa furore,
nondum illi flauum Proserpina uertice crinem
abstulerat Stygioque caput damnauerat Orco.
(IV.696–99 [M:958–63])

As I suggested in my opening chapter, these lines beg the question of Dido's
guilt by presenting her primarily as an object of sympathy. Neither blaming nor
exonerating her, Virgil proclaims her the victim of a sudden, irresistible fury.
The abundance of medieval and Renaissance commentary on this passage sug-
gests that its suspension of judgment perplexed readers trying to figure out
whether Dido was criminally responsible for her suicide. In general, commen-
tators attempted to resolve Virgil's ambiguities and apparent logical contradic-
tions. Servius, for example, found the notion of Dido's dying before her time

(*ante diem*) potentially problematic: after all, Virgil himself states in Book X that everyone's date of death is fixed (*stat sua cuique dies,* X.467).[14] Dismissing a death neither "merited" nor "fated" as a logical impossibility, Servius Auctus circumvents the enigmatic lines by introducing a distinction between decreed and conditional fate: Dido did not die necessarily, *fata denuntiativa,* but on the condition, *fata condicionale,* that the Trojans touched her shores. If they had not come to Africa, she would have presumably died at a riper age without any injury to her good fortune (*perveniret autem ad seram mortem sine ulla felicitatis offensa, si Troiana classis ad litus Africae non veniret*).[15]

In contrast to Servius, Spenser neither challenges Virgil's evasions nor tries to resolve his ambiguities but rather incorporates them in the Palmer's tentative pronouncement on Amavia's suicide:

> But temperance (said he) with golden squire
>> Betwixt them both can measure out a meane,
>> Neither to melt in pleasures whot desire,
>> Nor fry in hartlesse griefe and dolefull teene.
>> Thrise happie man, who fares them both atweene:
>> But sith this wretched woman ouercome
>> Of anguish, rather then of crime hath beene,
>> Reserue her cause to her eternall doome,
> And in the meane vouchsafe her honorable toombe.
>
> (i.58)

As in the *Aeneid,* the unequivocal assessment promised by seemingly straightforward antitheses ends only in suspended judgment. The stanza's first four lines analyze Amavia and Mordant's tragedy as a violation of the golden mean. Whereas Mordant melted concupiscently "in pleasures whot desire," Amavia surrendered to the "hartlesse griefe and dolefull teene" of irascibility.[16] But if the Palmer can classify her behavior as intemperate, he cannot decide whether that intemperance is damnable. The moment he broaches the question of her final doom, he falls into the same slippery distinction that characterizes Virgil's remarks on Dido's suicide. Just as a death might be pitiable as well as merited or fated, "anguish" and "crime" are not such clearly antithetical terms as his syntax suggests. If someone has been "ouercome / Of anguish," his or her actions may or may not be criminal. While the Palmer seems to argue that Amavia can be buried because she has not *committed* a crime, the passivity of being "ouercome . . . of crime" implies victimization rather than agency. Once again, his syntax draws a sharper antithesis than his ethical alternatives actually support. If Amavia had been the victim of a crime, she would surely deserve a burial no less than if she had been "ouercome / Of anguish."

Here on the threshold between holiness and temperance, the difficulties inherent in the Palmer's logic expose the limits of natural reason in questions of eternal destiny. In Virgil, heaven's clemency triumphs over the underworld's perplexed justice when Juno pities Dido's long sorrow (*Iuno omnipotens longum miserata dolorem*, IV.693) and sends Iris to release her spirit by cutting the lock consecrated to the Stygian gods. By reserving Amavia's cause to heaven, the Palmer raises the possibility that the Christian God might similarly pity her. He allows Guyon to perform the same office for her and Mordant that Iris performs in the *Aeneid*:

> The dead knights sword out of his sheath he drew,
> With which he cut a locke of all their heare,
> Which medling with their bloud and earth, he threw
> Into the graue.
> (i.61)

As Guyon and the Palmer lay Mordant and Amavia "tenderly" in their graves while "shedding many teares" (i.60–61), judgment yields to compassion even as it did at the close of Virgil's Book IV. By harkening back to the mercy that Book I upholds against both the Old Law and classical justice, such pity places the secular, Augustan virtue of temperance in the broader context of holiness. If Amavia is a type of Dido, she is also a type of Eve, the prototype of fallen humanity, in her final dependence on grace.[17]

As we have seen, later writers waived Virgil's tentativeness in assessing Dido's culpability. In an analogous way, Spenser abandons his own tentativeness about Amavia's guilt in the very next canto. When the stream flowing from Diana's nymph fails to wash Amavia's blood from her baby's hands, its perpetual stain occasions extreme, mutually incompatible interpretations of her character. Whereas the Palmer originally reserved her doom to heaven, he now unequivocally champions her innocence against the nymph's implicit accusations of her guilt. After explaining that the nymph rejects Amavia's blood because she cannot tolerate "any filth," he declares the same blood a "sacred Symbole" of Amavia's "innocence" (ii.9, 10). The question of whether it betokens filth or innocence underlies the ambiguity of his later description of Ruddymane's stained hands as "an endlesse moniment" for "all chast Dames" (ii.10). Given his commitment to Amavia's innocence, he presumably means that she will always be remembered for exemplary chastity. But the phrase carries the darker suggestion, more in tune with the nymph's revulsion, that Amavia's fate warns all chaste maids about the ensuing horrors "when raging passion with fierce tyrannie / Robs reason of her due regalitie" (i.57).

123

On one level, the conflicting interpretations of Amavia's blood continue to define the relationship between Book I's revealed truths and Book II's more natural values. Critics have tended to resolve its paradoxes and contradictions by evoking sacramental theology. As A. C. Hamilton has suggested, one explanation for the bloody hands that paradoxically betoken innocence may lie in Spenser's understanding of baptism.[18] To the extent that the innocence attributed to Amavia is the imputed innocence of baptism, the stain's persistence reveals the sacrament's limitations. If baptism exonerates us in the sight of God, the natural effect of original sin, our proneness to intemperance, nevertheless persists as long as we are "cloth'd with fleshly tyre" (i.57). Baptismal grace might render Amavia's blood a token of righteousness before God, but the nymph's more limited, temporal perspective allows her to see it only as "filth," a deviation from the rigorous, unswerving temperance she herself exemplified in fleeing Faunus.

Amavia's conspicuously Virgilian origins suggest an alternative, secular and literary historical source for the divergent interpretations of her blood. Her tragedy recasts the long-standing debate over Dido's responsibility for her passionate outrage. If the nymph's implicit condemnation of Amavia's intemperance recalls Neo-Latin repudiations of Dido's concupiscence, the Palmer follows vernacular writers who exonerated Dido because she was enraged by forces beyond her control. Immediately after declaring Ruddymane's bloody hands a token of Amavia's innocence, he also proclaims them an exhortation "to minde reuengement" against Acrasia as the true cause of her death (ii.10). Amavia is "innocent" precisely because she was inflamed with desperate passions by Acrasia, whose name identifies her as intemperance's allegorical essence.

Caxton's account in the *Eneydos* of Persephone's reluctance to release Dido's soul provides an authority within the Virgilian tradition for Spenser's transfer of responsibility for Amavia's actions onto Acrasia. Although Persephone maintains that Dido must suffer eternal punishment for her sins, Iris argues that they are not damnable because they were precipitated by "frawdulent induction."[19] Since Dido would not have killed herself if Venus and Cupid had not infected her with desire, the gods themselves are ultimately responsible for her crimes. In much the same way, Amavia's suicidal frenzy can be traced to her daimonization by Acrasia, who appears throughout the book as a kind of diabolic Venus. Both Caxton and Spenser defend their respective heroines by projecting the emotions that inflame them onto external forces, a deity or sorceress who overpowers them with her spells. While passion and intemperance, Eros and Acrasia, are condemned as abstract states, Dido and Amavia can be exonerated as their pitiable victims.

Acrasia's introduction draws on yet another strategy that early modern writers used in treating Dido sympathetically: the distinction between chaste and concupiscent Didos. Like Dido in the *Aeneid*'s Neo-Latin commentaries, Acrasia personifies intemperate passion luring men from honor. Although Acrasia's sorcery links her also to Circe, her involvement with Mordant follows the general outline of the *Aeneid* rather than the *Odyssey*.[20] Circe's charms have no effect on Odysseus, but Acrasia's influence, like Dido's, threatens Mordant's heroic identity. Just as Mercury discovers Aeneas wearing the Carthaginians' opulent garb and neglecting his vocation, Amavia finds Mordant, "transformed from his former skill" (i.54), languishing in Acrasia's Bower. When Amavia restores his former prowess "through wise handling and faire gouernance," she takes on Mercury's familiar allegorical role as an embodiment of eloquence's power to govern intemperance (i.54). Her disguise as a palmer links her to Guyon's squire, whose staff, carved "of that same wood . . . / Of which *Caduceus* whilome was made" (xii.41), reveals him as an explicit type of the god whom commentators like Bernard and Boccaccio equated with reasonable persuasion holding the passions in check.

Just as the Virgilian Dido's illicit passion for Aeneas served Renaissance commentators as a foil to the historical Dido's marital devotion, Acrasia's defining concupiscence sets off Amavia's chastity. Although Amavia does not kill herself to escape unwanted suitors, she is a widow whose suicide reveals her profound love for her murdered lord. While writers who evoked the two Didos vehemently condemned the one for her lasciviousness, they never condemned the other for her suicidal despair. They praised her instead as a model of wifely fidelity.[21] The contrasting example of Acrasia's utter depravity similarly diminishes the extent to which Amavia, despite the violence of her death, appears as an agent of intemperance. Like the noble Dido whom Lydgate claims was worshipped after her death as a "chast goddess," Amavia too, in her unswerving love for Mordant, becomes a model for all "chaste dames" to follow.

In Book I, Spenser recalled Dido solely along Fulgentian lines by casting Duessa as a temptress inflaming Redcrosse with illicit desire. His portrayal of Amavia recalls Dido as a more complex, potentially redeemable figure. Although Acrasia perpetuates the association of women with concupiscence, Amavia's rescue of Mordant from her spells creates a place in epic for women who foster rather than impede heroism. In a remarkably daring appropriation of the contradictory modes in which Dido's story was retold during the Renaissance, Spenser introduces a chaste Dido who liberates the hero from her concupiscent counterpart.

But Amavia's assumption of Mercury's role as a moral counselor only begins to counter the antifeminist bias of the *Aeneid*'s reception as a poem disciplining the passions. In contrast to Mercury's triumph over Dido, Amavia's victory over Acrasia proves only temporary. Her final submission to Acrasia's power may demonstrate humanity's need for grace, but it also reinforces a long-standing association of women with emotional instability. Amavia's capacity for "wise handling and faire gouernance," like Dido's when she first appears overseeing her city's construction, proves short-lived. She has escaped the Virgilian Dido's association with concupiscence and has joined the historical Dido as a model of wifely fidelity. But she has not demonstrated the definitive resistance to passion that would establish her as a surrogate of the Virgin Queen.

The only character in Book II's opening episodes who appears to any degree as a type of Elizabeth is the nymph who repudiates Amavia's blood. Her initial flight from Faunus anticipates Belphoebe's more militant repudiation of Braggadocchio, an episode that probably commemorates Elizabeth's final rejection of Alençon.[22] The nymph may seem insensitive to Amavia's tragedy, but her rigor accords with the severe sexual discipline that Elizabeth imposed on her court. As Paul Johnson and Christopher Haigh remind us, the queen banished courtiers and maids of honor from her presence and sometimes imprisoned them for indiscretions ranging from overly affectionate kisses to illegitimate pregnancies.[23] Those who conformed to her *pudor* shared the aura of her mythic chastity, but those who defied it, like Elizabeth Vernon, Ann Vavasour, and Elizabeth Throckmorton, faced imperial wrath. The next section of this chapter examines how Spenser overcomes epic's conventional biases against female sovereignty by transforming Dido into various figures who conform to Elizabeth's code of honor in all its austerity.

Temperate Dido: Medina and Alma

In the Siena-Sieve portrait discovered in the Sienese Pallazzo Reale in 1895, Elizabeth I appears before a pillar inset with nine medallions illustrating Dido's tragedy. Elizabeth herself holds a sieve, a conventional emblem of virginity that recalls how the maiden Tucchia proved her chastity by miraculously carrying water from the Tiber to the temple of Vesta. Roy Strong has argued that the portrait contrasts Aeneas, lured from his destiny by love, with Elizabeth, whose virginity protected her from similarly neglecting her imperial vocation.[24] But by contrasting Elizabeth with Dido, the portrait also honors her virginity for protecting her from Dido's fate as a queen undone by passion. The medallions trace the moral decay that differentiated the ancient queen from her Tudor counterpart. In the first, Dido appears as a commanding magistrate enthroned before Juno's temple. But the next illustrates her fatal infection by Cupid at the banquet hosted for Aeneas. Subsequent medallions depict her mad pursuit of Aeneas and her final suicidal frenzy. Meanwhile, Elizabeth herself stands before the ekphrastic pillar secure both in her chastity and in the "faire gouernance" that it sustains.

Like the painter of the Siena-Sieve portrait, Spenser presents Elizabeth's unswerving virginity as the primary factor shielding her from Dido's tragedy. But he does not simply contrast Dido and Elizabeth. He rewrites Dido's career in Guyon's encounters with Alma and Medina, surrogates of the queen herself in their personal chastity and in their rational government of their estates. Although their struggles against intemperance anatomize Dido's experiences on an allegorical level, their ultimately successful resistance establishes a place within the Virgilian tradition for effective female magistracy.

Medina's and Alma's virginity distinguishes them not only from Virgil's Dido but also from the virtuous widow of history, whom commentators inevitably praised for chastity rather than for her "faire gouernance." Since the good Dido kills herself to avoid a second marriage that might secure her newly established kingdom, her story could still be interpreted as evidence that women's passionate nature makes them unreliable rulers. Precisely because of her wifely fidelity, she refuses to subordinate her personal feelings to her people's welfare. Once again, Elizabeth's cultic status as the Virgin Queen provided Spenser an ideal counter to misgivings about female magistracy. Neither foreign suitors nor the obsessive memory of a dead husband distracted Elizabeth, metaphorically wed to the people of England, from her duties. In an analogous way, Medina's and Alma's virginity underwrites their estates' successful management in allegories equating the well-governed kingdom with reason's mastery of passion in the well-tempered soul.

By characterizing Medina and Alma as virginal Didos, Spenser rewrites several episodes from Book I of the *Aeneid*. Like Virgil's other Renaissance adaptors, he focuses in particular on Dido and Aeneas's first meeting at Juno's temple and on the banquet in Dido's palace. These episodes figure prominently in the Sieve portrait, the woodcuts illustrating Sebastian Brant's 1502 edition of Virgil's *Opera,* and the twenty-four silk engravings by Galle that were dedicated by Gandinus to the Archduke of Austria in 1595.[25] Whereas the encounter at Juno's temple presents Dido at the height of her magisterial authority, her submission to Cupid's spells at the banquet precipitates her madness. Spenser suppresses that peripeteia in transforming her into surrogates of Elizabeth: like the queen, Alma and Medina resemble Dido in her initially chaste magistracy but not in her later passion. Guyon's adventures at their respective houses revise Aeneas's truancy in Carthage as an allegory not of the hero's lapse into concupiscence but of his education in the moderation and self-restraint exemplified by his hostesses.

The Medina episode specifically recasts Dido's banquet with a noble hostess who provides the hero hospitality without falling in love with him. Something

of Dido's dignity in greeting Aeneas and Achates informs Medina's welcome to
Guyon and the Palmer:

> Medina was her name,
> A sober sad, and comely curteous Dame;
> Who rich arayd, and yet in modest guize,
> In goodly garments, that her well became,
> Faire marching forth in honorable wize,
> Him at the threshold met, and well did enterprize.
>
> (ii.14)

The description of Medina "marching forth" to meet her guests echoes Virgil's
description of Dido "marching forth" (*incessit,* I.497) to Juno's temple, where
she first receives Aeneas. The episode's Virgilian origin becomes increasingly
conspicuous when Medina hosts a banquet and asks Guyon to conclude it by
recounting his adventures. As scholars have often noted, Dido requests the same
favor from Aeneas.[26] In each case, the hero's tale lasts until dawn and provides
the poet's audience a flashback account of events preceding his own opening
narration in medias res.

While Medina's graciousness and hospitality link her to Dido, her "attem-
pered" feast (ii.39) contrasts with the lavish Carthaginian one. From late an-
tiquity, commentators treated Dido's banquet as an outward manifestation of
her emotional excess. Noting the difference between the simple repast enjoyed
by the Trojans after Aeneas kills the seven stags and the elaborate one in Dido's
palace, Macrobius praises Virgil for "shrewdly" contrasting "a riotous and a
sober meal."[27] John of Salisbury similarly distinguishes Dido's banquet, "where
the divinities are invited in flowing prayers to approve dissipation," from Evan-
der's frugal one, "where serious matters are treated and manly strength is stirred
to establish the republic."[28] For John, Aeneas's surrender to sexual temptation
is a natural consequence of his earlier overindulgence in food and drink. *Libido*
follows inevitably from *luxuria* since immoderation in eating and drinking makes
a man "slow of hearing, hasty of speech, quick to anger, prone to desire, and
inclined to whatever disgraceful acts."[29] Bernard also links the banquet to
Aeneas's later fornication by allegorizing the storm that drives Dido and Aeneas
into the cave as the humors that accumulate in "gluttonous eating and drinking"
and must be expelled as "sperm, that is, the male seed, for the stomach is cleared
out through the nearby and lower member" (*Affluentia humoris ciborum et potuum
taliter ad libidinis immundiciam ducit. . . . Purgatur enim venter per membrum proximum
et subditum,* 24).

Like the temperate meals advocated by Macrobius and John of Salisbury,
Medina's feast does not incline her guests to "disgraceful acts" but pleases them

"with meete satietie" (ii.39). In commending the Trojans' moderation in eating the stags killed by Aeneas, Macrobius focuses particularly on Virgil's remark that they ate only until their hunger was satisfied (*exempta fames*, I.216). Spenser likewise notes that Medina's guests eat only until "lust of meat and drinke was ceast" as a tribute to their judicious avoidance of gluttony (ii.39). By using the strikingly ambiguous word "lust," Spenser underscores the extent to which Medina's feast departs from its Virgilian prototype. "Lust" as "sexual appetite" figures prominently at the banquet where Cupid infects Dido with desire. But that sense of the word does not apply where Medina's "sober grace, and goodly carriage" dispel the traces of Dido's concupiscence (ii.38).

In creating his temperate version of Dido's banquet, Spenser alters both the content of the hero's flashback account and its effect upon his auditors. In the *Aeneid*, the conversation at Dido's table proves to be as effective an aphrodisiac as the food. While commemorating the Trojans' suffering, Aeneas inadvertently reinforces Dido's passion by reminding her of his personal virtues and his nation's honor (*ulta uiri uirtus animo multusque recursat / gentis honos*, IV.3–4). Spenser's later revision of her banquet in the Hellenore and Paridell episode suggests that he recognized the double effects of Aeneas's tale. When Guyon tells his story at Medina's table, however, its patriotic function is uncompromised by hints that it might kindle intemperate desires in its listeners. As a tribute to Gloriana, it dispels the Augustan association of women with political disaster. Whereas Aeneas relates the violence caused by Helen, "the common / Fury of Troy and of her homeland" (*Troiae et patriae communis Erinys*, II.573–74 [M:771–72]), Guyon celebrates Gloriana "that with her soueraigne power, and scepter shene / All Faery lond does peaceable sustene" (ii.40).

Guyon focuses on his experiences at Gloriana's "yearely solemne feast," which, like Medina's own banquet, provides an opportunity to honor "knights of worth and courage" and "to heare of straunge aduentures to be told" (ii.42). In this context of conspicuous Virgilian imitation, Gloriana's annual celebration, which the Letter to Raleigh treats as the fictional origin of *The Faerie Queene*'s action, appears as yet another revision of Dido's feast. At Dido's table, Cupid sparked the passion that would ultimately distract Aeneas from his quest. But at Gloriana's, each knight begins the quest distinguishing him as one of Spenser's titular heroes. Like Evander's temperate feast in John's commentary, both Gloriana's and Medina's banquets encourage the discussion of "serious matters" and inspire heroic valor. Medina's mastery of Elissa and Perissa throughout the banquet provides an abstract analysis of the moral conditions distinguishing her temperate house from Dido's Carthage. While she recalls Dido as a gracious and competent ruler, her warring sisters embody the extreme passions to which Dido later succumbs. Perissa's characterization incorporates the gluttony and concupiscence of the Carthaginian banquet. Like Dido's guests in Neo-Latin commentaries, she flows "in wine and meats . . . aboue the bancke" (ii.36). Her gastric overindulgence and "sumptuous tire" suggest her tendency toward "loue too lauish." If William Nelson is correct in conjecturing that the irascible Elissa's name derives not only from the Greek word for "deficiency" but also from Dido's Phoenician name "Elissa,"[30] the "lowring browes" with which she gazes on her lover "as she would threat" may recall Dido's rage after Aeneas deserts her. Medina's ability to moderate her sisters' "strong extremities" allows her to escape Dido's tragedy and to abet rather than to hinder the hero's quest (ii.38). She not only comforts Guyon but fosters a future heroic generation by promising to train Ruddymane's "tender youth" in temperance's "vertuous lore" (iii.2).

Guyon and Arthur's tour of Alma's House recalls a second major episode from the *Aeneid*'s opening book—Aeneas and Achates's exploration of the newly built Carthage. Their examination of Dido's walls, temples, theater, and harbor culminates when they discover murals depicting the Trojan war. Guyon and Arthur's tour of Alma's wondrous rooms ends in a similar confrontation with their own histories when they discover the Elfin and British chronicles stored in Eumnestes's cell. Once again, Spenser revises his Virgilian subtext so that Guyon's stay with his hostess corrects Aeneas's truancy in Carthage. Just as Aeneas first came to Dido's court seeking assistance for his shipwrecked crew, Guyon comes to Alma's after the trials of Mammon's Cave. Whereas Aeneas's refuge proved a greater threat to his enterprise than the disaster he escaped, however, Alma welcomes Guyon and Arthur without seducing them from their quests.

The moment Alma appears, Spenser characterizes her in ways that underscore her role as a temperate Dido:

> *Alma* she called was, a virgin bright;
> That had not yet felt *Cupides* wanton rage,
> Yet was she woo'd of many a gentle knight,
> And many a Lord of noble parentage,
> That sought with her to lincke in marriage.
>
> (ix.18)

The chaste lady pursued by "many a Lord of noble parentage" is a romance commonplace. But Book II's pervasive Virgilian allusion locates these suitors' particular origin in Iarbas and the North African princes rejected by Dido in her loyalty to Sychaeus. In retellings of Virgil's story during the later Middle Ages and Renaissance, Dido's suitors began to play an expanded role. Iarbas appears throughout Marlowe's *Tragedie of Dido, Queene of Carthage* as Aeneas's rival, and he himself commits suicide when he learns of his beloved Dido's death. The suitors figure most prominently in Boccaccio's, Lydgate's, and Caxton's accounts of the chaste Dido legend, where they drive her to suicide by threatening to crush her kingdom if she refuses them marriage.

In revising this feature of Dido's history, Spenser transforms the choice she is offered between her city's destruction and her chastity's surrender into the tenor and vehicle of a single allegorical image: Maleger's onslaught against the "fiue great Bulwarkes" of Alma's castle represents sensuality's threat against her chastity (xi.7). While the lords "of noble parentage" seeking her hand belong to a higher social class than the "villeins" besieging her, her castle's identification with her virginal body blurs the distinction in moral terms (xi.5). In a sense, both the lords and Maleger's troops seek to kindle in her "*Cupides* wanton rage." Virgil, Boccaccio, and Lydgate presented Dido's barbarian suitors as princes of noble descent and as marauding enemies of civilization. Perhaps Alma's resistance to lords as well as savages attempts to resolve contradictions potentially inherent in the notion of barbaric nobility.

In the *Aeneid*, Anna argues that a marital alliance with the Trojans would protect Dido against the barbarian threat (IV.38ff. [M:9ff.]). Given the episode's Virgilian background, Spenser's description of Alma as a virgin who has *not yet* felt Cupid's rage might foreshadow her infatuation with the knight who delivers her from Maleger. But this is precisely the point at which Spenser departs from Virgil. By equating the security of Dido's city with her body's chastity, the allegory of Alma's House suggests that Dido's surrender to passion accomplished what the barbarians set out to do. Spenser revises her tragedy so that Arthur helps Alma to defeat Maleger without launching his own assault on her virtue. The episode also revises the legend of the chaste Dido so that her struggle against the barbarian princes does not end in suicidal despair.

Spenser's definition of Alma's triumphant, Elizabethan chastity against the Virgilian Dido's concupiscence and the historical Dido's self-directed irascibility underlies the displacements that David Miller has traced in describing the allegory's swerve from erotic representation.[31] As Maurice Evans has remarked, the "only major human organs absent from the House of Alma are the sexual ones."[32] Spenser's descending survey of the body's organs raises expectations of their appearance near Port Esquiline only to surprise us with a sudden shift to the heart and the brain. This defeated expectation serves as a metonymy for the failure of any conjectures raised by the episode's subtexts that either Alma or her guests might yield to erotic desire. Spenser follows Virgil's narrative only until Dido's surrender to Cupid subverts her identity as her city's chaste and temperate guardian.

When Guyon and Arthur arrive in Alma's heart, its inhabitants' fawnings, giggles, frowns, and blushes identify them as the same affections that might become dangerous passions if they were not restrained by reason. Although the same Cupid that poisoned Dido with desire for Aeneas frolics among them, he has put away "his cruel bow, wherewith he thousands hath dismayd" (ix.34). Unlike her epic predecessor, Alma disarms eros and holds her affections in check:

> Soone as the gracious *Alma* came in place,
>   They all attonce out of their seates arose,
>   And to her homage made, with humble grace.
>
>   (ix.36)

Instead of joining her ladies in either their flirtations or their perverse coyness, she imposes on them her own modesty. As in the Medina episode, the spectacle of a female figure governing her private passions counters doubts about female sovereignty inherent in Spenser's Virgilian subtext. As a contrast to Dido's neglect of Carthage, Alma's expert management of her household compliments the Virgin Queen. Just as the sexual discipline that Elizabeth maintained among her maids of honour served as a synecdoche for her realm's effective government, the ladies' obedience to Alma signals the ascendancy of reason that shields her from Maleger's onslaughts.

Guyon and Arthur's encounters with Shamefastnesse and Prays-desire heighten the sense of Alma's House as a place where eros is either held in check or sublimated into forms promoting social stability. Behind the transparent fiction of a flirtation between two gallant knights and two attractive ladies lies an allegorical agenda precluding any passions that might tempt the heroes to reenact Aeneas's truancy. When the ladies speak, they reveal themselves as personified aspects of the knights' own temperaments rather than as external objects of desire.[33] Prays-desire introduces herself as an embodiment of Arthur's longing for heroic reputation:

> Pensiue I yeeld I am, and sad in mind,
>   Through great desire of glory and of fame;
>   Ne ought I weene are ye therein behind,
> That haue twelue moneths sought one, yet no where can her find.
>
>   (ix.38)

Her remarks immediately translate Arthur's erotic quest for Gloriana into an allegorical one, his "desire of glory and of fame." Alma similarly presents Shamefastnesse as an externalization of Guyon's innermost character trait: "She is the fountaine of your modestee; / You shamefast are, but *Shamefastnesse* it selfe is shee" (ix.43). Far from arousing any intemperate desire, Shamefastnesse is the precise virtue that Sir Thomas Elyot championed as the bridle with which youths might "rule as well their deeds as their appetites."[34]

The primary precedent for Arthur and Guyon's surprising discovery of a tribute to their own heroic nature while inspecting a noble woman's domain is Achates and Aeneas's discovery of Juno's murals. But even though Aeneas sees himself fighting valiantly on one panel, the murals focus more on his people's tragic history than on his personal character. Spenser postpones Guyon and Arthur's encounter with their national histories until they have left Alma's heart. His description of the tapestries covering the heart itself underscores this deferral through its teasing vagueness:

> Thence backe againe faire *Alma* led them right,
> And soone into a goodly Parlour brought,
> That was with royall arras richly dight,
> In which was nothing pourtrahed, nor wrought,
> Not wrought, nor pourtrahed, but easie to be thought.
>
> (ix.38)

Disagreements among critics and editors over what the tapestries actually depict attests to their enigmatic nature. The final line could mean that nothing was portrayed on them, even though a viewer might easily suppose that something could be. Berger, for instance, argues that nothing specific appears on the tapestries because Spenser wants to depict "the nature of the sensitive soul which is a potency unless moved." Yet as Jerry Mills has noted, the word "but" can mean "except" as well as "even though." The lines could mean that the tapestries portray nothing except those subjects that were "easie to be thought," whatever that means.[35] The ambiguity leaves us questioning not only what might be depicted on the tapestries but whether anything is actually depicted on them at all. We can only be sure of one thing: they do not contain the ekphrastic representation of national history that would complete the reenactment of Aeneas and Achates's experiences at the Temple of Juno. Spenser defers that narrative culmination until Arthur and Guyon discover the chronicles in Alma's head.

This displacement of historical representation from the heart to the head revises previous uses of the topos, as in *The Book of the Duchess, The House of Fame,* and the *Furioso,* to develop erotic as well as patriotic themes. In the *Aeneid* itself, the murals have both public and private, political and romantic significance. By commemorating the cataclysm that initiates Aeneas's quest for a new Troy, they establish the first term of the poem's historical myth. But by reminding Aeneas of Troy's destruction, they also heighten his awareness of the good fortune attending the Carthaginians "whose walls already rise" (*quorum iam moenia surgunt,* I.437 [M:621]). The nostalgia that they inspire possibly makes him more vulnerable to Dido's later offer of her own city as his new home.[36]

By placing the chronicles in Alma's head rather than her heart, Spenser signals that their public, epideictic purpose will not be compromised by their role in a private love story. Arthur and Guyon's delight in reading them is purely patriotic:

> At last quite rauisht with delight, to heare
> The royall Ofspring of his natiue land,
> [Arthur] cryde out, Deare countrey . . .
> How brutish is it not to vnderstand,
> How much to her we owe, that all vs gaue,
> That gaue vnto vs all, what euer good we haue.
>
> (x.69)

Unlike the murals on Juno's temple, which fed nostalgia for an irrecoverable past, Alma's chronicles spur their readers to future heroism. Although they too recount subjections to foreign rule, former British failures do not undermine confidence in the reestablishment of British glory. By grounding so much British suffering in past irascibility and concupiscence, in Cundah's "coles of cruell enmitie" (x.33) against his brother and in Locrine's "voluptuous disease" (x.17) for the Lady Estreldis, the chronicles equate governing a realm with disciplining individual passion.[37] The Legend of Temperance reaffirms Britain's capacity for an unassailable future *imperium* by insisting that each subject can learn to master his or her errant nature.

Readers have often denigrated the flatness of Spenser's writing in both the Alma and the Medina episodes. In 1888, Edward Dowden decried them as "the dullest portions of Spenser's poem," moments "where his love of beauty slumbers and his spirit of ingenuity awakes."[38] Commenting on the "tediousness" of Medina's House and the "dreadful allegory of the human body," Herbert Grierson lamented that "Clarion has been snared in the dusty web of the didactic, and can only rejoice when he escapes again to his favourite theme of love, or to expatiate in picturesque and musical irrelevancies."[39] Even modern critics who pride themselves on "objective" accounts of the poem's structure resort to evaluative language in anathematizing these episodes. For Graham Hough, Medina's house is "a frigid piece of allegory . . . built on [the] unpromising foundation" of Aristotle's Golden Mean. Hough similarly condemns the "antiquated physiological psychology" of Alma's castle as "a shock to the modern reader."[40]

In general, Medina and Alma's detractors perceive the contrast between the Bower's sensuous descriptions and the allegorical houses' explicit didacticism as a failure of "continuous decorum" (Hough, 158). But in a book analyzing human behavior as a continuum between the extremes of Medinan restraint and Acrasian abandonment, the contrast upholds temperance as an aesthetic as well as a moral virtue. Between "the dusty web of the didactic" and "picturesque irrelevancies" lies the perfect balance of the Horatian principle that literary works ought to teach and to delight simultaneously. On one level, Alma's resistance to her suitors and to Maleger's troops allegorizes Spenser's own resistance to art that merely pleases rather than instructs. In terms of the book's overall structure, he overcomes that threat by tempering the descriptiveness of Phaedria and Acrasia's bowers with the starker allegory of Medina and Alma's castles. My final section examines how Guyon's encounters with Phaedria and Acrasia figure aesthetic balance as a conflict between the allegorized *Aeneid*'s moral rigor and the sensuousness of the *romanzi*.

Dido and the Seductions of Italian Romance: Phaedria and Acrasia

By introducing Alma and Medina as unswervingly chaste Didos resisting both concupiscence and irascibility, Spenser counters Virgil's biases against female sovereignty. But he defines their chastity primarily against recollections of the unchaste Dido who hinders rather than abets heroic enterprise. Complex generic, political, and literary historical factors reinscribe the antifeminism of the *Aeneid* itself and of Dido's later dismissal as personified lasciviousness in the temptresses Phaedria and Acrasia. Angus Fletcher observes that allegorical agents of absolute virtue tend to generate subcharacters embodying their corresponding vices.[41] As the mean between two extremes, temperance can only be conceptualized in terms of deficiency and excess. Medina requires her sisters' irascibility and concupiscence to establish her own identity as a principle of rational restraint. Unless Guyon has a Phaedria or an Acrasia to resist, he cannot demonstrate his temperance.

Since *The Faerie Queene* is both an allegory and a national epic, its opposition of virtues to their corresponding vices reinforces imperial power structures. Just as societies create occasions for repressive force by stigmatizing "deviant" populations as threats to their existence, epic heroes seek antagonists to combat. As I suggested in the first chapter, Venus and Dido's appearance as foils to Aeneas's *pietas* reinforces the Augustan construction of Greek culture and of female participation in public life as joint threats to Roman civilization. In a now familiar reading of the Bower of Bliss, Stephen Greenblatt links Acrasia's identity as sexual excess to the Elizabethan construction of the New World as something mysteriously beautiful but dangerously alien to the social order.[42] For Greenblatt, the spectacle of the darkly maternal Acrasia sucking Verdant's spirit recalls contemporary descriptions of effeminacy, cannibalism, and incest among the African and North American natives. In the same way that such descriptions sanctioned the subjugation of aboriginal populations in the name of civility, Acrasia's malice justifies Guyon's rampage.

But if allegory generates a vice for every virtue, and if epic introduces antisocial forces as justifications for imperial violence, Phaedria and Acrasia cannot fully be understood without considering Spenser's ambition to enter the Virgilian succession. The fact that Spenser and Virgil both portrayed the conflict between civilization and its enemies may be explained as the historical coincidence of two poets writing for analogous court cultures. But Spenser's decision to center his fiction around a hero's resistance to a seductress results from explicit literary imitation. As scholars have long recognized, Acrasia comes to him from Dido, mediated through allegorical commentary and Italian romance. A densely allusive passage like the Bower of Bliss defies attempts to establish the priority of socio-political or literary historical origins. The power structures that the text validates, questions, and ultimately recuperates exist not only in contemporary society but in the texts that society upholds as canonical.

Spenser's adoption of a Virgilian poetic is more complex than the mere appropriation of topoi and character types. The strikingly parallel reception histories of Dido's abandonment and the Bower's destruction suggest that he followed Virgil in testing his hero's merits through the sacrifice of something profoundly desirable but incompatible with civilization. While Acrasia, or at least her Bower, has enjoyed as many champions as Dido, Guyon has found as many detractors as has Aeneas. In general, critics defending Guyon have raised the same arguments that classicists have used to justify Aeneas's desertion of Dido. Both Carthage and the Bower have been denounced as demonic parodies that must be rejected for the truths they travesty. If Carthage falsely imitates the new Troy, the Bower "falsely imitates the Divine Creation" or perverts the values later celebrated in the Gardens of Adonis.[43] Virgil's readers have condemned the opulence of Dido's palace as often as Spenser's readers have decried the splendor of Acrasia's gardens. Opposing critics have cited Dido's tragic pathos and the Bower's allure to argue that both poets covertly rejected the imperial values that their works ostensibly upheld.[44]

The specific points of debate as well as the general argumentative intensity distinguish the controversies over Dido and the Bower from those generated by abandoned temptresses in Italian romance. Critics continue to question whether Ariosto identifies himself more with Alcina as a poet of sensuous surfaces or with Logistilla as a didactic allegorist. But no one treats Ruggiero's abandonment of Alcina as harsh and inhumane.[45] Armida's conversion and reconciliation to Rinaldo at the end of the *Liberata* precludes debate altogether, although controversy resurfaces when Tasso cancels his earlier happy ending in the 1593 *Conquistata*. In the remainder of this chapter, I will argue that Guyon's violence provokes critical ambivalence precisely because it resists Ariosto's and Tasso's mitigation of the sacrifices validating their heroes' public commitments. Book II of *The Faerie Queene* reestablishes epic as a genre valorizing the surrender of whatever one holds most alluring and precious. Its cataclysmic denouement indicts the clemency of Italian romance as a deviation from the "rigour pittilesse" with which Virgil exhorted his readers to self-denial.

Before turning to Acrasia as an apotropaic embodiment of Italian influence, I want to consider Spenser's preliminary critique of the *romanzi* through the transformation of Tasso's Armida into Phaedria. Scholars have often noted the episode's general Italianate character as well as its specific origins in Rinaldo's arrival on Armida's island. Martha Craig has argued that Spenser endows the laughing raconteuse with an aura of Italian hedonism by deriving the word "gondelay" for her boat from "gongolare," which Florio translates as a verb meaning "to laugh till ones heart be sore."[46] Everything about Phaedria aligns Italian culture with concupiscible delights distracting men from valiant enterprise. While the "inland sea" on which she sails literally translates the word "Mediterranean," its identity as the Idle Lake may derive from an association of the Adriatic with *adraneia,* or "inactivity" (Craig, 464). From Phaedria's stereotypically Mediterranean perspective, work and pleasure are antithetical phenomena. All labor is "fruitlesse toile" and "present pleasures" alone are the purpose of our existence (vi.17).

The aesthetic counterpart of Phaedria's contempt toward work is her implicit denial of the Horatian tenet that artistic pleasure ought to accompany ethical instruction. For her, the laureate's struggle to fashion his auditors by gentle discipline is nothing but "fruitlesse toile." If her songs and stories are *dulce,* they are emphatically not *utile*:

> For she in pleasant purpose did abound
> And greatly ioyed merry tales to faine,
> Of which a store-house did with her remaine,
> Yet seemed, nothing well they her became;
> For all her words she drowned with laughter vaine.
>
> (vi.6)

Instead of teaching sound moral principles, her "merry tales" merely elicit the "laughter vaine" that characterizes her throughout the episode. If her song about the lilies of the field teaches anything at all, it is a lesson in idleness. Her false analogies about nature's spontaneous perfection suggest that humanity has no reason to seek its own ethical perfection. Phaedria's Italianate demeanor, as well as her conspicuously Tassean origins, associate her art divorced from moral instruction with Italian romance. Throughout the episode, Spenser recalls the *romanzi* as a genre of superficial wonder and delight to set off his own identity as a didactic, Virgilian poet. This strategy becomes particularly apparent when the episode is read against its Tassean subtext. As we have seen, the Armida episode itself has an emphatic moral agenda. By distinguishing Armida's sorcery from the marvelous effects of reason in collaboration with grace, Tasso affirms humanity's power to overcome sensual temptation with providential assistance. But when Spenser recalls the *Liberata* in this section of *The Faerie Queene*, he ignores Tasso's didactic distinctions between the miraculous and the diabolical to dismiss him as a poet of sensuous surfaces and fantastic effects. In essence, Spenser denies Tasso's status as a moralist in the Virgilian tradition by identifying Tasso's own art entirely with Armida's.

The intertextual genealogy of Phaedria's magical "gondelay" exemplifies the strategies through which Spenser stigmatizes Tassean romance as antithetical to Virgilian moral instruction. Spenser bases the boat on two separate vessels in the *Liberata*. When Guyon abandons his Palmer on first boarding it, the passage recalls Rinaldo's dismissal of his squires on first boarding the boat that transports him to Armida's island (*GL* XIV.58; *FQ* II.vi.19). Although that boat is part of Armida's trap, it is neither piloted by her nor inherently magical. It is only an ordinary boat that Rinaldo rows himself. The marvelous aspects of Phaedria's "gondelay" that flits along unhindered by either "swelling *Neptune,* ne loud thundring *Ioue*" (vi.10) come from a second Tassean boat, the one piloted by Fortuna, which carries Carlo and Ubaldo to rescue Rinaldo from Armida's island. Like Phaedria's skiff, Fortuna's is "swift beyond the order of nature" (*veloce sovra il natural costume,* XV.8) and unaffected by storms and swelling tides. But it is emphatically an instrument of Armida's defeat rather than her own diabolical invention. Throughout the episode, Tasso presents Fortuna as a faithful servant of Providence who eventually ferries Rinaldo back to the Holy Land to resume his fight against the Infidel.[47]

But when Spenser rewrites Rinaldo's adventures, he retrospectively transforms the magical skiff into the vessel ferrying the hero into the sorceress's domain. Whereas Fortune's boat proved instrumental in recalling Rinaldo to his quest, Phaedria's "gondelay," as Spenser's spelling suggests, delays his campaign against Acrasia. By inverting the moral function of Tasso's providential skiff, Spenser dissolves his precursor's distinction between diabolical effects and divine wonders. From his perspective, nothing in Tasso's fiction is ethically sound. The enticing music, the birdsong, and the luxuriance of Armida's garden blur to-

gether with the tranquil sea to evoke an indolence antithetical to heroic am-
bition. Everything becomes part of Phaedria's seductive art.

By diabolizing Fortune's vessel and inverting its role in the hero's career,
Spenser suppresses Tasso's didactic purpose. In the *Liberata,* Tasso presents the
allure of Armida's gardens as a test of his hero's inner virtue. Although Rinaldo
temporarily succumbs to temptation, Carlo and Ubaldo teach him how to over-
come his vulnerability to sensuous enticement the moment they arrive on the
magical skiff. Spenser rejects that denouement for the time being and substitutes
for the fallible but ultimately educable Rinaldo a Guyon who never seems par-
ticularly tempted. The latter scorns Phaedria's pleasantries as invitations to in-
temperance: "But when he saw her toy, and gibe, and geare / . . . / Her
dalliance he despisd, and follies did forsake" (vi.21). In contrast to Rinaldo's
arrival on Armida's island, Guyon's adventures on Phaedria's stress not his sus-
ceptibility to deception but his ability to recognize and overcome it.

Guyon's power to see through Phaedria's courtesies becomes a metonymy
for Spenser's own ability to expose the *romanzi*'s ostensible didactic agenda as a
screen for a poetry whose primary end is wonder and delight. From Spenser's
revisionary perspective, Rinaldo succumbs to the temptations that Guyon scorns,
not so much to illustrate a point about concupiscence, but because Tasso himself
is enamored of Armida's enchantments. As in the Belphoebe episode, Spenser
challenges his Italian precursor for being too indulgent toward his hero's lapses.
In the same way that Spenser retrospectively equates Ruggiero with the would-
be rapist Braggadocchio, he equates Rinaldo with Cymochles: Cymochles falls
into a fast sleep listening to an imitation of the same song that hypnotizes Rin-
aldo. Like Braggadocchio's pretensions, Cymochles's farcical languor casts his
predecessor's actions in a ridiculous light. Once more, Spenser suggests that a
hero who succumbs to concupiscent impulse is not really a hero at all. A true
hero, like Guyon, triumphs over temptation through his temperate commitment
to the Golden Mean.

Spenser's critique of Tasso is nowhere more apparent than in the destruction
of the Bower, where Guyon's violence overturns the clemency extended toward
Armida at the *Liberata*'s conclusion. Spenser himself introduced a pardonable
Dido in the Amavia episode to establish a boundary between Book I's emphasis
on divine forgiveness and Book II's emphasis on natural perseverance. While
mercy is privileged over justice on the order of grace, pity is stigmatized on the
order of nature for diminishing the rigor necessary to prevail against carnal temp-
tation. Spenser saw Tasso as a lesser threat to his Virgilian identity in Book I
because Spenser too was expanding the epic paradigm to embrace forgiveness
and conversion. But with Book II's recuperation of epic primarily as a genre
fortifying natural reason and will against intemperance, Tassean clemency be-

comes the chief temptation Spenser himself must overcome in creating a place for himself in the Virgilian succession.

Aligning himself with Virgilian rigor against Tasso's lenity, Spenser overturns the *Liberata*'s reconciliation of love with heroic enterprise. If passion distracts Rinaldo temporarily from the conquest of Jerusalem, it also saves his life by making Armida abandon her initial, murderous intentions. Her conversion at the poem's conclusion suggests that even the most extravagant desire can be perfected in the higher love of God. By accommodating epic to a more positive representation of passion, Tasso writes a poem in which Dido no longer has to be irrecoverably lost. In Book II of *The Faerie Queene,* Spenser restores a fundamental opposition between duty and desire by casting Acrasia as a one-dimensional agent of intemperance rather than as a more fully developed character capable of moral regeneration. Unlike Armida, she must be repudiated once and for all in accordance with the Palmer's general condemnation of love as "a monster fell" that "filth did breede" (II.iv.35).

In distancing himself from what he treats as Tasso's greater indulgence toward passion, Spenser focuses on the passage in which Armida first falls in love with Rinaldo and abandons her intention of killing him:

> But when she fixed her gaze upon him and saw how calm of countenance he breathes, and how charming a manner laughs about his lovely eyes, though they be closed (now what will it be if he opens them?), first she stands still in suspense, and then sits down beside him, and feels her every wrath becalmed while she gazes upon him; and now she bends so above his handsome face that she seems Narcissus at the spring.
>
> And those trembling drops of sweat that welled up there she softly takes off into her veil and with a gentle fanning tempers for him the heat of the summery sky. So (who would believe it?) the slumbering warmth of his hidden eyes dissolved that frost that had hardened her heart even more than adamant, and from his enemy she became his lover.
>
> (XIV.66–67)

> Ma quando in lui fissò lo sguardo vide
> come placido in vista egli respira,
> e ne' begli occhi un dolce atto che ride,
> benché sian chiusi (or che fia s'ei li gira?),
> pria s'arresta sospesa, e gli s'asside
> poscia vicina, e placar sente ogn'ira
> mentre il risguarda; e 'n su la vaga fronte
> pende omai sì che par Narciso al fonte.

E quei ch'ivi sorgean vivi sudori
accoglie lievemente in un suo velo,
e con un dolce ventillar gli ardori
gli va temprando de l'estivo cielo.
Così (chi 'l crederia?) sopiti ardori
d'occhi nascosi distempràr quel gelo
che s'indurava al cor più che diamante;
e di nemica ella divenne amante.

Fixing her eyes on her intended victim, Armida herself suffers an erotic wound
that prepares her for her ultimate conversion. Spenser recalls her gazing on her
sleeping lover when Guyon and the Palmer discover Verdant and Acrasia:

And all that while, right ouer him she hong,
With her false eyes fast fixed in his sight,
As seeking medicine, whence she was stong,
Or greedily depasturing delight:
And oft inclining downe with kisses light,
For feare of waking him, his lips bedewd,
And through his humid eyes did sucke his spright.

(xii.73)

Although Spenser derives his parodic *pietà* conspicuously from Tasso, he alters
its moral force so that Acrasia's malignancy, unlike Armida's, remains unaffected
by the young man's beauty. At the same time, the unexpected wound that
opened Armida's heart to love's redemptive powers becomes a kind of sado-
masochistic thrill, a stinging rather than a healing medicine that Acrasia delib-
erately seeks. In identifying himself with Virgil as a quintessentially antierotic
poet, Spenser presents sexual desire as something inherently destructive. From
the perspective that Spenser adopts at this stage, Tasso's dramatic peripeteia
hinges on a false distinction. The lover's gaze is itself a fatal instrument, the
ghoulish medium through which Acrasia consumes Verdant's spirit.[48]

By denying Acrasia the conversions through which Armida becomes first
Rinaldo's lover and later a Christian, Spenser distances himself not only from
Tasso's pity toward Armida but also from Virgil's toward Dido in the *Aeneid*.
Much of the sympathy with which Tasso endows Armida in later episodes de-
rives directly from Virgil's characterization of Dido. Armida quotes Dido's lines
when Rinaldo abandons her; just before her conversion, she threatens to reenact
Dido's suicide. But if Armida and Dido rise to tragic status through their in-
vectives against the hero who betrays them, Acrasia maintains a deadly, forbid-
ding silence throughout the episode. While the pathos of Dido's speeches

provoked later writers to condemn Aeneas, and the poignancy of Armida's reveal a fundamental humanity capable of regeneration, Acrasia's silence marks her as a monstrous moral condition rather than a pitiable individual. The Dido she ultimately recalls is not the *Aeneid*'s tragic heroine but the Dido of Neo-Latin commentary, a daimonized embodiment of concupiscence. Just as the Fulgentian Dido dissolves silently into ashes when reason confronts her in the guise of Mercury, Acrasia submits without any pitiable lamentation to Guyon and the Palmer. Spenser underscores the episode's allegorical origin by giving the Palmer a staff made of the same wood as Mercury's caduceus (xii.41).

In every other epic in the Virgilian succession, the hero overcomes a temptress so that he can fulfill his mission of founding an empire, establishing a dynasty, or liberating the Holy City. Even in works that counsel against concupiscence as vehemently as do the *Confessions* and the *Divine Comedy,* sexual restraint is championed primarily as a means to greater joys that more than compensate for abandoned carnal pleasures. In both Augustine and Dante, libido is ultimately sublimated in the higher love of God. In the Bower of Bliss, it is sublimated only into "the tempest of [Guyon's] wrathfulnesse" as he defaces Acrasia's garden, fells her groves, spoils her arbors, razes her palace, and burns her "banket houses" to the ground (xii.83). Overcoming eros is not something that Guyon must do to resume an interrupted quest but is itself the goal of his quest. Acrasia stands finally not just as a potential Dido who might distract him from his mission but also as his Turnus, the final antagonist through whose destruction he achieves his destiny.

Although epics in the Virgilian tradition often culminate in displays of violence, coercive or repressive force usually appears as a necessary means to more constructive, even creative ends. With Turnus's death, Aeneas establishes a glorious future for his people; Rinaldo's *aristeia* achieves the liberation of Jerusalem. At the beginning of Guyon's voyage to the Bower, his mission too appears as a constructive act:

> Now gins this goodly frame of Temperance
> Fairely to rise, and her adorned hed
> To pricke of highest praise forth to aduance,
> Formerly grounded, and fast setteled
> On firme foundation of true bountihed.
>
> (xii.1)

But if Aeneas's triumph over Turnus establishes an empire, Guyon's destruction of the Bower paradoxically completes "this goodly frame of Temperance." As Guyon's experiences at Medina's House remind us, temperance is inevitably defined in terms of control, compulsion, and restraint. What Guyon ultimately builds up by suppressing Acrasia is the capacity to continue suppressing her in a constant valorization of his governing virtue.

Guyon's final display of "rigour pittilesse" distances Spenser not only from the clemency concluding the *Liberata* but also from the happy endings imposed on the *Aeneid* itself by its sixteenth-century editors (xii.83). As we have seen, the Renaissance sense of the *Aeneid* as an unfinished work encouraged writers like Decembrio, Forestus, and Vegius to write thirteen books depicting Aeneas's dynastic marriage to Lavinia. While Spenser turned to Vegius's *Supplementum* as a model for Redcrosse's betrothal to Una, he returns to the starker, more abrupt ending of the *Aeneid* itself in Book II.[49] Yet unlike the *Aeneid*, Book II is clearly a complete, self-contained work: Guyon has neither a bride to marry nor an empire to establish. His career ends with Acrasia's defeat not because Spenser failed to finish his story but because his victory over concupiscence is the ultimate purpose of his existence.

Associating Virgilian writing with both sexual and aesthetic restraint reinforces Spenser's concept of temperance as a virtue opposing concupiscence and irascibility. But this particular construction of Virgil does not necessarily accommodate the poem's other titular virtues. As we have already seen, Book I indicts the Virgilian commentators' confidence in human agency as a presumptuous blindness to grace. From the perspective of holiness, Guyon's "rigour pittilesse" leads only to despair. In Book III, Spenser's emphasis on eros as a force that inspires rather than hinders heroic enterprise leads to yet another interpretation of what it means to write a poem in the Virgilian tradition.

"Diverse Folk Diversely They Demed":
Virgilian Alternatives in Book III

Scholars have often debated why Spenser replaces the single heroes and the comparatively linear action of his first two books with Book III's multiple heroes and interlaced plots. Those who prefer the earlier books' allegorical clarity have blamed the latter book's looser structure on everything from the presence of insufficiently revised juvenilia to Spenser's incompetence as a love poet.[1] In response to these critiques, Book III's champions have defended its *entrelacement* as the perfect structural correlative of the virtue that it anatomizes. Thomas Roche, for instance, argues that its digressive, multiple plots reflect love's complexity. Although Spenser explores holiness and temperance through the adventures of a single knight, he cannot do the same for chastity "because of the variety and multiplicity of forms inherent in that virtue."[2] A. C. Hamilton similarly maintains that exchanging the Bible and classical epic for Italian romance as Book III's principal model reinforces Spenser's emphasis on erotic diversity.[3]

In this chapter, I want to suggest that the structural and stylistic contrasts between Book III and the earlier books arise less from such thematic pressures than from contemporary arguments over the nature of Virgilian writing. Twentieth-century critics might describe the shift from single to multiple heroes as a turn from classical epic to Italian romance. Renaissance readers, however, would have recognized this shift as an exchange between alternative notions of what poetic forms inherited Virgil's cultural authority. In the earlier books, Spenser joined Minturno, Sassetti, and others in rejecting the interlaced adventures of multiple heroes as a distraction from the Virgilian goal of fashioning people in virtuous and gentle discipline. In Book III, he joins Pigna and Fornari in embracing them as the best means to achieve that didactic end. Not surprisingly, debates among Spenserians over Book III's relationship to the poem's earlier books replicate humanist arguments over the *Furioso*'s relationship to the *Aeneid*. If Bennett's contention that Book III's organization is unclear recalls Minturno's complaints about Ariosto's rambling plots, Roche's defense that its digressive structure best displays the polymorphousness of love echoes Giraldi's argument that the *Furioso*'s variety enhances its effectiveness as a vehicle of moral instruction.

Other Renaissance poets either sanctioned or rejected the notion that romance conventions might be compatible with Virgilian poetry. Tasso's response to the question shifted throughout his career, but he revised his views by writing separate poems. Spenser's originality lies in his incorporating both stances toward romance in a single poem. Like Tasso's *Conquistata,* Books I and II of *The Faerie Queene* discredit Ariostan influence as an impediment to the didactic rigor associated with Virgilian epic by commentators from Fulgentius to Petrarch, Boccaccio, and Sidney. Like Tasso's earlier *Liberata,* Spenser's Book III rejects the skepticism underlying Ariosto's abandonment of Virgilian structure while embracing Ariosto's formal innovations as compatible with Virgil's didactic ideals. But in contrast to Tasso, Spenser does not assume that one understanding of Virgilian poetry invalidates the other. Instead of endorsing different views in discrete works written at different points in his career, he brings them into deliberate confrontation in a single work so that each illuminates the other. The transition from Book II to Book III transforms epic from a monologic into a dialogic form, containing alternative conceptions of even its own generic nature.

Reconceiving epic form leads in turn to redefining the education that epic achieves as a quintessentially didactic genre. Earlier in the poem, Spenser joined Virgil's Neo-Latin commentators in couching its lessons primarily in terms of discipline and restraint. His conspicuous resistance to Italian romance reinforced those lessons by demonstrating an aesthetic restraint paralleling his heroes' sexual restraint. In contrast, Book III exhorts its readers less to a particular behavior than to a greater consciousness of moral complexities. Spenser reinforces this alternative understanding of epic's didactic ends by transforming it into a genre that incorporates rather than excludes other modes of writing. Assessing his characters according to the competing conventions of allegorized epic and of romance or fabliau, he exposes the limitations of judging human actions from any single perspective.

As I will later argue, Spenser's concept of epic as an exchange between alternative ethical and aesthetic perspectives is indebted principally to Chaucer. In *The Shepheardes Calender,* he discredited the more dialogic aspects of Chaucer's poetry as a threat to his laureate identity. He endorsed instead the sententiousness that Hoccleve and Lydgate sanctioned as truer to the Virgilian didactic spirit. In the 1590 *Faerie Queene,* however, the more ludic Chaucer of the fabliaux provides Spenser a model for balancing the conflicting claims of allegorical epic and Italian romance. Spenser rarely adopts Chaucer's solution of associating diverse genres and points of view with individual narrators. But he does create a poem that foregrounds collisions between antithetical influences. Behind the confrontations between Virgil and Ariosto in the Malecasta episode, or between epic and fabliau in the Hellenore episode, lie the confrontations between Virgil and Ovid in *The House of Fame* and between the Knight's idealism and the Miller's earthiness in *The Canterbury Tales.*

In departing from his earlier conception of epic as a genre that teaches restraint by excluding alternative poetic influences, Spenser transforms the central topos through which his predecessors established their Virgilian identities. In Books I and II, he figured his resistance to idioms deemed incompatible with his laureate vocation through his heroes' resistance to temptresses patterned on the concupiscent Dido of Neo-Latin commentary. In Book III, he finds an image of epic's dialectic engagement with these previously stigmatized influences in the erotic unions sought by Arthur, Britomart, Florimell, and other characters. Sexuality continues to be the principal metaphor for Spenser's relationship to diverse poetic forms. Yet in privileging consummation as the goal of epic labor, he casts the sorcerer who opposes youthful desires, rather than the temptress, as the hero's chief antagonist. Britomart's triumph over Busirane marks Spenser's final turn against his earlier association of epic with exclusion and restraint.

Ariosto Revisited: Britomart at Castle Joyeous

Words, motifs, and images conspicuously associated with the Bower of Bliss haunt Book III's opening canto and present Britomart's confrontation with Malecasta as a revision of Guyon's with Acrasia. In the first stanza of Book II, canto xii, for instance, Spenser describes the Bower as

> that same perilous sted,
> Where Pleasure dwelles in sensuall delights,
> Mongst thousand dangers, and ten thousand magick mights.
>
> (xii.1)

He subsequently draws on this passage's vocabulary in portraying the "wastefull wayes, / Where daungers dwelt, and perils most did wonne" through which Guyon and Arthur pass before their encounter with Britomart (III.i.3). The "hideous horror and sad trembling sound" (III.i.14) of the forest surrounding Castle Joyeous echo the "hideous roaring" of the Gulfe of Greedinesse, which Guyon hears just as the morning spreads "her trembling light" on the waves (II.xii.2). The bears, lions, and bulls of Malecasta's forest, associated emblematically with concupiscence, recall Acrasia's "many beasts, that roard outrageously" as if "*Venus* sting / Had them enraged with fell surquedry" (II.xii.39). Inside Castle Joyeous itself, the tapestry of Venus holding the sleeping Adonis recalls Acrasia cradling the sleeping Verdant.[4]

By recalling the Bower on the threshold of chastity, Spenser interrogates alternative understandings of the ethical vision that authorizes epic in the Virgilian tradition. As I argued in the previous chapter, Guyon's victory over Acrasia reaffirms the commentators' view of Dido's tragedy as a lesson in passion's submission to the higher mental faculties. But when Spenser recasts Aeneas's rejection of Dido yet again in Britomart's confrontation with Malecasta, he no longer presents passion as something inherently incompatible with virtue.[5] Malecasta's longing for Britomart might be condemned as concupiscence, but Britomart's desire for Arthegall has a heroic dimension resisting the unqualified antieroticism of Neo-Latin commentary.

Expanding the Virgilian paradigm to encompass a more positive view of sexuality is synecdochic of Spenser's greater openness to Italian romance. Throughout the episode, asides and narrative digressions patterned on the *Furioso* qualify the Neo-Latin commentators' ethical premises. When Guyon attacks Britomart in the book's opening stanzas, for instance, touches of Ariostan urbanity reinforce Spenser's retrospective critique of the Bower's antieroticism. Guyon's aggression conspicuously resembles his earlier violence against Acrasia:

> . . . then the Faery quickly raught
> His poinant speare, and sharpely gan to spurne
> His fomy steed, whose fierie feete did burne
> The verdant grasse, as he thereon did tread.
>
> (III.i.5)

The "fomy steed" with "fierie feete" recalls Book III's juxtaposition of fire and water, flame and froth, as an emblem of intemperance in its twin forms of concupiscence and irascibility. By modifying the trampled grass with the adjective "verdant," Spenser subtly evokes the memory of Verdant, the young man whom Guyon rescued from Acrasia's spells.

But in Book III, Spenser no longer privileges Guyon's "rigour pittilesse." Opposing a woman who embodies the erotic figured as chaste desire rather than as concupiscence, Guyon becomes an enemy rather than an agent of virtue. As Spenser suggests in a narrative aside more typical of the *Furioso* than of the Legend of Temperance, Britomart is leagued with forces that Guyon cannot fathom:

> Ah gentlest knight, that euer armour bore,
> Let not thee grieue dismounted to haue beene,
> And brought to ground, that neuer wast before;
> For not thy fault, but secret powre vnseene,
> That speare enchaunted was, which layd thee on the greene.
>
> (III.i.7)

In the commentary tradition dominating Guyon's world, there is no place for the "secret powre" of a chastity whose end is sexual consummation in marriage rather than perpetual restraint. But from the perspective of Book III, Guyon's ethical vision is dangerously incomplete. His repressiveness proves just as threatening as Acrasia's ghoulish languor to the promises of sexual awakening and new birth etymologically associated with Verdant as "the giver of spring."

When Arthur and the Palmer try to check Guyon's anger after Britomart unseats him, Spenser raises Ariostan suspicions that reason might not even be capable of subduing passion:

> By such good meanes [the Palmer] him discounselled,
>> From prosecuting his reuenging rage;
>> And eke the Prince like treaty handeled,
>> His wrathfull will with reason to asswage,
>> And laid the blame, not to his carriage,
>> But to his starting steed, that swaru'd asyde,
>> And to the ill purueyance of his page,
>> That had his furnitures not firmely tyde:
> So is his angry courage fairely pacifyde.
>
> (III.i.11)

Spenser seems to endorse reason's primacy over emotion when Arthur and the Palmer urge Guyon to assuage "his wrathfull will with reason." Nevertheless, Guyon is appeased less by exhortations to rational behavior than by Arthur's discrete lies about his careless page and "starting steed." Arthur's slide from reasonable appeal to urbane dissimulation recalls one of Ariosto's typical ploys against the confidence in reason underlying the *Aeneid*'s humanist canonization. Melissa's resort to disguise and promises of Bradamante's affections suggest that reasonable castigations alone might not quell Ruggiero's lust for Alcina. Arthur's fib similarly implies that reason might not fully assuage the complementary passion of wrath. As in Melissa's conversation with Ruggiero, emotional excess is controlled not by suppression and self-denial but by a temporizing accommodation to social norms.[6]

Throughout Britomart's visit to Castle Joyeous, quasi-Ariostan doubts about humanity's ability to master its passions continue to subvert the didactic program attributed to Virgil by humanist commentators.[7] Her androgyny allows Spenser to construct the episode around a retelling of Aeneas's encounter with Dido from two antithetical perspectives. In repudiating Malecasta, Britomart plays the commentators' Aeneas rejecting an embodiment of unbridled passion. But the narrator's Ariostan asides cast her simultaneously as a type of Dido herself yearning for an errant hero. In the balance between competing notions of what constitutes a heroic poem in the Virgilian tradition, she stands both as Malecasta's allegorical antagonist and as her fellow sufferer from a desire that cannot be disciplined by either internal reason or external persuasion. Spenser previously opposed chaste to unchaste Didos in contrasting the temptresses Phaedria and Acrasia and the virgins Alma and Medina. But Book III's reconciliation of epic and romance decorums develops the chaste Dido not as a perpetual virgin but as a young woman called like Bradamante to a marriage fulfilling both private desire and imperial destiny.

Like Dido's Carthage in Neo-Latin commentary, Castle Joyeous stands primarily as a seat of carnal indulgence seducing its visitors from virtue. The Venus and Adonis tapestries that Britomart examines before meeting Malecasta parallel the gate illustrating Jason's tragic affair with Medea that Guyon passes on entering the Bower. Both artworks recall the murals on Juno's temple that Aeneas sees just before he meets Dido. As I have already argued, the original Virgilian ekphrasis could be interpreted either as a public commemoration of Trojan history or as a private stimulus to Aeneas's love for Dido. But like Acrasia's gate, Malecasta's tapestries reduce epic and mythic history entirely to private, erotic intrigue. Everything in Malecasta's house, like the attractions both of the Bower and of Dido's Carthage as John of Salisbury and others interpreted them, exists to stir desires presumably incompatible with heroic enterprise:

> She caused them be led in curteous wize
> Into a bowre, disarmed for to bee,

> And cheared well with wine and spiceree:
> The *Redcrosse* Knight was soone disarmed there,
> But the braue Mayd would not disarmed bee.
>
> (i.42)

While the "bowre" where Malecasta disarms her guests recalls the Bower where Acrasia disarms hers, the "wine and spiceree" recall the Carthaginian *deliciae* that Bernard, Salisbury, and others condemned as provocations to lasciviousness. Once again, aristocratic hospitality masks amorous solicitation. The same Cupid who inflames Dido with illicit desire kindles "lustfull fires" among Malecasta's guests (i.39).

Throughout the canto, Spenser heightens Malecasta's association with Dido by recalling the images of fire, wounds, and poison through which Virgil depicted her passion for Aeneas:

> The queen is caught between love's pain
> and press. She feeds the wound within her veins;
> she is eaten by a secret flame.

> At regina graui iamdudum saucia cura
> uulnus alit uenis et caeco carpitur igni.
>
> (*Aen.* IV.1–2 [M:1–3])

> But yet her wound still inward freshly bled,
> And through her bones the false instilled fire
> Did spred it selfe, and venime close inspire.
>
> (*FQ* III.i.56)

But the "sighes, and sobs, and plaints, and piteous griefe, / The outward sparkes of [Malecasta's] in burning fire" reduce Dido's tragic grief to bawdry (i.53). Medieval and Renaissance commentators anticipated this reduction by dismissing Dido as lust personified. In the *Aeneid* itself, Dido struggles to conceal her desire. When she finally succumbs to it and becomes an object of scandal, she provides a terrifying, Euripidean spectacle of passion's power to corrupt even the noblest human. Spenser distances himself from the *Aeneid*'s pathos and aligns himself with the commentators' harsher judgment by emphasizing Malecasta's alacrity in abandoning herself to her desires. The fire that ultimately consumes Dido remains secret (*caeco . . . igni,* IV.2) until fanned by Anna's encouragements, but Malecasta's "fickle hart" bursts immediately into a "hasty fire, / Like sparkes of fire, which fall in sclender flex" (i.47). The commentators' sense of Dido as less a human being than an abstract vice underlies Malecasta's characterization as Britomart's allegorical antagonist. Like Guyon, Britomart appears as an Aeneas who successfully resists the Dido threatening to distract her from her quest. By rebuffing Malecasta's nocturnal advances and confronting Gardante, Parlante, Noctante, and the other allegorized stages of a seduction, she too emerges as an agent of temperance and chastity:

> Wherewith enrag'd she fiercely at them flew,
>   And with her flaming sword about her layd,
>   That none of them foule mischiefe could eschew,
>   But with her dreadfull strokes were all dismayd:
>   Here, there, and euery where about her swayd
>   Her wrathfull steele, that none mote it abide.
>   (i.66)

In an unsettling return to Guyon's violence, a daimonized virtue once more vanquishes its opposite to provide a lesson primarily on resisting temptation. As at the end of Book II, Spenser appears to present himself as Virgil's heir by advocating the antieroticism attributed to the *Aeneid* by commentators from Fulgentius through Petrarch and Boccaccio.

But throughout the episode, his narrative asides challenge the commentators' understanding of what lessons must be taught by poetry endowed with Virgil's cultural prestige. By revealing Britomart's own status as a victim of Cupid's oppression, Book III's narrator modifies the rigid allegorical distinctions between concupiscence and chastity conceived solely as restraint. Spenser suggests that the boundaries between love and lust are not so clear as those between temperance and intemperance by establishing a potential bond of sympathy between Britomart and Malecasta. Unlike Guyon and Acrasia, they are not utterly antithetical characters:

> Full easie was for her to haue beliefe,
>   Who by self-feeling of her feeble sexe,
>   And by long triall of the inward griefe,
>   Wherewith imperious loue her hart did vexe,
>   Could iudge what paines do louing harts perplexe.
>   (i.54)

Nothing like this could have occurred in Book II. The stanza not only grants Britomart an interiority distinguishing her from Guyon but also places her in a moral world that cannot be neatly compartmentalized. Spenser asserts that Britomart is mistaken in believing Malecasta's "outward smoke" stems from an "inward fire" like hers for Arthegall (i.55). But his later insistence on the diversity with which "loue doth his pageants play" (v.1) suggests that their passions may have more in common than he acknowledges here on the threshold between Books II and III. Whereas temperance and intemperance are antithetical by definition, love and lust can be seen as diverse manifestations of the same fundamental instinct.

The long digression recounting Britomart's love for Arthegall grounds her sympathy for Malecasta in their common Virgilian origin. Although scholars have often cited the pseudo-Virgilian *Ciris* as the digression's primary source, Spenser describes Britomart's infatuation in terms that also recall Dido's first stirrings of passion for Aeneas.[8] Like Aeneas, Arthegall appears to Britomart as a warrior who "restlesse walketh all the world around, / Ay doing things, that to his fame redound" (ii.14). By possessing Achilles's arms, he acquires not only a general aura of classical heroism but also a direct link to the Trojan war. The same "false archer" (ii.26) who wounds Dido while she listens to Aeneas's narrative of Troy's fall wounds Britomart while she gazes on the image of Achilles and his ancient armor in Merlin's mirror. Like Dido, Britomart suffers sleepless nights and endures the pains and "poysnous gore" (ii.39) typical of Cupid's secret mastery. If Glauce's counsels conspicuously imitate those offered Scylla by her nurse Carme in the *Ciris,* they also owe something to Anna's encouragement of Dido's interest in Aeneas.

From the perspective of the Neo-Latin commentators, Dido's agonies attest to the destructiveness of a desire inherently opposed to virtue. But in redefining Virgilian ideals, Spenser recasts them as the initial stages of a passion that inspires rather than impedes noble enterprise. Eros does not have to be the degrading fury that it becomes for Malecasta and the commentators' Dido. As Merlin informs Britomart when she reenacts Aeneas's descent into the underworld, Cupid's wound does not hinder her destiny but leads to its fulfillment:

> It was not, *Britomart,* thy wandring eye,
>> Glauncing vnwares in charmed looking glas,
>> But the streight course of heauenly destiny,
>> Led with eternall prouidence, that has
>> Guided thy glaunce, to bring his will to pas.
>
> (iii.24)

Abandoning Dido proved Aeneas's worthiness to achieve the glorious future revealed in the underworld. The *Aeneid*'s Christian commentators saw his rejection of passion as a necessary step toward the *vita contemplativa* and ultimate salvation. By introducing Britomart's love for Arthegall as a force reconciling these oppositions between public and private, transcendent and temporal commitments, Spenser accommodates the Virgilian paradigm to the Protestant idealization of marriage as the highest sexual state.

Creating a place in epic for a love that fosters virtuous enterprise typifies

Book III's tendency to recast the genre along Ariostan lines. In earlier books, Spenser's portrayal of eros as a threat to the hero's quest paralleled his construction of Italian influence as a threat to his laureate vocation. Here in Book III, depicting desires that strengthen the hero's public commitments recuperates romance as a set of conventions reinforcing the epic poet's commitment to "vertuous and gentle discipline." Merlin's assertion that Britomart's "wandring eye / Glauncing vnwares in charmed looking glas" secretly obeyed the "streight course of heauenly destiny" implicitly dissolves theoretical distinctions between epic and romance itineraries. Just as Spenser no longer equates sexual consummation with dereliction from duty, he no longer associates narrative digression and *entrelacement* with moral error. Throughout Book III, they become his primary strategies for accommodating Virgilian paradigms with a more comprehensive ethical vision.

Merlin's revelation that apparent error and caprice actually serve "heauenly destiny" echoes Melissa's insistence that Bradamante's seemingly fortuitous arrival at Merlin's tomb fulfills the will of God (*non giunta qui senza voler divino, OF* III.9). Spenser's acceptance of Italian romance as a positive influence culminates in his sustained patterning of Britomart's career on Bradamante's. Although Ariosto preceded him in presenting erotic desire as the instrument of an imperial *fatum,* Spenser establishes an intertextual dialogue between the *Furioso* and the allegorized *Aeneid* that modifies the final ethical implications of both toward the Virgilian past. If he appeals to the *romanzi* in challenging the commentators' antieroticism, he rejects Ariostan skepticism by maintaining the commentators' confidence in humanity's capacity for lasting commitments. Whereas Ruggiero's sudden passion for Angelica unsettles his idealized relationship with Bradamante, nothing in *The Faerie Queene* suggests that Britomart and Arthegall's commitment will be compromised by errant desires. Even in the Radigund episode of Book V, Arthegall is never "to his owne absent loue . . . vntrew" (V.v.56).

In earlier books, Spenser figured the *romanzi* as influences antithetical to epic in the Virgilian tradition. His revisions of Italian subtexts in the Bower of Bliss suggest that he found the *Liberata*'s reconciliation of martial and erotic themes as generically subversive as the *Furioso*'s more radical doubts about human educability. Although he never embraces the latter cynicism, his admission of "faithfull loues" as a suitable heroic subject alters his earlier conception of epic as a genre that stigmatizes romance conventions unsuited to its didactic ends. In the next section, I want to examine how this greater toleration of alternative influences affects his tributes to a queen whose virginity exemplifies the lessons of Neo-Latin commentary rather than of vernacular romance.

From Imperial Panegyric to Royal Critique: The Changing Fortunes of Belphoebe

As long as Spenser imitated the *Aeneid* as a Neoplatonic diatribe against carnality, he bolstered the cult of the queen's virginity. By recalling it as a dynastic romance associating eros with imperial destiny, however, he challenged the myth equating her virginity with effective government. In revising his understanding of the Virgilian tradition, Spenser revises his commitment to courtly celebration. Whereas Book II hails Elizabeth's chastity as the virtue shielding her against Dido's vulnerability to foreign princes, Book III links it to anxieties about the succession. Elizabeth resembled Augustus not only in punishing sexual indiscretions at court but also in failing to produce an heir. Like Virgil, Spenser found himself in the awkward position of composing a dynastic epic for a sovereign whose barrenness threatened to extinguish the dynasty.

Anxiety about the darker consequences of Elizabeth's virginity first surfaces when Spenser adapts Virgil's principal topos of dynastic celebration, Anchises's underworld procession of future Roman heroes. After initial tributes to Numa, Mummius, Gracchus, and others who prepared the way for Augustus, Anchises's vision concludes with an allusion to Marcellus's premature death. Renaissance editors linked this personal tragedy to national anxieties about the succession by identifying Marcellus as "Augustus sisters son, that should haue ben his heir in the empier."[9] The passage's particular pathos arises from a rift between two models for describing historical experience that any work of dynastic complement must reconcile. For the imperial poet, history exists as a linear progression, ordained by fate, that culminates in the present sovereign's accession. But by cataloguing a particular family's marriages, births, and deaths, he raises an alternative, potentially subversive view of history as a recurrent process lacking a clearly distinguishable goal. As time unfolds, this process proves subject more to chance than to destiny. The caprices of family history may ultimately disrupt the public myth of time ending in an *imperium sine fine*. Anchises might hail the *Pax Augustana* as the culmination of a linear progression, for instance, but Marcellus's death hints that empire itself may be subject to the natural cycles of birth, maturation, and death. With no clear successor to Augustus, there is no assurance that the line running from him back to Aeneas will survive.

When Merlin describes his vision of Britomart's future descendants, private and imperial, cyclical and linear histories once more converge in problematic ways. Spenser models his tribute to Elizabeth as the ruler destined to establish "sacred peace" on Virgil's compliments to Augustus for restoring the Saturnian Golden Age (III.iii.49; *Aen.* VI.791ff.). Stretching "her white rod ouer the *Belgicke* shore" and smiting "the great Castle," the "royall virgin" achieves a victory as decisive and apocalyptic as Actium (*FQ* III.iii.49). But Spenser also joins Virgil in realizing that time does not stop when the sovereign-patron reaches the height of power:

> But yet the end is not. There *Merlin* stayd,
> As ouercomen of the spirites powre,
> Or other ghastly spectacle dismayd,
> That secretly he saw, yet note discoure.
>
> (iii.50)

A. C. Hamilton's gloss that Merlin's "ecstatic trance" indicates "a vision of England's domination over Europe"[10] suppresses the darker possibility that "the ghastly spectacle" may be a return to civil strife or some other national disaster. One precedent for a "ghastly" vision that a prophet sees but refuses to "discoure" is Anchises's reluctance to reveal the great sorrow (*ingentem luctum,* VI.868) of Marcellus's death. Merlin's dismay, like Anchises's, may arise from fears that Elizabeth's barrenness might limit the Golden Age to a single, mortal life.

By surveying only the highlights of Roman history, Virgil underplays the private history of generational succession until he recounts Marcellus's death. Spenser, by contrast, provides a more continuous genealogy in which the record of military conquests repeatedly intersects with the dynastic history of deaths and births. This shift in prophetic strategy reinforces Book III's Ariostan recuperation of eros as a vehicle of imperial destiny. In the passage from the *Furioso* that stands between the *Aeneid* and *The Faerie Queene,* Ariosto's Merlin recounts Estense history primarily as a genealogy of Bradamante's descendants. Since the accession of one Estense son after the other establishes continuity between apparently disparate descriptions of wars and foreign invasions, procreation emerges as history's principal driving force. In this context, Bradamante's love for Ruggiero readily acquires a public, patriotic significance.

Although Spenser follows Ariosto in upholding eros as an instrument of destiny, Elizabeth's virginity precludes the confidence with which Ariosto imagined the Estense dynasty enduring through future centuries. Since Alfonso d'Este had five sons when the *Furioso* first appeared, Ariosto had no reason to present his reign as the possible terminus of a grand historical process. His Merlin can reassure Bradamante that "light and darkness would have to succeed each other many times" before he could finish recounting the accomplishments of her race (*bisognerà che si rischiari e abbui / più volte prima il ciel,* III.59). By 1590, Elizabeth's commitment to virginity had cost her the opportunity ever to produce an heir. In imagining the Tudor future, Spenser yielded Ariosto's Estense confidence to the uncertainty and trepidation with which Virgil imagined the fate of Rome after Augustus's death.

In earlier books of *The Faerie Queene,* Spenser restored the *Aeneid*'s darker tonalities in characterizing himself as a more faithful Virgilian than Ariosto or Tasso. But this reassertion of Virgil's original dynastic anxiety contradicts Book III's general openness to romance influence. Elizabeth's "rare chastitee" impedes Spenser's revisionary understanding of what constitutes writing in the laureate tradition. By disrupting the private, cyclical history of marriage and maternity, it short-circuits his attempt to reconcile private desire and civic responsibility. In Book II, her mythic marriage to her realm appeared as an exemplary surrender of personal to public commitments. But judged by Book III's championship of eros as the source of "all noble deeds and neuer dying fame," it appears as an obstinate resistance to natural instinct (iii.1). Like the chaste Dido's refusal to remarry, Elizabeth's virginity can be indicted as selfish indifference to her realm's future welfare.

Judith Anderson and David Lee Miller have traced Spenser's increasingly critical stance toward the queen in his ambivalent portrayal of Belphoebe's relationship to Timias.[10] I want to suggest that their peculiar courtship reinscribes the political threat posed by Elizabeth's barrenness as an aesthetic threat to Spenser's transformation of epic decorums. Timias's thwarted longings mirror Spenser's own frustrations in reconciling Ariostan influence with Tudor myth. Belphoebe's refusal to grant Timias the consummation he desires freezes him in the bachelorhood that Arthur, Marinell, Arthegall, and Scudamour are destined to outgrow. In an analogous way, Spenser's commitment to the queen's "rare chastitee" rigidifies his earlier sense of epic as a genre advocating temperance and restraint.

In order to appreciate more fully how Spenser situates himself in literary history, I want to consider his principal subtext for Timias's encounter with Belphoebe: Angelica's discovery of the wounded Medoro in Canto XIX of the *Furioso.* As scholars have long noted, Ariosto conspicuously bases the episode on Nisus and Euryalus's tragic death in Book IX of the *Aeneid.* Thomas Greene has explored how Ariosto substitutes a witty pragmatism for the pathos characterizing Virgil's original account of two soldiers ambushed while attempting to cross the enemy's camp at night. More recently, Barbara Pavlock has argued that Ariosto's portrayal of Cloridano and Medoro suppresses the narcissism and materialism that characterized Nisus and Euryalus.[12] But Ariosto does not simply correct his subtext so that epic *pietas* might be freed from its associations with greed and bloodlust. In his most conspicuous departure from Virgil—Medoro's recovery and subsequent union with Angelica—Ariosto dismisses the *Aeneid*'s masculine, militarist values as an adolescent homosociality that his hero eventually outgrows. Like Ariosto's opening parody of the *Aeneid* 's invocation, the

Cloridano and Medoro episode suggests that Virgil's devaluation of heterosexual attachment impoverishes his epic vision.

In the *Aeneid*, Nisus and Euryalus's willingness to die for each other and for their country earns them an immortal reputation. As Virgil proclaims in a rare apostrophe, his poetry will commemorate them throughout time:

> If there be any power
> within my poetry, no day shall ever
> erase you from the memory of time;
> not while Aeneas' children live beside
> the Capitol's unchanging rock nor while
> a Roman father still holds sovereignty.

> si quid mea carmina possunt,
> nulla dies umquam memori uos eximet aeuo
> dum domus Aeneae Capitoli immobile saxum
> accolet imperiumque pater Romanus habebit.
> (IX.446–49 [M:592–97])

Given the poem's official, patriarchal ethos, this guarantee of fame as long as "a Roman father still holds sovereignty" stands as valor's perfect reward. Although Nisus and Euryalus will die without biological heirs, their heroic example will foster generations of future Roman patriots.

Ariosto corrects Virgil's narrative by bringing its exclusively masculine heroic code into conflict with an alternative view of human experience advocating procreation as the privileged means to transcend mortality. Like the Nisus and Euryalus episode, the Cloridano and Medoro story begins by glorifying military, homosocial bonding. But Medoro's unprecedented recovery after the ambush overturns the *Aeneid*'s masculine values. Angelica's ability to cure him implicitly condemns Virgil's exclusion of women from heroic enterprise, with the exceptions of Amazonian figures like Penthesilea and Camilla who renounce the feminine arts of nursing and of motherhood in their "endless / love of . . . arms and of virginity" (*aeternum telorum et uirginitatis amorem,* XI.583 [M:768–69]). Once more, Ariosto suggests that *le donne* and *gli amori* are just as central to the heroic poem as the accomplishments of *i cavallier.*

Nisus and Euryalus might achieve renown, but Medoro wins what throughout the *Furioso* is a far more elusive prize, Angelica's love. Abandoning Virgilian precedent, Ariosto shifts attention from Medoro's physical wounds to the equally life-threatening erotic wound suffered by Angelica the moment she sees him:

Her wound enlarged and festered in measure as his dwindled and healed. The boy grew better, she languished with a strange fever which made her

hot and cold by turns. Day by day, beauty flowered in him, while the
poor damsel wasted away.

> La sua piaga più s'apre e più incrudisce,
> quanto più l'altra si ristringe e salda.
> Il giovine si sana: ella languisce
> di nuova febbre, or agghiacciata, or calda.
> Di giorno in giorno in lui beltà fiorisce:
> la misera si strugge.
> (XIX.29)

If Medoro remained insensitive to Angelica's plight in his devotion to Clori-
dano's memory, she would perish. But unlike his classical predecessors, he not
only survives his enemies' ambush but repudiates the battlefield's homosocial
ethos by plucking "the first rose, hitherto untouched," of Angelica's virginity
(*la prima rosa / . . . non ancor tocca inante,* XIX.33). The moment he yields to
Cupid's power, his earlier love for Cloridano appears as an adolescent attachment
destined to develop into a more mature heterosexuality. By introducing a char-
acter who transcends the homosocial limits of Virgilian heroism, Ariosto declares
his own more comprehensive understanding of human experience. He also es-
tablishes himself as a champion of vital, generational energies that expose Virgil's
idealization of death as a perversion of natural instinct.

When Spenser adopts the Medoro episode as a model for Timias's encounter
with Belphoebe, he begins with the elusive virgin's discovery of the wounded
youth in the forest. At precisely this point in the narrative, Ariosto transformed
Virgil's story about masculine comradeship into one about heterosexual passion.
Like Medoro, Timias is injured in an ambush, but he is alone rather than ac-
companied by a devoted friend. Only a trace of the distant Virgilian subtext's
homosocial emphases remains in the passing description of him as Arthur's "gen-
tle Squire, / That Ladies loue vnto his Lord forlent" (iv.47).[13] In a book where
the mature, heterosexual desire for marriage repeatedly subsumes adolescent at-
tachments, the episode might be expected to reenact its Ariostan subtext by
establishing a union between the youth and the woman who discovers him. But
since Belphoebe's virginity stands as an explicit compliment to Elizabeth's, it
cannot be surrendered. In contrast to the unequivocal endorsement of the
queen's chastity in Book II, Spenser evokes it here as a source of both narrative
and intertextual impasse. Timias's failure to achieve a mature, marital relationship
with Belphoebe provides an image of Spenser's difficulties in trying to accom-
modate Book III's Ariostan emphasis on dynastic marriage to the fact of Eliza-
beth's virginity.

Spenser reinforces this sense of intertextual impasse through two conspicuous departures from the episode's Italian model. He reverses the gender of the character suffering the incurable wound of love and then heightens the symbolic value of the rose associated with the woman's virginity. In the *Furioso*, Angelica's psychological wound that "enlarged and festers" (*s'apre e . . . incrudisce, XIX.29*) as Medoro's physical wound begins to heal signals that she has renounced her selfishness and finally sympathizes with male anguish.[14] Their mutual suffering forms an immediate basis for mutual devotion. Belphoebe too experiences "soft passion and vnwonted smart" (v.30) when she sees Timias, but those feelings never develop into the pain of erotic longing. The man, rather than the woman who discovers him, suffers the internal wound that gets worse while his external wound gets better: "Still as his wound did gather, and grow hole, / So still his hart woxe sore, and health decayd" (v.43). In contrast to Medoro, whose physical suffering is answered by Angelica's emotional suffering, Timias alone feels the pains both of battle and of love. Since he and Belphoebe are never united in mutual anguish and reciprocal compassion, their relationship never matures into a conjugal one. While Timias lies paralyzed in the solipsistic interiority of Petrarchan complaint, Belphoebe never sees that she has caused his pain.[15]

Spenser never explicitly charges Belphoebe with unkindness for failing to relieve Timias's suffering. But as Miller has observed, his tribute to the rose of her virginity allows "an implicit criticism to emerge from within what is ostensibly a language of praise" (233). When the passage is read against its subtexts, it appears as a troubled retreat from the *Furioso*'s integration of public and private histories into the *Aeneid*'s characteristic privileging of public experience. While Nisus and Euryalus's loyalty to each other and to their country distinguishes them as noble examples for later Romans to follow, they have no offspring. When Angelica yields her previously untouched rose to Medoro, she opens the possibility that they, like Bradamante and Ruggiero, may live on in their children. Yet when Belphoebe denies her rose to Timias and everyone else, she deprives herself of that compensation for her ultimate mortality. Like Nisus and Euryalus, she will always remain a "faire ensample" (v.54). Since that "ensample" is one of "vertue virginall" (v.53), she too will never enjoy any other perpetuity.

Anderson and Miller have detected several verbal ambiguities that qualify Spenser's ostensible praise throughout the encomium to her rose. This subversive countertext centers on the inadequacy of fame alone to transcend time. The opening reference to Belphoebe's rose as "the daughter of her Morne" (v.51) paradoxically hails the quality that will prevent her from ever having children through a metaphor of filial relationship. Her tendency to tender her rose "more deare then life" can be read either as an empty superlative or as an indictment of her alienation from life and its natural rhythms. If her "vertue virginall" distinguishes her as a model of perfect chastity, it also sets her apart from the ordinary cycles of generation. The ostensible compliment that "none liuing may compaire" with her in "spotlesse fame / Of chastitie" (v.54) covertly suggests that Belphoebe is not really a "liuing" being but an abstract type. This ironic countertext culminates in the final observation that "Ladies all may follow her ensample dead" (v.54). Hamilton is correct in noting that the line's primary meaning is that ladies may follow her example when she is dead.[16] But as Anderson has remarked, Spenser's praise is compromised by hints that Belphoebe is "a dead example," a woman whose virtues will not live on in her offspring (54–58).

Spenser amplifies these darker resonances by placing his paean to Belphoebe's "ensample dead" just one canto before the Gardens of Adonis, his most extensive tribute to sexual generation. Although the philosophical sources and analogues for this climactic celebration of nature's fecundity are innumerable, the most striking precedent for such a vision in an epic poem is the sermon on metempsychosis preceding Anchises's procession of future Roman heroes. As in the *Aeneid,* references to cyclical generation unsettle overt compliments to a sovereign who does not produce an heir. In contrast to the Gardens' inhabitants, Elizabeth fails to heed "the mightie word, / Which first was spoken by th'Almightie lord" in bidding all creation "to increase and multiply" (vi.34). The perpetuity that nature achieves by generative "succession" (vi.47) mirrors the stability a realm enjoys through dynastic succession. Elizabeth has denied her subjects that security by fetishizing the flower of a virginity that will never bear fruit of living offspring.

Exposing virginity's darker consequences marks a crucial stage in Spenser's interrogation of the educational program long attributed to epic poetry. By substituting the biblical injunction "to increase and multiply" for the commentators' emphasis on erotic restraint, he qualifies Elizabeth's status as a moral example. In the Gardens of Adonis, he departs even further from the didactic *labor* conventionally attributed to epic by focusing not only on successive generation but also on natural diversity. His stance is less hortatory than celebratory. Instead of teaching his readers how to act, he helps them find consolation for individual mortality in the mystery of an ever-varying universe. In the next section, I want to examine how the Gardens' lesson in cosmic diversity manifests itself in a renewed intertextual dialogue between the moralized *Aeneid* and Chaucerian fabliau.

The Epic Recovery of Chaucerian Fabliau

In discussing Book III's idealization of desire, Spenserians almost inevitably cite the opening stanzas of cantos iii and v. At first glance, their similar Neo-platonic imagery seems to reinforce a common distinction between love and lust.[17] Canto iii locates the emotions' origins in two separate, prototypical fires whose emanations govern human behavior:

> Most sacred fire, that burnest mightily
>> In liuing brests, ykindled first aboue,
>> Emongst th'eternall spheres and lamping sky,
>> And thence pourd into men, which men call Loue;
>> Not that same, which doth base affections moue
>> In brutish minds, and filthy lust inflame,
>> But that sweet fit, that doth true beautie loue,
>> And choseth vertue for his dearest Dame,
> Whence spring all noble deeds and neuer dying fame.
>
>> (iii.1)

From the narrator's perspective here, the "sacred fire" inspiring heroic enterprise differs entirely from the flames of "filthy lust." His taxonomy implies that Britomart's love for Arthegall has nothing in common with Malecasta's sudden passion for her. By introducing the two women as respective agents of chastity and concupiscence, Spenser presumably achieves an unequivocal didactic end: just as Britomart exemplifies virtuous behavior, Malecasta reveals the degeneracy of "base affections."

Canto v ostensibly underwrites a similar distinction between heroic love and lust:

> Wonder it is to see, in diuerse minds,
>> How diuersly loue doth his pageants play,
>> And shewes his powre in variable kinds:
>> The baser wit, whose idle thoughts alway
>> Are wont to cleaue vnto the lowly clay,
>> It stirreth vp to sensuall desire,
>> And in lewd slouth to wast his carelesse day:
>> But in braue sprite it kindles goodly fire,
> That to all high desert and honour doth aspire.
>
>> (v.1)

The lasciviousness of the "baser wit" still sets off the "braue sprite"'s honorable desire, but the narrator's tone has shifted dramatically. Both his reverence before love's "sacred fire" and his revulsion from the flames of "filthy lust" begin yielding to detached wonder. This shift in tone reinforces an alternative view of the relationship between Britomart and Malecasta's apparently antithetical desires. According to Spenser's revised etiology, love and lust no longer arise from two completely distinct fires but from a single cosmic force manifesting itself differently in diverse personalities. The stanza broadens the significance of "loue" so that the word no longer refers exclusively to heroic, Britomartian passion but to desire in general. From this alternative perspective, Britomart and Malecasta become fellow players in a single erotic pageant.

As wonder before love's "powre in variable kinds" qualifies denunciations of lust, Spenser transforms epic's didactic purpose. By this point in his narrative, he calls his readers less to virtuous action than to a more sophisticated awareness of erotic diversity. Although he continues to make ethical pronouncements, he tempers them with a less prescriptive view of humanity's capricious nature. From this modified perspective, a character like Malecasta is the subject more of wit than of opprobrium.[18] Britomart provides a better example to those "that to all high desert and honour doth aspire," but Malecasta is not evil. In a text analyzing moral experience along a continuum rather than as a set of fixed oppositions, a woman who falls for another woman disguised as a man might appear ridiculous. But even as a representative of *stultus amor,* she will not harbor Acrasia's malice.

In recharacterizing epic as a genre that explores the range of human experience, Spenser subordinates both the commentators' moralizations and Ariosto's cynicism to the more ludic, dialogic tendencies of Chaucer. The English Tityrus reduced to a mere fabulist in *The Shepheardes Calender* returns in Book III as Spenser's primary guide in balancing divergent cultural and poetic influences. The polyptoton "in *diuerse* minds, / . . . *diuersly* loue doth his pageants play" (emphasis mine) associates wonder at love's protean nature with Chaucer by echoing several passages from *The Canterbury Tales.* Chaucer first uses the figure to describe the Pilgrims' reactions to the Miller's Tale:

> Whan folk hadde laughen at this nyce cas
> Of Absolon and hende Nicholas,
> Diverse folk diversely they seyde,
> But for the moore part they loughe and pleyde.
>
> (3855–58)

When Cambyuskan's courtiers examine the brass steed, the Squire similarly emphasizes the diversity of their comments: "Diverse folk diversely they demed; / As many heddes, as manye wittes ther been" (202–3). In the Man of Law's Tale, "Diverse men diverse thynges seyden" about the possibility of the Suldan's marriage to Constance (211). These local instances of divergent opinion typify Chaucer's general insistence on the variable ways in which people perceive, describe, and interpret their experience.

Accommodating the epic paradigm to a Chaucerian plurality of voices and ethical stances precipitates the often bewildering shifts in tone and genre that critics have associated more with Book III than with any other section of *The Faerie Queene*. Whereas the Squire of Dames' tale would have occasioned a homily on the monstrosity of sexual desire in Book II, it provokes only Satyrane's hearty laughter in Book III. His guffaws might betoken his subhuman coarseness. But they might also be taken as a generic signpost inviting the reader to suspend ethical judgment in accordance with fabliau convention.

What most aligns Spenser with Chaucer at such moments is not fabliau amorality per se but its juxtaposition with a more exalted, conventional moral vision. This play of alternative ethical perspectives underlies the interpretive difficulties posed by the Hellenore episode, which immediately follows Satyrane's laughter over the Squire of Dames' misfortunes. Scholars have long recognized that the intrigue at Malbecco's table revises Dido's banquet. Spenser complicates the Virgilian situation by introducing two wandering heroes, Paridell and Britomart, and two women suffering Cupid's wound, Britomart and Hellenore. As in the Malecasta episode, Britomart's androgyny allows her to play both Dido and Aeneas. While her patriotism contrasts with Paridell's private, erotic obsession, her chastity counters Hellenore's lasciviousness.

Berger and Suzuki have linked the episode's implicit championship of Britomart at Hellenore and Paridell's expense to Spenser's contempt for Ovid's urbane poetry of adultery and its medieval descendant, the *amour courtois*.[19] While such interpretations point to Spenser's overarching concern with genre, they do not explain the bawdy humor that distinguishes this episode from the rest of *The Faerie Queene*. Nor do they account for the similarities between Hellenore, "unfitly yokt" with a senescent husband, and virtuous women like Florimell and Amoret who suffer the advances of hoary gods, ancient fishermen, and sorcerers.

These aspects of Hellenore's story arise from its relationship to fabliau, Chaucer's preferred genre for subverting courtly pretensions. If Spenser is trying to distance himself from the adulteries of the *amour courtois*, he does so rather perplexingly by toying with the equally adulterous fabliau. Instead of consistently discrediting genres and conventions undercutting his epic idealization of marriage, he evokes them to resist the ethical rigidity associated with epic by Renaissance commentators. Above all, he uses them to qualify the traditional condemnation of women seducing the hero from his quest. From the moment the episode begins, the joint presence of epic and fabliau motifs encourages antithetical assessments of Hellenore's character. If she stands as a lascivious foil to Britomart's chastity, she also appears as a fabliau heroine duping her jealous husband in a triumph of youthful ingenuity over restrictive social custom.

Although Hellenore's name identifies her as a second Helen, the circumstances of her meeting with Paridell associate her with Dido, interpreted along Fulgentian lines as lust incarnate. As Suzuki has noted, Spenser models the storm that brings both Paridell and Britomart to her house on the one that drives Aeneas to Carthage (160–61). Like Petrarch and Landino, Spenser treats the storm as an allegory of passion's insurgence against reason. When Hellenore later spills her wine to signal her sexual availability, the incident specifically recalls the *Amores*.[20] But this Ovidian detail enhances a more general debt to Dido's Carthaginian banquet interpreted by commentators like Macrobius and John of Salisbury as a prelude to debauchery. Just as Aeneas's narration fell on Dido's ears as an aphrodisiac, Paridell's account of the same Trojan matter increases Hellenore's infatuation.

As in the Malecasta episode, Spenser balances a character based on a lascivious Dido against Britomart, who reappears as a virtuous Dido reconciling love and heroism. While Hellenore follows Dido in responding to Paridell's narrative as an erotic lure, Britomart hears it as a commemoration of her people's past sufferings:

> Whenas the noble *Britomart* heard tell
> Of *Troian* warres, and *Priams* Citie sackt,
> The ruefull story of Sir *Paridell*,
> She was empassiond at that piteous act,
> With zelous enuy of Greekes cruell fact,
> Against that nation, from whose race of old
> She heard, that she was lineally extract.
>
> (ix.38)

Although Britomart listens to the same story that fanned Dido's secret longing for Aeneas, the passion that it stirs in her is not destructive. Nostalgic recollections of defeat may seduce Virgil's characters into the false comfort of present, personal relationships, but Paridell's history reinforces Britomart's commitment to her nation's future glory by bolstering her faith in the continuity between Trojan, Roman, and British cultures.

In privileging Britomart's behavior over Hellenore's, Spenser seems to reaffirm canto iii's distinction between love's sacred fire and lust's debased flames. Once again, he apparently casts his epic as an exhortation against the passion leading to Hellenore's degradation as a second Helen and a second Dido. But he simultaneously modifies the rigor of Virgilian commentary by associating

Hellenore with May and other fabliau heroines. Whereas Dido betrayed the memory of the deceased husband she adored, Hellenore betrays a living husband whom she detests for depriving her "of kindly ioy and naturall delight" (ix.5). Like Chaucer in the Merchant's Tale, Spenser stresses his adulterous heroine's sufferings at the hands of a husband whose jealousy is aggravated by a goading consciousness of his own incapacity. As the episode unfolds, Hellenore's career attests less to the dangers of lust than to the absurdity of marriages violating "natural" erotic inclinations.[21]

Spenser's turn toward Chaucerian fabliau ultimately shields Hellenore from repeating her epic predecessors' greatest crime. Unlike Dido, Alcina, and Armida, Hellenore cannot be condemned for distracting a hero from his public destiny. Paridell's resemblance to Aeneas, like Braggadocchio's in Book II, is merely superficial; he apes Aeneas's words without inheriting his *pietas*. While he proclaims his descent from Paris, the intersection between epic and fabliau convention reveals his primary literary ancestor as the lusty clerk or squire who liberates the heroine from her senescent husband. Hellenore cannot distract him from his heroic vocation because he really does not have one to fulfill. As a descendant of Squire Damien and the "hende Nicholas," his only "duty" is to free her from from a jealous *vieillard*.

By transforming the heroine's abandonment, Spenser departs most from his Virgilian subtext's canonization as a call to continence. If Hellenore resembles the commentators' Dido at dinner, she recalls the pitiable Dido of Chaucer's *Legend of Good Women* and of vernacular romance when Paridell jilts her. Suzuki has speculated that Paridell deliberately omits the events at Carthage in retelling the *Aeneid* precisely because he plans to reenact Aeneas's treachery (170).[22] Although this interpretation may attribute too much premeditation to an allegorical character, Spenser himself undoubtedly deletes references to Dido as an oblique reminder that Hellenore has replaced her. But omitting the Dido story has an even more complex impact on subsequent poetic history. In suppressing it, Spenser rejects Virgil's portrayal of eros as a temptation that the hero must overcome. Just as Paridell's involvement with Hellenore betrays no higher vocation, his abandonment of her does not valorize his recommitment to noble enterprise. When he casts her "vp . . . / To the wide world" (x.35), his treachery recalls neither Aeneas's devotion to duty in the *Aeneid* nor his triumph over passion in the commentaries. It reflects only the callousness attributed to "traytour" Aeneas in vernacular romance.

Nevertheless, Spenser identifies Hellenore no more consistently with the vernacular Didos than with the concupiscent Didos of the commentaries. Rejecting all previous versions of the story, he suppresses the tragic consequences of female abandonment. Hellenore wanders "like a forelorn weft" for less than a stanza

before joining the jolly satyrs (x.36). Critics who see her only as a foil to Bri-
tomart's virtue have dismissed her life among the satyrs as a punishment for her
bestial nature (x.44).[23] But such readings dampen her comic triumph over both
the husband who imprisoned her and the carouser who jilted her. As John
Bernard and Theresa Krier remind us, we see the scene entirely through Mal-
becco's eyes. Any horror or shame associated with Hellenore properly belongs
to Malbecco, whose jealousy and desiccation exclude him from the satyrs' primal
joys.[24] His outrage in watching her copulate nine times with a satyr recalls
January's when he recovers his sight and catches his wife copulating with Squire
Damian in the pear tree. Spenser even surpasses Chaucer in allowing the youth-
ful wife the last word of the quarrel. After ingeniously convincing January of
her fidelity, May presumably has to remain "vnfitly yokt" with him. Hellenore,
by contrast, discards Malbecco once and for all. Nor does she have to renounce
her newly discovered sexual fulfillment.

Spenser's reversal of Dido's tragedy culminates in Malbecco's metamorphosis.
In Virgil, Aeneas's rejection of Dido for the greater good of Rome precipitates
the suicidal frenzy that associates her forever with intemperance. Hellenore
drives Malbecco to similar despair when she rejects him for the greater delights
of her life in the forest. Just as Dido was dehumanized by later commentators
into a personification of concupiscence, Malbecco is transformed into an em-
blem of jealousy:

> There dwels he euer, miserable swaine,
> Hatefull both to him selfe, and euery wight;
> Where he through priuy griefe, and horrour vaine,
> Is woxen so deform'd, that he has quight
> Forgot he was a man, and *Gealousie* is hight.
>
> (xi.60)

Revising Dido's fate involves more than the obvious gender reversal substituting
an abandoned man for an abandoned woman as the embodiment of destructive
emotion. By judging Malbecco more harshly than Hellenore, Spenser also priv-
ileges Chaucerian fabliau over Virgilian commentary. In the final analysis, the
vieillard's envy is more degrading than the heroine's concupiscence.

Throughout the Hellenore episode, Spenser rejects female abandonment both
as a test of his heroes' virtue and as a topos signaling his own repudiation of
styles, conventions, and attitudes incompatible with more rigid notions of epic.
He discovers an alternative image for his poem's genesis in the conjunction of
disparate voices and manners at Malbecco's table. Britomart's and Hellenore's
antithetical responses to Paridell's narrative identify them not only as subjects of
eros manifesting "his powre in variable kinds" but as inhabitants of divergent

poetic realms. By foregrounding the discrepancy between heroic and fabliau conventions, Spenser ultimately preserves their generic autonomy. Britomart might be inspired to patriotic service and Hellenore only to bawdy intrigue. But instead of stigmatizing Hellenore for betraying epic destiny, Spenser licenses her as a prototypical fabliau heroine. Both characters are free to coexist as representatives of antithetical, but not necessarily incompatible, poetic modes.

Although the Hellenore episode marks *The Faerie Queene*'s most conspicuous recollection of Chaucerian fabliau, Book III repeatedly privileges youthful, procreative energies over the desiccation of old age. Archetypal critics are correct in seeing Florimell's struggles against the Fisherman and Proteus, as well as Amoret's against Busirane, as revisions of the Pluto and Proserpina myth.[25] Nevertheless, these classical stories are mediated directly through Chaucer, who acknowledged the mythic patterns underlying his fabliaux by introducing Pluto and Proserpina as characters in the Merchant's Tale. By incorporating them into Book III's erotic myth, Spenser revises Virgilian convention more drastically than at any other point in *The Faerie Queene*. Imperial destiny, the force drawing Britomart to Arthegall, is subordinated to the general erotic magnetism drawing Florimell to Marinell, Amoret to Scudamour, and even Hellenore to Paridell and the Satyrs. Spenser still upholds Arthegall and Britomart as Elizabeth's fictional progenitors. But a Chaucerian sanction of diversity as a final aesthetic and perhaps even moral end continually qualifies the ethical dichotomies underlying his earlier epideictic.

"Neither of idle shewes, nor of false charmes aghast": Busirane and the Black Art of Reading Classical Texts

Whereas Book II concludes with a woman bound in chains and carried into captivity, the 1590 version of Book III ends with a woman released from chains and restored to her lover's arms. Overturning Book II's final stanzas, Amoret and Scudamour's embrace establishes erotic consummation as a principal goal of epic action. Whereas Temperance equates the conquest of Latium with perpetual restraint, Chastity equates it with the marriage bond that Protestantism privileged as the basis of social harmony. Book III's antagonists are not temptresses luring the heroes from their quests but guardians or prison keepers blocking their unions with destined lovers. In less threatening forms, these antagonists appear as overprotective mothers like Cymoent, who warns Marinell "euery day, / The loue of women not to entertaine" (iv.26).[26] They acquire more menacing aspects when Spenser recasts the fabliau's *vieillard* as the Fisherman, Proteus, and Busirane. These blackguards force their victims to relive Proserpina's nightmare by abducting them from a world of vernal, erotic possibility and subjecting them to their own senescent desires.

I want to conclude this study by examining how the Busirane episode revises the fabliau triangle by casting the *vieillard* as an opponent of hermeneutic diversity. Spenser associates Busirane's threat to Amoret with the antieroticism that commentators like Fulgentius, Bernard, Petrarch, and Boccaccio found in the *Aeneid*. The episode refutes their approach to classical texts and Spenser's use of it in earlier books. At the conclusion of the 1590 *Faerie Queene*, Amoret's release signals epic's liberation from a limited range of didactic stances and aesthetic possibilities.

Spenserians have often associated Busirane's art with poetic discourses that Spenser renounces in constructing Book III's erotic myth. Isabel MacCaffrey, Thomas Roche, and others have developed C. S. Lewis's seminal contention that Britomart's triumph over Busirane's illusions repudiates the *amour courtois* and the Petrarchan tradition stemming from it.[27] More recently, Lauren Silberman has argued that the episode indicts the dualist, Platonic metaphysics underlying European Petrarchanism.[28] For Susanne Wofford, Busirane's spectacles expose the limitations of allegory itself as Spenser's dominant compositional mode.[29] In general, such critics have focused more on Busirane's masque than on his tapestries. But the tapestries foreground yet another literary discourse Book III repudiates: the interpretation of classical texts as exhortations against desire. Busirane's retellings of Ovid expound the same lesson that Virgilian commentators found in Dido's tragedy. As in the *Aeneid*, Cupid's wound prefaces individual despair, public disgrace, and imperial disaster. As an implicit rejection of this lesson, Britomart's triumph distances Spenser's own text from the *Aeneid*'s reception as an allegorical call to continence.

Since the episode compounds the problem of interpreting Virgil with parallel questions about reading Ovid, I want to begin by examining how Busirane's tapestries revise Arachne's in the *Metamorphoses*.[30] In Ovid, Arachne weaves her tapestries in an ill-fated competition against Minerva. Busirane suppresses that narrative context to bolster a myth of erotic tyranny that is more his invention than Ovid's. Arachne's theme is not how love has debased the gods but how the gods have deceived and tormented humanity. She depicts Europa, Leda, and other mythological heroines as the victims of deities exulting in their power over defenseless human beings:

> There was Europa, cheated
> By the bull's guise; you would think him real, the creature,
> Real as the waves he breasted, and the girl
> Seems to be looking back to the lands of home,

Calling her comrades, lifting her feet a little
To keep them above the lift and surge of the water.

(VI.115–20)

Maeonis elusam designat imagine tauri
Europam: verum taurum, freta vera putares;
ipsa videbatur terras spectare relictas
et comites clamare suas tactumque vereri
adsilientis aquae timidasque reducere plantas.

(VI.103–7)[31]

Busirane preserves Arachne's emphasis on victimization, but he narrows her condemnation of the gods to an indictment of Cupid alone. According to him, love's tyranny unites both gods and mortals in common suffering. Arachne's tapestries, for instance, do not depict the agonies of desire that compel Jove to transform himself into a bull and ravish Europa. But when Busirane recasts the myth, Jove's pain figures more prominently than does Europa's horror:

> Therein was writ, how often thundring *Ioue*
>   Had felt the point of his hart-percing dart,
>   And leauing heauens kingdome, here did roue
>   In straunge disguize, to slake his scalding smart;
>   Now like a Ram, faire *Helle* to peruart,
>   Now like a Bull, *Europa* to withdraw:
>   Ah, how the fearefull Ladies tender hart
>   Did liuely seeme to tremble, when she saw
> The huge seas vnder her t'obay her seruaunts law.

(xi.30)

Whereas Arachne presents Jove's metamorphoses as cold-blooded stratagems, Busirane portrays them as desperate attempts to slake the same erotic anguish experienced by mortals. Cupid alone retains the chilling deviousness of Arachne's pantheon. In Busirane's redaction, Cupid infects everyone and everything with the same debilitating madness.

In interpreting the *Metamorphoses* as antierotic exempla, Busirane suppresses what Renaissance commentators recognized as a characteristically Ovidian emphasis on the diversity of erotic experience.[32] Ovid does not always designate love as a destructive force. The Ceyx and Alcyone episode, for instance, honors it as an ennobling, transcendental virtue. Arthur Golding's introductory epistle upholds Ceyx and Alcyone as exemplars of marital chastity not unlike the various couples in Book III of *The Faerie Queene*: "In Ceyx and Alcyone appeeres most constant love, / Such as betweene the man and wyfe too bee it dooth behove."³³ Chaucer's allusions to the episode in *The Book of the Duchess* suggest that he too saw Ovid as a champion of wedded love, a view that Spenser confirms when he recalls Ceyx and Alcyone via Chaucer in the *Daphnaïda*.

Ovid's appreciation of love's diversity is precisely what Busirane's tapestries resist. While portraying Europa's rape and Jove's degradation, they ignore Ceyx and Alcyone's mutual commitment and the generosity of Baucis and Philemon. Nor do they allow myth to be read as anything but an indictment of Cupid's savagery. Busirane's monolithic hermeneutic distorts not only Ovid's many-sided representations of desire but also the Chaucerian diversity that Spenser embraces throughout Book III. The tapestries' portrayal of how *"Ioue* these pageaunts playd" (xi.35) superficially echoes Spenser's own tributes to the diversity with which "loue doth his pageants play" (v.1). But where the earlier passage suggests comic wonder before the capriciousness of human sexuality, Busirane's tapestries express only disgust and horror. Their misprisions of Ovid reduce love's variable and wondrous pageants to "mournfull Tragedyes," teaching Busirane's victims to mistrust their own sexual natures (xi.45).

Although the *Metamorphoses* is the episode's most conspicuous subtext, its revision of Ovid masks an underlying concern with Virgil. Spenser bases only the tapestries' content on an Ovidian subtext. He bases their form, an ekphrasis threatening to sidetrack a hero from his or her quest, on the *Aeneid*. Busirane's temptation to what Spenser presents as a false view of eros and a distorted interpretation of classical texts derives from Juno's murals. In the House of Alma, Spenser appropriated the ekphrasis principally as a revelation of personal and political history. Here at *The Faerie Queene*'s 1590 conclusion, he uses it as an invitation to emotions incompatible with the hero's imperial destiny.

As I noted in discussing Chaucer's *House of Fame*, medieval commentators often glossed the murals as a temptation Aeneas must learn to overcome. This interpretation figures prominently in several commentaries often reprinted in Renaissance editions of Virgil's *Opera*. Readers like Servius and Badius Ascensius noted the ironic fact that a depiction of Trojan suffering, located in a temple dedicated to a hostile goddess, somehow allays Aeneas's fears (*hoc primum in luco noua res oblata timorem / leniit, Aen.* I.450–51). Badius notes that the murals transform Trojan anguish into an occasion for Carthaginian rejoicing (*oblectationis causa*, 183 recto). Servius recognizes that Virgil's description of Aeneas feeding his soul on an empty picture (*animum pictura pascit inani, Aen.* I.464) identifies the murals either as portrayals of things not really there or as vain displays.³⁴ In either case, Servius's remarks, which are echoed by Donatus and Badius, suggest that Aeneas's comfort may be grounded in illusion.

Like Aeneas, Britomart experiences an interpretive crisis in a shrine dedicated to a hostile deity responsible for her past suffering. In each case, the ekphrastic trap lies in its falsification of history. Although Britomart does not literally discover her own picture, Busirane's spectacles metaphorically mirror aspects of her continually frustrated longing for Arthegall. She has experienced firsthand the vicissitudes of hope and fear, fury and grief depicted in the masque. Cupid's "scalding smart," which forced Jove to disguise himself as an animal, drives Britomart to disguise herself as a man. Like Virgil, Spenser presents the deceptive art through the hero's eyes and emphasizes its hold on her imagination:

> The warlike Mayde beholding earnestly
> The goodly ordinance of this rich place,
> Did greatly wonder, ne could satisfie
> Her greedy eyes with gazing a long space.
>
> (xi.53)

Just as Juno's temple tempts Aeneas with an incomplete vision of Trojan history, Busirane's tapestries, bas-reliefs, and masque offer Britomart a one-sided view of sexual experience that excludes the joyful, faithful consummation prophesied for her.

But in contrast to Aeneas, Britomart finally resists her enemy's images and rejects their limited perspective on human experience. The moment she bursts into the inner room and challenges Busirane to reverse his spells, she stands "neither of idle shewes, nor of false charmes aghast" (xii.29). The phrase "idle shewes" aptly translates Virgil's *pictura inani,* the vain displays with which Aeneas feeds his soul before surrendering himself to Dido. By spurning Busirane's art, Britomart escapes an analogous fate. She perseveres in her championship of marital chastity by forcing Busirane to "reuerse" the spells holding Amoret captive (xii.36). To the extent that Amoret's restoration to Scudamour adumbrates Britomart's own future union with Arthegall, her victory over Busirane provides an image of her quest's completion.

On one level, Busirane's reversal of his charms points to several intertextual reversals repudiating Spenser's earlier use of classical texts as antierotic exempla. In Book II, where the Palmer characterizes love as a "monster fell" whom "filth did breede" (II.iv.35), Guyon emerges as a better Aeneas by never yielding to sexual desire. In Book III, Britomart emerges as a better Aeneas by never yielding to antierotic counsels. As a reversal of Acrasia's binding, Amoret's release challenges the earlier book's recollection of Dido's tragedy as a warning about passion's incompatibility with noble endeavor. The spectacle of Dido pierced by Aeneas's sword and consumed by her pyre's rising flames concludes Virgil's Book IV. But the 1590 *Faerie Queene* ends with Amoret's Cupid-inflicted wound made "perfect hole" and the flames suppressed that divided her from her awaiting lover (xii.38).

Scudamour and Amoret's embrace marks Book III's final intertextual reversal. As we have seen, Busirane's tapestries reduce Ovid's complex erotic vision to a single lesson in love's destructiveness. But when Spenser recalls the *Metamorphoses* in comparing the reunited lovers to the Hermaphrodite, he transcends Busirane's exegesis. The hermaphroditic fusion of male and female identities provides a classical emblem for his own poetry, now conceived as an exchange between competing and divergent voices:

> Had ye them seene, ye would haue surely thought,
>> That they had beene that faire *Hermaphrodite,*
>> Which that rich *Romane* of white marble wrought,
>> And in his costly Bath causd to bee site.
>
> (xii.46 [1590])

As a marble redaction of Ovid, the statue foregrounds Spenser's concern with the ways that classical texts had been interpreted by later readers and recast by later artists. Busirane might agree with Golding that the Salamacis and Hermaphroditus story proves that "idlenesse / Is cheefest nurce and cherisher of all volupteousnesse" ("Epistle," ll. 113–14). Spenser himself endorsed that interpretation in tracing the origin of the fountain that emasculates Redcrosse. But at the end of the 1590 poem, he reads it differently as a tribute to matrimony.

As Donald Cheney has argued, however, the concluding stanzas of the 1590 poem draw on a long hermeneutic and iconographic tradition associating the hermaphrodite not only with a new synthesis but also with the destruction of individual essences.[35] The hermaphrodite achieves its perfect union of opposites by reducing autonomous personalities to "senceles stocks" (xii.45 [1590]). Spenser no longer stigmatizes eros as a deflection from the hero's quest, but he does present it as a threat to individual identity. His description of Amoret melting "in pleasure" echoes earlier passages portraying Acrasia's victims dissolving in concupiscent bliss. A similar recollection of Redcrosse "pourd out in loosnesse on the grassy grownd" (I.vii.7) unsettles the "sweete rauishment" with which Amoret "pour[s] out her spright" (xii.45 [1590]) with Scudamour.[36] Although Book III transvalues eros as heavenly chastity, it does not dispel desire's ability to overpower individual volition and intelligence. Love's agents are just as subject to a mastering daimon as are Acrasia's.

Twentieth-century readers have overwhelmingly preferred Book III's sanction of erotic desire to Book II's insistence on restraint. But the suggestions of personal annihilation inherent in Scudamour and Amoret's metamorphosis have made more than a few critics uncomfortable. In abandoning the Neo-Latin commentators' contempt for carnal desire, which generally characterized Book II's allegory, Spenser also challenges their belief in humanity's free moral agency.

As we have seen, the Legend of Redcrosse espoused their antieroticism but qualified their didactic vision in terms of a Protestant theology of grace. By bracketing questions of spiritual merit, the Legend of Guyon partially recuperates their confidence in natural virtue. Spenser aligns himself more with the commentators here than anywhere else in *The Faerie Queene* by urging his readers to discipline their passions and by suggesting that they are capable of doing so on their own initiative. Unlike temperance, however, chastity is a heavenly virtue "ykindled first aboue" (III.iii.1). The Legend of Britomart departs both from the moralized *Aeneid*'s attitude toward sexuality and from its emphasis on rational choice. Spenser so endows *amor* with the aura of *caritas* that a single logic of grace governs both: Britomart's projected union with Arthur rests just as much on divine decree as does Redcrosse's salvation.

Nowhere is Spenser's departure from the commentary tradition clearer than in his account of Britomart's "education" in chastity. Scholars have generally treated her education as a linear progression from girlish ignorance toward a mature understanding of sexuality.[37] Spenser's recurrent imitations of the *Aeneid*, however, challenge the notion that her virtue develops in direct proportion to her increasing cognitive and hermeneutic sophistication. The commentators' Aeneas becomes a better person by learning to look beyond the deceptions of Juno's temple and to appreciate the origins of all things in God. Britomart, by contrast, never acquires such transcendent insight. From the moment she first misreads the significance of Arthegall's appearance in Merlin's looking glass, she is subject to misprision and dangerous sensory enthrallments that recall Aeneas's.

Even at the end of her quest, in the poem's most conspicuous reenactment of the episode in Juno's temple, Britomart experiences interpretive blind spots. She neither shares the reader's appreciation of Busirane's art as a corruption of Ovid's nor does she understand the threat that its dark erotic vision poses to her quest. Spenser repeatedly reminds us of her failures as an interpreter:

> And as she lookt about, she did behold,
> How ouer that same dore was likewise writ,
> *Be bold, be bold,* and euery where *Be bold,*
> That much she muz'd, yet could not construe it
> By any ridling skill, or commune wit.
>
> (xi.54)

In her inability to "satisfie / Her greedy eyes with gazing a long space" on Busirane's tapestries and bas-reliefs (xi.53), she comes perilously close to repeating Aeneas's surrender to the spell of Juno's frieze. If she accepted their portrayal of tragedy as the final end of human action, she could no longer believe in a future, joyful union with Arthegall.

But in contrast to her epic prototype, Britomart's hermeneutic limitations never lead to deviation from her quest. When the time comes for decisive action, Busirane's art and pageantry cannot stop her. A Neoplatonic commentator would insist that nothing but a cognitive awareness of their fraudulence would enable someone to resist their spell. Yet even at the end of her titular Legend, Britomart cannot interpret such spectacles "by any ridling skill, or commune wit" (xi.54). Spenser attributes both her triumph over Busirane and her subsequent rescue of Amoret to her powers not as a reader but as an agent of heavenly chastity. Although the "good endeuours" of individuals "*ought* . . . [to] confirme, / And guide the heauenly causes to their constant terme," Book III finally insists that "the fates are firme" (iii.25, emphasis mine). Divine inspiration underwrites whatever Britomart accomplishes.

The allegorical commentators to whom Spenser responds in his Virgilian imitations established a complex analogy between Virgil's hero and his poetry's implied audience. Fulgentius, Bernard, and Landino repeatedly suggested that reading the *Aeneid* could offer one the metaphysical insights that finally redeemed Aeneas from his subjection to carnal misprisions. But in reconciling allegorical convention with the darker epistemology of Protestantism, Spenser severs the bond between reader and hero so that Britomart never shares the former's privileged knowledge. Susanne Wofford sees the gap between the characters' hermeneutic impasse and the implied reader's knowledge as a source of pervasive pathos: by denying his characters a full understanding of their moral situation, Spenser suggests that the heroic life "requires the strength to undertake one's quest without any certainty of what it means or where it will lead."[38] But an even greater pathos marks the situation of the reader of a moral allegory repeatedly hinting at its own futility. While Spenser urges his readers to follow his characters' virtuous examples, he also reminds them that those examples cannot be followed outside a state of similar, inimitable election. By suggesting that only those called to virtue can be virtuous, Spenser brings the Virgilian allegorical tradition to an end.

⟮⟯ A F T E R W O R D ⟮⟯

As Barbara Bono has observed, "generalized allusion to the *Aeneid* becomes more diffuse" in the three books added to *The Faerie Queene* in 1596.[1] Spenser no longer explicitly proclaims himself a laureate following the progression from pastoral to epic. Nor does he adopt the *Aeneid* as his principal subtextual model. In general, classical influence yields to native, medieval examples: Chaucer dominates Book IV's retelling of the Knight's and Squire's Tales, and Malory arises as a principal voice in Book VI. The classical poet with whom the later Spenser enjoys the most affinity is Ovid. The longer he stayed in Ireland, the more he identified himself with the exiled poet glancing toward the court from a skeptical distance. Since the Leicesterian party had not recovered from the losses it suffered during the late 1580s, the Protestant appropriation of Virgil's *imperium sine fine* seemed less and less feasible. Above all, Spenser seems to have had increasing qualms about the ethos of stigmatization and sacrifice that formed the basis of Virgil's moral vision. The Virgil who finally does play a major role in *The Faerie Queene*'s last three books is the poet of pastoral *otium* rather than of epic *labor*.

Significantly, one of the 1596 poem's rare Virgilian imitations occurs "in the middest" of its most jingoistic section: Arthegall's bondage to Radigund conspicuously recalls Aeneas's subservience to Dido. Although Arthegall's transvestism links the episode more immediately to Hercules's encounter with Omphale, it owes something as well to Virgil's description of an effeminized Aeneas wearing Carthaginian robes and working on Dido's city. As in the moralized *Aeneid,* Arthegall's escape from feminine authority marks the central crisis in his moral education. But such apparent sanctions of patriarchal *rigor* are rare in the poem's second half. Book IV challenges Book V's emphasis on retributive justice with the River Marriage's evocation of natural harmonies underlying all human civilization. Book VI challenges Book V with the Acidalian vision of a world ordered more by internalized grace than external compulsion. In neither of these surrounding and subsuming books does a hero prove his virtue by sacrificing an alluring woman.

Spenser's 1596 departure from Virgil manifests itself most strikingly in his rejection of female abandonment as a topos for defining himself in opposition to nonepic modes and genres. In Books I or II, Arthegall's liberation from Radigund might have signalled an aesthetic liberation from romance influence. Like Redcrosse's subservience to Duessa, the episode juxtaposes classical and Italian subtexts. While Radigund's "Camis light of purple silke" (V.v.2) recalls the *purpuream . . . vestem* worn by Dido during the royal hunt (IV.139), her role as an Amazon queen links her to Ariosto's *femine omicide,* who also force their menfolk to dress in feminine attire and to perform women's work.[2] But in the 1596 *Faerie Queene,* Spenser does not reject an Ariostan denouement for a conventionally moral Virgilian ending. As Susannah Jane McMurphy notes, he patterns Radigund's defeat at Britomart's hands on Bradamante's victory over Marfisa.[3] Instead of a Virgilian hero spurning an Italianate temptress, we find in Britomart a heroine whose Ariostan origins remain as salient as those of the woman she defeats.

Pastorella provides an even more significant departure from the paradigm that Spenser followed earlier. More than any other figure in his poem, she embodies a genre defined in explicit contrast to epic. The moment Calidore falls for her, heroic action yields to pastoral stasis. The narrator censures Calidore just as Mercury rebuked Aeneas:

> Who now does follow the foule *Blatant Beast,*
>   Whilest *Calidore* does follow that faire Mayd,
>   Vnmyndfull of his vow and high beheast,
>   Which by the Faery Queene was on him layd,
>   That he should neuer leaue, nor be delayd
>   From chacing him, till he had it attchieued?
>   (VI.x.1)

On a metapoetic level, this passage indicts Spenser's own abandonment of epic's higher strains. But as his fiction unfolds, he figures a more complex relation between epic and pastoral than unequivocal opposition.[4] The disappearance of Colin's graces suggests that the pastoral vision cannot be sustained indefinitely; the ultimate destruction of Melibee's kingdom argues for a reassertion of epic's martial values against the enemies of civilization. Pastorella's own fate, however, reminds us that the pastoral need not be wholly abandoned. It can exist on the margins of epic itself as a source of aesthetic recuperation "after the stubborne stroke of stronger stounds" ("October," 49). It can also develop into more overtly heroic forms. The discovery of Pastorella's identity as a romance heroine abandoned in infancy hints at such an overarching myth of generic transvaluation. If she once distracted Calidore from his epic vocation, she now becomes the reward awaiting him when he fulfills his quest.[5]

The later work that conforms most fully to Spenser's earlier generic hierarchies is one whose relationship to *The Faerie Queene*'s final structure cannot be determined: *The Two Cantos of Mutabilitie.* Much as the scheming Duessa demonizes the complex plotting of Ariostan romance, Mutabilitie captures the polymorphousness of Ovidian storytelling. The moment Jove himself succumbs to her allure, Spenser projects his own anxieties about trespassing the boundaries between epic and more mythic, archetypal narrative:

> But, when he looked on her louely face,
> In which, faire beames of beauty did appeare,
> That could the greatest wrath soone turne to grace
> (Such sway doth beauty euen in Heauen beare)
> He staide his hand.
> (VII.vi.31)

Like Arthegall's surrender to Radigund, the passage constructs female beauty as the supreme threat to patriarchal authority. But here, as in Books I and II, the passage uses gender conflict to indict a specific kind of poetry. The resources at Mutabilitie's command threaten to subsume the Tudor myth of history in a broader myth of cosmic flux. From Mutabilitie's perspective, an *imperium sine fine* is impossible: all things are doomed to pass away in time. Were Cynthia, a surrogate for the Virgin Queen, to fall under her sway, Elizabeth's ascendancy would be exposed as merely a phase in a directionless historical process. Nature's judgment resists this threat by reimposing hierarchical order on the chaos of spontaneous mythic generation.

At first, Mutabilitie's defeat seems as decisive as Dido's, Radigund's, or Acrasia's. Although the fragment's general outline recalls those fictions of female repudiation, however, its final lines reopen moral and aesthetic ambiguities.

Nature's judgment ostensibly endorses an exclusionary model of epic more typical of Books I and II. But a nostalgia for Mutabilitie's pageantry resurfaces when Nature's decree makes the speaker

> . . . loath this state of life so tickle,
> And loue of things so vaine to cast away;
> Whose flowring pride, so fading and so fickle,
> Short *Time* shall soon cut down with his consuming sickle.
>
> (VII.viii.1)

The speaker seemingly welcomes a stasis transcending Mutabilitie's reign by rejecting "this state of life so tickle" and by casting away the "loue of things so vaine." But as Berger has noted, the syntax is so ambiguous that it establishes an ironic countertext.[6] The lines could also be construed as expressing the speaker's loathing to cast away the love of transitory things and unwillingness to embrace an eschaton devoid of pleasing diversity. By simultaneously renouncing and reaffirming Ovidian variation, Spenser brings the *Cantos* to an unstable conclusion.

This suspension of final aesthetic, moral, or political judgment constitutes Spenser's most significant contribution to the history of epic. As we have seen throughout this study, *The Faerie Queene*'s formal and thematic evolution follows from his continual reassessment of the competing claims of "ancients" and "moderns," Neo-Latin allegorists and writers of vernacular romance, as to what constitutes writing in the Virgilian tradition. Other vernacular laureates responded to the debate about the heroic poem's character by aligning themselves with one set of aesthetic and thematic criteria to the exclusion of all others. Spenser, by contrast, never commits himself permanently to one concept of epic's formal nature or didactic aims. His impact on later poets from Milton to Wordsworth, Blake, and Byron depends on his reconception of it as a form that continually revises its relationship to alternative literary influences.

ᛅ N O T E S ᛏ

Introduction

1. Rpt. in J. E. Spingarn, *Critical Essays of the Seventeenth Century: 1685–1700* (Oxford: Clarendon Press, 1909), 3:238. Emphasis in original.

2. Joseph Spence, *Polymetis: or, An Enquiry Concerning the Agreement Between the Works of the Roman Poets, and the Remains of the Antient Artists* (London, 1755), 307.

3. Preface to Rymer's translation of R. Rapin's *Reflections on Aristotle's Treatise of Poesie*, 1674, in *The Critical Works of Thomas Rymer*, ed. Curt A. Zimansky (New Haven: Yale Univ. Press, 1956), 5.

4. See Paul J. Alpers's discussion of the "limitations" of eighteenth-century Spenserian criticism in *Edmund Spenser: A Critical Anthology* (Harmondsworth, Middlesex: Penguin, 1969), 64–67.

5. Throughout this study, I am indebted to the extensive literature on epic's long-standing conflict with romance. See especially W. P. Ker, *Epic and Romance: Essays on Medieval Literature* (1908; rpt. New York: Dover, 1957); James Nohrnberg, *The Analogy of* The Faerie Queene (Princeton: Princeton Univ. Press, 1976), 5–22; Patricia A. Parker, *Inescapable Romance: Studies in the Poetics of a Mode* (Princeton: Princeton Univ. Press, 1979); David Quint, *Epic and Empire: Politics and Generic Form from Virgil to Milton* (Princeton: Princeton Univ. Press, 1993). Quint anticipates my concern with the way epic poets create "romance" as a genre opposing their own aesthetic and ideological commitments. See especially *Epic and Empire*, 31–41, 248–67. I extend Quint's thesis by noting that romance is only one of the genres that epic writers portray as a threat to their careers.

179

NOTES TO PAGES 4–11

6. Lawrence Lipking, *Abandoned Women and Poetic Tradition* (Chicago: Univ. of Chicago Press, 1988), xv.

7. Barbara Pavlock, *Eros, Imitation, and the Epic Tradition* (Ithaca: Cornell Univ. Press, 1990).

8. Mihoko Suzuki, *Metamorphoses of Helen: Authority, Difference, and the Epic* (Ithaca: Cornell Univ. Press, 1989).

9. See "Toward a Methodology for the Study of the Novel," in *The Dialogic Imagination: Four Essays by M. M. Bakhtin*, ed. Michael Holquist, trans. Caryl Emerson and Michael Holquist, Univ. of Texas Press Slavic Series, 1 (Austin: Univ. of Texas Press, 1981), 3–40.

10. See Gian Biagio Conte's discussion of the "dialectic of contamination" that characterizes Virgilian epic in *The Rhetoric of Imitation: Genre and Poetic Memory in Virgil and Other Latin Poets*, ed. Charles Segal, Cornell Studies in Classical Philology, 44 (Ithaca: Cornell Univ. Press, 1986), 141–84.

11. Merritt Y. Hughes, *Virgil and Spenser*, Univ. of California Publications in English, 2 (Berkeley: Univ. of California Press, 1929), 263–418. For typical discussions of Spenser as a syncretist, see Kathleen Williams, *Spenser's World of Glass: A Reading of* The Faerie Queene (Berkeley: Univ. of California Press, 1966), 97–98; Angus Fletcher, *The Prophetic Moment: An Essay on Spenser* (Chicago: Univ. of Chicago Press, 1971), 90. See also Thomas Greene's characterization of Spenser as "a poet whose loyalty to his own medieval roots limits his room for poetic maneuver, as one unconcerned with the exercise of bridging a rupture and playing with the differences between . . . separated worlds" (*The Light in Troy: Imitation and Discovery in Renaissance Poetry* [New Haven: Yale Univ. Press, 1982], 274).

I am grateful to the many previous scholars who have commented on Spenser's relationship to Virgil. Michael O'Connell notes how the Servian commentary tradition allowed Spenser to appropriate the *Aeneid* as the supreme model of an epic grounded in a specific historical situation (*Mirror and Veil: The Historical Dimension of Spenser's* Faerie Queene [Chapel Hill: Univ. of North Carolina Press, 1977]). I share my general interest in the hermeneutic conditions governing Virgil's Renaissance reception with William Sessions ("Spenser's Georgics," *English Literary Renaissance* 10 [1980]: 202–38). Building on Nohrnberg's initial suggestions about the Renaissance interpretation of Aeneas as "the whole man in all his parts" (*Analogy*, 29), Sessions sees *The Faerie Queene*'s individual quests coalescing in a Protestant reenactment of Aeneas's civilizing *labor*. I situate Spenser in a more ambivalent relationship to the Augustan past by focusing more on his retellings of Dido's abandonment than on his recollections of Aeneas's triumphs. Despite this fundamental difference in perspective, I am indebted to Sessions's essay as the richest extant treatment of the problems addressed in this study. More specific debts will be acknowledged in the course of my argument.

12. My emphasis on the *Aeneid*'s reception history as a means of de-essentializing modern categories of authorship is indebted in part to Hans Robert Jauss, "Literary History as a Challenge to Literary Theory," in *Toward an Aesthetic of Reception*, trans. Timothy Bahti, Theory and History of Literature, 2 (Minneapolis: Univ. of Minnesota Press, 1982), 3–45.

Chapter 1: From Homeric Romance to Augustan Epic

1. See Quint's discussion of how the shield's ideological program centers around intersecting binary oppositions that support a fundamental generic opposition between epic and

romance (David Quint, *Epic and Empire: Politics and Generic Form from Virgil to Milton* [Princeton: Princeton Univ. Press, 1993]).

2. My interpretation of the principate is indebted to Ronald Syme's seminal discussion in *The Roman Revolution* (Oxford: Oxford Univ. Press, 1939). For modifications of Syme's thesis, see the essays by H. Galsterer, Z. Yavetz, J. Linderski, and C. Meier in *Between Republic and Empire: Interpretations of Augustus and His Principate,* ed. Kurt A. Raaflaub and Mark Toher (Berkeley: Univ. of California Press, 1990). For more sympathetic views of the *renovatio* as a genuine attempt to preserve continuity with the Republic, see Alban Dewes Winspear and Lenore Kramp Geweke, *Augustus and the Reconstruction of Roman Government and Society,* Univ. of Wisconsin Studies in the Social Sciences and History 24 (1935; rpt. New York: Russell and Russell, 1970); Mason Hammond, "The Sincerity of Augustus," *Harvard Studies in Classical Philology* 69 (1965): 139–62; W. Eder, "Augustus and the Power of Tradition: The Augustan Principate as Binding Link between Republic and Empire," in Raaflaub and Toher.

3. For discussion of the evolving social status of Roman women, see Percy Ellwood Corbett, *The Roman Law of Marriage* (Oxford: Clarendon Press, 1930); J. P. V. D. Balsdon, *Roman Women: Their History and Habits* (London: Bodley Head, 1962); M. I. Finley, "The Silent Women of Rome," in *Aspects of Antiquity: Discoveries and Controversies* (New York: Viking, 1960), 129–42; Ramsay MacMullen, *Roman Social Relations: 50 B.C. to A.D. 284* (New Haven: Yale Univ. Press, 1974); Sarah B. Pomeroy, *Goddesses, Whores, Wives, and Slaves: Women in Classical Antiquity* (New York: Schocken, 1975), 149–204; MacMullen, "Woman in Public in the Roman Empire," *Historia* 29 (1980): 208–18; Mary R. Lefkowitz, "Influential Women," in *Images of Women in Antiquity,* ed. Averil Cameron and Amélie Kuhrt (London: Croom Helm, 1983), 49–64.

4. For background on Roman anti-Hellenism, see Charles Norris Cochrane, *Christianity and Classical Culture: A Study of Thought and Action from Augustus to Augustine* (Oxford: Oxford Univ. Press, 1940), 94–95; Nicholas Petrochilos, *Roman Attitudes to the Greeks* (Athens: National and Capodistrian Univ. of Athens Press, 1974); J. P. V. D. Balsdon, *Romans and Aliens* (London: Duckworth, 1979), 30–58. On Cato's anti-Hellenism in particular, see Theodor Mommsen, *The History of Rome,* trans. William P. Dickson, 4 vols. (1911; rpt. London: J. M. Dent, 1921), 2:446; Alan E. Astin, *Cato the Censor* (Oxford: Clarendon Press, 1978), 157–81.

5. Ralph Hexter argues that Roman anxiety about the deceptiveness of Greek art informs Aeneas's relationship to Odysseus, the great teller of tales, throughout the *Aeneid* ("What Was the Trojan Horse Made Of?: Interpreting Vergil's *Aeneid,*" *Yale Journal of Criticism* 3 [1990]: 109–31). Hexter develops this argument at greater length in his forthcoming study, *The Gate of Ivory: A Reader's Aeneid.* See also John P. Lynch's discussion of the association of Greek rhetoric with insincerity, "Laocoön and Sinon: Virgil, *Aeneid* 2.40–198," *Greece & Rome,* 2nd. ser. 27 (1980): 170–79.

6. See Donald Earl, *The Moral and Political Tradition of Rome,* Aspects of Greek and Roman Life (Ithaca: Cornell Univ. Press, 1967), 36–37.

7. *Sed virtus, vigilantia, labor apud Graecos nulla sunt* (Letter to Caesar on the State) in *Sallust,* trans. J. C. Rolfe (London: Heinemann, 1921), 478–79.

8. For modern discussion of Virgil's debt to Homer, see Georg Nicolaus Knauer, *Die Aeneis und Homer: Studien zur poetischen Technik Vergils mit Listen der Homerzitate in der Aeneis,* Hypomnemata: Untersuchungen zur Antike und zu Ihrem Nachleben, 7 (Göttingen: Vandenhoeck & Ruprecht, 1964); Brooks Otis, "The Originality of the Aeneid," in *Virgil,* ed. D. R. Dudley (London: Routledge, 1969), 27–66; W. R. Johnson, *Darkness Visible: A Study*

of Vergil's Aeneid (Berkeley: Univ. of California Press, 1976); Gordon Williams, *Technique and Ideas in the* Aeneid (New Haven: Yale Univ. Press, 1983), 82–119; Francis Cairns, *Virgil's Augustan Epic* (Cambridge: Cambridge Univ. Press, 1989), 177–214.

9. Thomas Greene, *The Light in Troy: Imitation and Discovery in Renaissance Poetry* (New Haven: Yale Univ. Press, 1982), 40–41.

10. *Virgil's* Aeneid: Cosmos *and* Imperium (Oxford: Clarendon Press, 1986), 362. See also Carl Becker, "Der Schild des Aeneas," *Wiener Studien* 77 (1964): 111–27.

11. All quotations are from the translation by Richmond Lattimore, *The Odyssey of Homer* (New York: Harper and Row, 1965). Line numbers are Lattimore's, which follow those of the Greek original.

12. Robert Lamberton, *Homer the Theologian: Neoplatonist Allegorical Reading and the Growth of the Epic Tradition* (Berkeley: Univ. of California Press, 1986), 208–15. See also Michael Murrin's discussion of the Aeolus episode's relationship to allegorizations of Zeus's deception in *The Allegorical Epic: Essays in Its Rise and Decline* (Chicago: Univ. of Chicago Press, 1980), 3–25. For a more general discussion of Virgil's debt to scholiastic misgivings about the morality of Homer's poetry, see Robin R. Schlunk, *The Homeric Scholia and the* Aeneid: *A Study of the Influence of Ancient Homeric Literary Criticism on Vergil* (Ann Arbor: Univ. of Michigan Press, 1974).

13. Barbara J. Bono, *Literary Transvaluation: From Vergilian Epic to Shakespearean Tragicomedy* (Berkeley: Univ. of California Press, 1984), 16–17; Mihoko Suzuki, *Metamorphoses of Helen: Authority, Difference, and the Epic* (Ithaca: Cornell Univ. Press, 1989), 105.

14. Theresa M. Krier grounds the Virgilian pathos in an illuminating contrast between the relative clarity of perception in the *Odyssey* and the murkiness of perception in the *Aeneid* (Krier, *Gazing on Secret Sights: Spenser, Classical Imitation, and the Decorums of Vision* [Ithaca: Cornell Univ. Press, 1990], 18–26).

15. X.46–49 (M:65–67). See Quint's discussion of Venus's offer (*Epic and Empire,* 84–86).

16. As Quint has noted, Virgil "redefines the epic hero, whose heroic virtue now consists in the sacrifice of his own independent will—a will independent from his national mission" (*Epic and Empire,* 83). Quint's entire discussion of heroic self-abnegation in the Palinurus episode's transformation of Odyssean subtexts (83–96) is profoundly relevant to my remarks on Virgil's nostalgia for Homer.

17. Lillian Robinson, *Monstrous Regiment: The Lady Knight in Sixteenth-Century Epic* (New York: Garland, 1985), 22–52; Suzuki, *Metamorphoses of Helen,* 93.

18. Barbara Pavlock, *Eros, Imitation, and the Epic Tradition* (Ithaca: Cornell Univ. Press, 1990), 72–87; Sarah Spence, *Rhetorics of Reason and Desire: Vergil, Augustine, and the Troubadours* (Ithaca: Cornell Univ. Press, 1988), 35–36.

19. On the conflict between public and private interests in the *Aeneid,* see Susan Ford Wiltshire, *Public and Private in Vergil's* Aeneid (Amherst: Univ. of Massachusetts Press, 1989).

20. On the distinction between Homeric and Virgilian similes, see David West, "Multiple-Correspondence Similes in the *Aeneid,*" *Journal of Roman Studies* 59 (1969): 40–49.

21. Classicists have noted dozens of verbal and structural correspondences between Odysseus's visit to the Phaeacian court in Books V–VII of the *Odyssey* and Aeneas's visit to Dido in Book I of the *Aeneid.* See Knauer, *Die* Aeneis *und Homer,* 152–77.

22. For complementary and alternative discussion of the Artemis-Diana similes, see Viktor Pöschl, *The Art of Vergil: Image and Symbol in the* Aeneid, trans. Gerda Seligson (Ann Arbor: Univ. of Michigan Press, 1962), 63–65; M. K. Thornton, "The Adaptation of Homer's Artemis-Nausicaa Simile in the *Aeneid*," *Latomus* 44 (1985): 615–22; Pavlock, *Eros, Imitation, and the Epic Tradition*, 72–73.

23. Angus Fletcher, *The Prophetic Moment: An Essay on Spenser* (Chicago: Univ. of Chicago Press, 1971), 90.

24. See Gordon Williams's discussion of the *univira* ideal in *Tradition and Originality in Roman Poetry* (Oxford: Clarendon Press, 1968), 377–81. For alternative views, see Richard C. Monti, *The Dido Episode and the* Aeneid: *Roman Social and Political Values in the Epic* (Leiden: E. J. Brill, 1981), 54–55; Niall Rudd, "Dido's *Culpa*," in *Oxford Readings in Vergil's* Aeneid, ed. S. J. Harrison (Oxford: Oxford Univ. Press, 1990), 145–66.

25. See Knauer, *Die Aeneis und Homer*, 214–18. Despite the fact that the Calypso episode opens the poet's account of Odysseus's adventures in Book v and falls immediately after the *Telemachia* (i–iv), his stay in Ogygia follows chronologically, if not narratively, both the Circe episode (x) and the *Nekyia* (xi). We learn about these earlier adventures through his first-person narrative in Alcinous's house.

26. For an alternative account of how Virgil's characterization of Dido revises Homeric and Apollonian representations of sexual passion, see Pavlock, *Eros, Imitation, and the Epic Tradition*, 72–87.

27. See Greene's seminal discussion of how Virgil charges the Homeric topos with "new moral and symbolic richness" (*The Descent from Heaven: A Study in Epic Continuity* [New Haven: Yale Univ. Press, 1963], 74–85).

28. For discussion of the second half of the *Aeneid* as an imitation of the *Iliad*, see Henry W. Prescott, *The Development of Virgil's Art* (Chicago: Univ. of Chicago Press, 1927), 428–29; Brooks Otis, *Virgil: A Study in Civilized Poetry* (Oxford: Clarendon Press, 1963); K. W. Gransden, *Virgil's Iliad: An Essay on Epic Narrative* (Cambridge: Cambridge Univ. Press, 1984); Quint, *Epic and Empire*, 65–76.

29. Noting that "all the images of Lavinia are negative: not speaking, not demonstrating individual traits, not showing deep feeling," Robinson concludes that she is "the model bride for the Roman state, dedicated to hearth and home, subject to the authority of both father and husband" (*Monstrous Regiment*, 55–56).

30. See R. O. A. M. Lyne, "Lavinia's Blush: Vergil, *Aeneid*, 12.64–70," *Greece and Rome*, 30 (1983): 55–64; Michael C. J. Putnam, *The Poetry of the* Aeneid: *Four Studies in Imaginative Unity and Design* (Cambridge: Harvard Univ. Press, 1966), 159; William S. Anderson, *The Art of the* Aeneid (Englewood Cliffs, N.J.: Prentice-Hall, 1969), 116; Johnson, *Darkness Visible*, 50–59.

31. On Renaissance objections to the poem's conclusion, see Andrew Fichter, *Poets Historical: Dynastic Epic in the Renaissance* (New Haven: Yale Univ. Press, 1982), 12–13; Joseph C. Sitterson, Jr., "Allusive and Elusive Meanings: Reading Ariosto's Vergilian Ending," *Renaissance Quarterly* 45 (1992): 10–13.

32. See Rudd's discussion of recent debates over the question of Dido's guilt ("Dido's *Culpa*," 145–66).

33. See Gordon Williams's discussion of the moral ambiguity inherent in Virgilian representation in *Technique and Ideas*, 82–119.

Chapter 2: Remembrances of Dido

1. The most complete general account of Virgil's medieval reception remains Domenico Comparetti's *Vergil in the Middle Ages,* trans. E. F. M. Benecke (London: Swan Sonnenschein, 1895). For general discussion of his reception in the Renaissance, see Vladimiro Zabughin, *Vergilio nel Rinascimento italiano da Dante a Torquato Tasso* (Bologna: Zanichelli, 1921); Craig Kallendorf, *In Praise of Aeneas: Virgil and Epideictic Rhetoric in the Early Italian Renaissance* (Hanover, N.H.: Univ. Press of New England, 1989). See also Gilbert Highet, *The Classical Tradition: Greek and Roman Influences on Western Literature* (Oxford: Oxford Univ. Press, 1949); R. D. Williams and T. S. Pattie, *Virgil: His Poetry through the Ages* (London: The British Library, 1982).

2. On the dialectic that Virgil himself establishes between individual points of view, like that of Dido, and those of other figures in the poem, see Gian Biagio Conte, *The Rhetoric of Imitation: Genre and Poetic Memory in Virgil and Other Latin Poets,* ed. Charles Segal, Cornell Studies in Classical Philology, 44 (Ithaca: Cornell Univ. Press, 1986), 153–63.

3. Ovid, *Heroïdes,* in *Heroïdes and Amores,* ed. Grant Showerman (London: William Heinemann, 1931). Subsequent references to Ovid's *Heroïdes* are to this edition; the English text is Showerman's facing-page translation.

4. On Ovid's suppression of Dido's curse, see Siegmar Döpp, *Virgilischer Einfluss im Werk Ovids* (Munich: Verlag UNI-Druck, 1968), 17–20.

5. M. Owen Lee discusses the theme of paternity in the *Aeneid* in *Fathers and Sons in Virgil's* Aeneid: Tum Genitor Natum (Albany: State Univ. of New York Press, 1979).

6. Barbara J. Bono, *Literary Transvaluation: From Vergilian Epic to Shakespearean Tragicomedy* (Berkeley: Univ. of California Press, 1984), 42. Several scholars have seen the *Metamorphoses* as a critique of the *Aeneid* and of its apparent endorsement of the *renovatio.* I am especially indebted to Brooks Otis, *Ovid as an Epic Poet* (Cambridge: Cambridge Univ. Press, 1966). See also Leo C. Curran, "Transformation and Anti-Augustanism in Ovid's *Metamorphoses,*" *Arethusa* 5 (1972): 71–91; and three articles by Charles Segal, "Ovid's *Metamorphoses*: Greek Myth in Augustan Rome," *Studies in Philology* 68 (1971): 371–94; "Narrative Art in the *Metamorphoses,*" *Classical Journal* 66 (1971): 331–37; "Ovid's Orpheus and Augustan Ideology," *Transactions of the American Philological Association* 103 (1972): 473–94; W. S. Anderson, "The Orpheus of Virgil and Ovid: *flebile nescio quid,*" in *Orpheus: The Metamorphoses of a Myth,* ed. John Warden (Toronto: Univ. of Toronto Press, 1982), 25–50.

7. See G. Karl Galinsky's discussion of Ovid's retelling of the *Aeneid* in *Ovid's* Metamorphoses: *An Introduction to the Basic Aspects* (Oxford: Basil Blackwell, 1975), 217ff.

8. Richard Lanham, *The Motives of Eloquence: Literary Rhetoric in the Renaissance* (New Haven: Yale Univ. Press, 1976), 48–64.

9. Peter Brown discusses the social and political conditions underlying Augustine's thought in *Augustine of Hippo: A Biography* (Berkeley: Univ. of California Press, 1967).

10. On the *Aeneid*'s early reception as grammatical and rhetorical text, see Comparetti, *Vergil in the Middle Ages,* 28–49.

11. *Confessions,* ed. John Gibb and William Montgomery (Cambridge: Cambridge Univ. Press, 1927). Subsequent references to the *Confessions* are to this edition and are cited according to the standard division into books and chapters. English references are to Rex Warner's translation of *The Confessions of St. Augustine* (New York: Signet, 1963).

12. See H. C. Coffin, "The Influence of Vergil on St. Jerome and on St. Augustine," *Classical Weekly* 17 (1924): 170–75; Harald Hagendahl, *Augustine and the Latin Classics*, 2 vols. (Göteborg: Elanders Boktryckeri Aktiebolag, 1967), 2:384–463; John J. O'Meara, "Augustine the Artist and the *Aeneid*," *Mélanges offerts à Mademoiselle Christine Mohrmann* (Utrecht: Anvers, 1963), 252–61; Andrew Fichter, *Poets Historical: Dynastic Epic in the Renaissance* (New Haven: Yale Univ. Press, 1982), 40–69; Bono, *Literary Transvaluation*, 45–50.

13. A. J. Minnis, *Medieval Theory of Authorship: Scholastic Literary Attitudes in the Later Middle Ages* (London: Scolar Press, 1984), 20–21. Michel Foucault addresses the fluidity of earlier conceptions of authorship in "What Is an Author?", in *Language, Counter-Memory, Practice: Selected Essays and Interviews*, ed. Donald F. Bouchard, trans. Bouchard and Sherry Simon (Ithaca: Cornell Univ. Press, 1977), 113–38.

14. For general discussion of Fulgentius's *Expositio*, see Don Cameron Allen, *Mysteriously Meant: The Rediscovery of Pagan Symbolism and Allegorical Interpretation in the Renaissance* (Baltimore: The Johns Hopkins Press, 1970), 137–39; O. B. Hardison, Jr.'s Introduction to the translation of Fulgentius in *Classical and Medieval Literary Criticism: Translations and Interpretations*, ed. Alex Preminger et al. (New York: Frederick Ungar, 1974), 324–29.

15. See Rita Copeland's discussion of medieval *allegoresis* in *Rhetoric, Hermeneutics, and Translation in the Middle Ages: Academic Traditions and Vernacular Texts* (Cambridge: Cambridge Univ. Press, 1991), 80–82.

16. For recent discussion of the disputed authorship of the *Commentary* ascribed to Bernard, see Julian Ward Jones, Jr., "The So-Called Silvestris Commentary on the *Aeneid* and Two Other Interpretations," *Speculum* 64 (1989): 835–48. Throughout this study, I refer to the unknown author as "Bernard" for the sake of convenience. See also J. Reginald O'Donnell, "The Sources and Meaning of Bernard Silvester's Commentary on the *Aeneid*," *Mediaeval Studies* 24 (1962): 233–49.

17. Jon Whitman discusses the ways allegorical interpretation bridged the gap between pagan and Christian cultures in *Allegory: The Dynamics of an Ancient and Medieval Technique* (Cambridge: Harvard Univ. Press, 1987), 104–12. See also A. G. Jongkees, "Translatio Studii: les avatars d'un thème médiéval," in *Miscellanea Mediaevalia in memoriam Jan Frederik Niermeyer* (Groningen: Wolters, 1967), 41–51.

18. *The Exposition of the Content of Virgil*, in *Fulgentius the Mythographer*, ed. and trans. Leslie George Whitbread (Columbus: Ohio State Univ. Press, 1971), 127. Subsequent references to Fulgentius are to this translation and are cited according to page number in the text.

19. *Expositio Virgilianae Continentiae Secundum Philosophos Moralis*, in *Fabii Planciadis Fulgentii V. C. Opera*, ed. Rudolf Helm (Leipzig, 1898), 94–95.

20. *Commentum Quod Dicitur Bernardi Silvestris Super Sex Libros Eneidos Virgilii*, ed. Julian Ward Jones and Elizabeth Frances Jones (Lincoln: Univ. of Nebraska Press, 1977), 25. English references are to *Commentary on the First Six Books of Virgil's Aeneid*, trans. Earl G. Schreiber and Thomas E. Maresca (Lincoln: Univ. of Nebraska Press, 1979), 27.

21. For discussion of the general character of such romances, see Louis Brewer Hall, "Caxton's 'Eneydos' and the Redactions of Vergil," *Mediaeval Studies* 22 (1960): 136–47, and "Chaucer and the Dido-and-Aeneas Story," *Mediaeval Studies* 25 (1963): 148–59; David J. Shirt, "The Dido Episode in *Enéas*: The Reshaping of Tragedy and Its Stylistic Consequences," *Medium Æ vum* 51 (1982): 3–17; Jerome E. Singerman, *Under Clouds of Poesy: Poetry and Truth in French and English Reworkings of the Aeneid, 1160–1513* (New York: Garland, 1986). As Chris-

topher Baswell argues, the romances depart from Virgil's text in stressing "personality rather than political identity, swift and intense sexual response, and an almost fevered preoccupation with the linkage between passion and death" ("'Figures of Olde Werk': Visions of Virgil in Later Medieval England," [Ph.D. diss., Yale Univ., 1983], 240–41).

22.   Il m'a ocise a molt grant tort;
            ge li pardoins ici ma mort;
            par nom d'acordement, de pais
            ses guarnemenz et son lit bais. (2063–66)

From *Eneas: Texte Critique,* ed. Jacques Salverda de Grave, Bibliotheca Normannica, 4 (Halle, 1891), 77. In the text I have supplied the English translation by John A. Yunck, *Eneas: A Twelfth-Century French Romance,* Records of Civilization: Sources and Studies, 93 (New York: Columbia Univ. Press, 1974), 98.

23. *Primera Crónica General de España,* ed. Ramón Menéndez Pidal, in *Nueva Bibliotheca de Auctores Españoles* (Madrid, 1955), 39.

24. See Minnis's discussion of this transition in *Medieval Theory of Authorship.*

25. I am indebted to Copeland's extensive investigation of the boundaries between academic and vernacular appropriations of classical texts in *Rhetoric, Hermeneutics, and Translation.*

26. Although the secondary literature on the Francesca episode is voluminous, the following studies are particularly helpful in assessing Dante's relationship to his precursors: J. H. Whitfield, *Dante and Virgil* (Oxford: Basil Blackwell, 1949); Antonino Pagliaro, "Il canto di Francesca," in *Ulisse: richerche semantiche sulla* Divina Commedia, 2 vols. (Messina and Florence: D'Anna, 1967) 1:115–59; A. C. Charity, *Events and Their Afterlife: The Dialectics of Christian Typology in the Bible and Dante* (Cambridge: Cambridge Univ. Press, 1966); Giuseppe Mazzotta, *Dante, Poet of the Desert: History and Allegory in the* Divine Comedy (Princeton: Princeton Univ. Press, 1979), 159–77; Bono, *Literary Transvaluation,* 51–61.

For more general treatments of Virgilian influence in Dante's works, see Colin Hardie, "Virgil in Dante," in *Virgil and His Influence,* ed. Charles Martindale (Bristol: Bristol Classical Press, 1984), 37–69; Robert Hollander, *Il Virgilio Dantesco: Tragedia nella "Commedia"* (Florence: Olschki, 1983); Teodolinda Barolini, *Dante's Poets: Textuality and Truth in the* Comedy (Princeton: Princeton Univ. Press, 1984).

27. "Paolo and Francesca," in *Dante: A Collection of Critical Essays,* ed. John Freccero (Englewood Cliffs, N.J.: Prentice-Hall, 1965), 61–77.

28. All references to Dante are to *The Divine Comedy of Dante Alighieri,* 3 vols., ed. and trans. John D. Sinclair (London: Bodley Head, 1939). The English text is Sinclair's facing-page translation.

29. John M. Fyler suggests that Chaucer's stance toward Dante recapitulates Ovid's revisionary stance toward Virgil (*Chaucer and Ovid* [New Haven: Yale Univ. Press, 1979], 1–22). On Chaucer's relationship to Dante, see also Howard H. Schless, *Chaucer and Dante: A Revaluation* (Norman: Pilgrim Books, 1984); Karla Taylor, *Chaucer Reads* The Divine Comedy (Stanford: Stanford Univ. Press, 1989); Richard Neuse, *Chaucer's Dante: Allegory and Epic Theater in* The Canterbury Tales (Berkeley: Univ. of California Press, 1991).

30. Several studies have examined how *The House of Fame* problematizes the concepts of truth and authority by suggesting the origins of all "certain" knowledge in rumor. See especially Sheila Delany, *Chaucer's* House of Fame: *The Poetics of Skeptical Fideism* (Chicago: Univ. of Chicago Press, 1972); Taylor, *Chaucer Reads,* 20–49.

31. The one exception is Baswell's "'Figures of Olde Werk.'" Reading the *House of Fame* in terms of an intertextual confrontation between Virgilian and Boethian figurations of the quest, Baswell also locates the poem's origins in Aeneas's experiences at Juno's temple.

32. For further discussion of Chaucer's relationship to medieval readings of the Juno's temple episode, see my article, "'Neither of idle shewes, nor of false charmes aghast': Transformations of Virgilian *Ekphrasis* in Chaucer and Spenser," *Journal of Medieval and Renaissance Studies* 23 (1993): 345–63.

33. See Edgar Finley Shannon, *Chaucer and the Roman Poets* (Cambridge: Harvard Univ. Press, 1929), 48–119; Louis Brewer Hall, "Chaucer and the Dido-and-Aeneas Story"; Fyler, *Chaucer and Ovid*, 23–64.

34. All references are to *The Riverside Chaucer*, ed. Larry D. Benson et al. (Boston: Houghton Mifflin, 1987).

35. Several Chaucerians have argued that the dreamer grows in moral knowledge over the course of the poem. See especially Charles P. R. Tisdale's account of it as "a reconstruction of the setting of Book IV of Virgil's poem coupled with an amplified resolution in Boethian philosophy" ("*The House of Fame*: Virgilian Reason and Boethian Wisdom," *Comparative Literature* 25 [1973]: 261). I find more persuasive Baswell's point that Chaucer's satiric wit argues against such attempts to read the poem as a progress toward genuine Boethian consolation.

36. I am indebted throughout to Donald W. Rowe's discussion of narrative contradictions (*Legend of Good Women*, in *Through Nature to Eternity: Chaucer's* Legend of Good Women [Lincoln: Univ. of Nebraska Press, 1988]).

37. Lisa Kiser argues that Chaucer's entire cycle subverts its apparent genre as a collection of exempla celebrating female virtue by its conspicuous omission of evidence contrary to the conclusions that Cupid desires (*Telling Classical Tales: Chaucer and the* Legend of Good Women [Ithaca: Cornell Univ. Press, 1983]).

38. "The Proloug of the First Buik of *Eneados*," in *The Poetical Works of Gavin Douglas, Bishop of Dunkeld*, ed. John Small, 4 vols. (Edinburgh, 1874), 2:16. For further discussion of Douglas's stance toward Virgil, see Singerman, *Under Clouds of Poesy*, 217–85.

39. For a discussion of Douglas's anachronisms, see Thomas Greene, *The Light in Troy: Imitation and Discovery in Renaissance Poetry* (New Haven: Yale Univ. Press, 1982), 242–43.

40. See Allen, *Mysteriously Meant*, 135–62; Michael Murrin, *The Allegorical Epic: Essays in Its Rise and Decline* (Chicago: Univ. of Chicago Press, 1980), 3–25.

41. Badius, *P. Virgilii Maronis Aeneida Commentarium*, in Giunta's edition of Virgil's *Opera* (Venice, 1544), 267, verso, translation mine. Subsequent references to Badius's commentary are to this edition and are cited in the text according to page number. Badius summarizes Fulgentius's allegory of the stages of a man's life both in his general introduction to the *Aeneid* (147, recto) and at the opening of his commentary on Book IV (267, verso).

42. Melanchthon, Introduction to Book IV in *P. Vergilii Maronis Opera Philippi Melanchthonis illustrata scholiis* (Lyons, 1533), 192.

43. Girolamo Balbi, *De civili et bellica fortitudine liber ex mysteriis poetae Vergilii nunc depromptus* (Rome, 1526).

44. *Maphei Vegii Laudensis De Educatione Liberorum Et Eorum Claris Moribus Libri Sex*, ed. Sister Maria Walburg Fanning (Washington, D.C.: Catholic Univ. of America, 1933). In the text, I provide my translation of Vegius's Latin: ". . . ita per Didonem feminas etiam, quibus

vitam rationibus instituere deberent vel praemio laudis vel metu infamiae ac tristissimi demum interitus, omni illa sui poematis editione admonere studuit" (87). Vegius continues by asking how anyone hearing Dido's story would not prefer "embracing a rather austere chastity than a rather flattering desire" (*non pudicitiam licet austeriorem malit amplecti quam blandiorem libidinem*) (87).

45. *Disputationes Camaldulenses*, ed. Peter Lohe (Florence: G. C. Sansoni, 1980), 180–83. Landino's *Allegorica Platonica*, which first appeared in the Basel edition of Virgil's *Opera* in 1577, tends to repeat many of the allegorizations that figure in the last two books of the *Disputationes*, which were first published in Venice about 1505. For further discussion of Landino, see Allen, *Mysteriously Meant*, 143; Murrin, *Allegorical Epic*, 27–50; William Sessions, "Spenser's Georgics," *English Literary Renaissance* 10 (1980): 211–17.

46. See Kallendorf, *In Praise of Aeneas*, 58–76.

47. *Amorosa visione*, ed. Vittore Branca, trans. Robert Hollander et al. (Hanover: Univ. Press of New England, 1986), 114.

48. II.55.1. Brian Anslay published an English translation of Christine's work, *The Boke of the Cyte of Ladyes*, in 1521.

49. For a comprehensive account of Dido on the Renaissance stage, see Bono, *Literary Transvaluation*, 83–139.

50. Latin references to Boccaccio are to *De Genealogia Deorum Gentilium Libri*, ed. Vincenzo Romano, 2 vols. (Bari: Laterza, 1951), 2:722. I have supplied the English translation by Charles G. Osgood, *The Genealogy of the Gentile Gods*, in *Boccaccio on Poetry: Being the Preface and the Fourteenth and Fifteenth Books of Boccaccio's* De Genealogia Deorum Gentilium, ed. and trans. Charles G. Osgood (Princeton: Princeton Univ. Press, 1930), 68.

51. Henry Parker, "The Bridle," in *Recusant Poets*, ed. Louise Imogen Guiney (New York: Sheed and Ward, 1939), 1:22.

52. Sidney, *A Defence of Poetry*, ed. J. A. Van Dorsten (Oxford: Oxford Univ. Press, 1966), 47. See Sessions's discussion of Sidney's Virgilian heritage ("Spenser's Georgics," 207–11).

53. Albert Ascoli, *Ariosto's Bitter Harmony: Crisis and Evasion in the Italian Renaissance* (Princeton: Princeton Univ. Press, 1987). I am indebted throughout this study to Ascoli's discussion of Ariosto's skepticism toward the didactic defense of poetry. For further discussion of the sixteenth-century crisis in humanist educational theory and its impact on the reception and imitation of classical texts, see Timothy Hampton, *Writing from History: The Rhetoric of Exemplarity in Renaissance Literature* (Ithaca: Cornell Univ. Press, 1990).

54. Italian references are to *Orlando Furioso*, ed. Cesare Segre, 2 vols. (Milan: Arnoldo Mondadori, 1976). English references are to *Orlando Furioso*, trans. Guido Waldman (Oxford: Oxford Univ. Press, 1974).

55. David Quint characterizes the San Giovanni passage as a "mock 'defense of poetry' " (*Origin and Originality in Renaissance Literature: Versions of the Source* [New Haven: Yale Univ. Press, 1983], 85).

56. Patricia A. Parker, *Inescapable Romance: Studies in the Poetics of a Mode* (Princeton: Princeton Univ. Press, 1979), 40–44.

57. David Quint argues that Ariosto eventually abandons Boiardo's influence but associates that repudiation with the destruction of Atlante's palace ("The Figure of Atlante: Ariosto and Boiardo's Poem," *Modern Language Notes* 94 [1979]: 77–91).

58. For a complementary account of the erotics of Ariostan narrative, see Eugenio Donato, " '*Per Selve e Boscherecci Labirinti*': Desire and Narrative Structure in Ariosto's *Orlando Furioso*," *Barroco* 4 (1972): 17–34.

59. For more extensive discussion of the controversy over the *Furioso*, see Giuseppina Fumagalli, *La fortuna dell'* Orlando Furioso *in Italia nel secolo XVI* (Ferrara: Zuffi, 1910); Bernard Weinberg, *A History of Literary Criticism in the Italian Renaissance*, 2 vols. (Chicago: Univ. of Chicago Press, 1961), 2:954–1073; Daniel Javitch, *Proclaiming a Classic: The Canonization of* Orlando Furioso (Princeton: Princeton Univ. Press, 1991), 21–47.

60. "Il discorso contro l'Ariosto, di Filippo Sassetti. Edito per la prima volta di su l'originale magliabechiano. . . . Nota di Giuseppe Castaldi," *Rendiconti della Reale Accademia dei Lincei, Classe di scienze morali, storiche e filologiche* 22 (1913): 473–524. See also *L'Arte poetica del Sig. Antonio Minturno* (Venice: G. A. Valvassori, 1564).

61. *Giraldi Cinthio: On Romances,* trans. Henry L. Snuggs (Lexington: Univ. of Kentucky Press, 1968), 39.

62. *Allegoria di Gioseffo Bononome sopra il* Furioso *di M. Lodovico Ariosto,* in the Ruscelli edition of the *Furioso* (Venice, 1584).

63. See Porcacchi's annotations to Canto XI in his edition of the *Furioso* (Venice, 1568). See also Toscanella's annotations in his *Bellezze del* Fvrioso (Venice, 1574).

64. *Torquato Tasso: Discourses on the Heroic Poem,* trans. Mariella Cavalchini and Irene Samuel (Oxford: Clarendon Press, 1973), 78.

65. Margaret Ferguson, *Trials of Desire: Renaissance Defenses of Poetry* (New Haven: Yale Univ. Press, 1983), 54.

66. See especially Fichter's chapter on Tasso in *Poets Historical,* 112–55.

67. Critics have charged Tasso with implausibility and violations of decorum for the suddenness of Armida's conversion. See A. Bartlett Giamatti, *The Earthly Paradise and the Renaissance Epic* (Princeton: Princeton Univ. Press, 1966), 209–10. See also Greene's similar complaint that Tancredi and Rinaldo's redemptions are not "psychologically authentic" (*The Descent from Heaven: A Study in Epic Continuity* [New Haven: Yale Univ. Press, 1963], 213).

68. Italian references are to *Gerusalemme Liberata,* ed. Lanfranco Caretti (Milan: Arnoldo Mondadori, 1983). English references are to *Jerusalem Delivered,* trans. Ralph Nash (Detroit: Wayne State Univ. Press, 1987).

69. See Weinberg, *History of Literary Criticism,* 2:954–1073; Eugenio Donadoni, *Torquato Tasso: Saggio Critico,* 2 vols. (Florence, 1920), 2:7–53. See also Ferguson's chapter on Tasso in *Trials of Desire,* 54–136. Ferguson reads Tasso's defenses as an extended dialogue with his detractors.

70. See Quint's discussion of the *Conquistata* in *Origin and Originality,* 117–32.

71. See Thomas Cain, *Praise in* The Faerie Queene (Lincoln: Univ. of Nebraska Press, 1978), 40.

Chapter 3: Paulo maiora canamus

1. Richard Helgerson, *Self-Crowned Laureates: Spenser, Jonson, Milton and the Literary System* (Berkeley: Univ. of California Press, 1983), 25–35; David Lee Miller, "Spenser's Vocation, Spenser's Career," *ELH* 50 (1983): 197–231. I follow Helgerson in using the term

laureate for poets who see their art as "a means of making a contribution to the order and improvement of the state" (29).

2. See Ezio Raimondi, "Dalla natura alla regula," in *Rinascimento inquieto,* Saggi di varia cultura, 5 (Palermo: Manfredi, 1965), 7–21; Thomas Greene, *Light in Troy: Imitation and Discovery in Renaissance Poetry* (New Haven: Yale Univ. Press, 1982), 171–96.

3. Lynn Johnson, The Shepheardes Calender: *An Introduction* (University Park: Pennsylvania State Univ. Press, 1990), 1.

4. Patrick Cullen, *Spenser, Marvell, and Renaissance Pastoral* (Cambridge: Harvard Univ. Press 1970), 25.

5. Harry Berger, *Revisionary Play: Studies in the Spenserian Dynamics* (Berkeley: Univ. of California Press, 1988), 277–78.

6. Richard Halpern, *The Poetics of Primitive Accumulation: English Renaissance Culture and the Genealogy of Capital* (Ithaca: Cornell Univ. Press, 1991), 176–214.

7. For complementary and alternative discussions of "October" 's ambivalence, see Cullen, *Spenser, Marvell, and Renaissance Pastoral,* 68–76; Johnson, The Shepheardes Calender: *An Introduction,* 84–86.

8. See Thomas Cain's introduction to "October," in *The Yale Edition of the Shorter Poems of Edmund Spenser,* ed. William Oram et al. (New Haven: Yale Univ. Press, 1989), 167. As Ruth Luborsky suggests, the woodcuts to each of the eclogues recall those in humanist editions of Virgil's *Opera* ("The Allusive Presentation of *The Shepheardes Calender,*" *Spenser Studies* 1 [1980]: 29–67).

9. Jane Tylus sees Piers's suppression of Orpheus's failure as an attempt to set Orpheus's poetry above materialist concerns about poetic compensation ("Spenser, Virgil, and the Politics of Poetic Labor," *ELH* 55 [1988]: 53–77).

10. William Kennedy, "The Virgilian Legacies of Petrarch's *Bucolicum Carmen* and Spenser's *Shepheardes Calender,*" in *The Early Renaissance: Virgil and the Classical Tradition,* Acta 9 (1982): 98.

11. Several critics have read the *Calender* as a covert critique of the French marriage negotiations. See Paul E. McLane, *Spenser's* Shepheardes Calender: *A Study in Elizabethan Allegory* (Notre Dame: Univ. of Notre Dame Press, 1961); David Norbrook, *Poetry and Politics in the English Renaissance* (London: Routledge and Kegan Paul, 1984), 69–90; Annabel Patterson, *Pastoral and Ideology: Virgil to Valéry* (Berkeley: Univ. of California Press, 1987), 118–27; Johnson, The Shepheardes Calender: *An Introduction,* 144–56.

12. Helgerson (*Self-Crowned Laureates,* 72–75) and Miller ("Spenser's Vocation," 209–10) have focused on Cuddie's allusions to Maecenas and Augustus as a thinly veiled commentary about Spenser's own dependence on patronage as an aspiring poet.

13. Louis Montrose, " 'The perfecte paterne of a Poete': The Poetics of Courtship in *The Shepheardes Calender,*" *Texas Studies in Literature and Language* 21 (1979): 49.

14. Both Helgerson (*Self-Crowned Laureates,* 67ff.) and Montrose (" 'The perfecte paterne of a Poete,' " 37–39) have focused on Petrarchanism's fundamentally amateurish character as a threat to Spenser's laureate vocation.

15. John Freccero, "The Fig Tree and the Laurel: Petrarch's Poetics," *Diacritics* 5 (1975): 34–40; Giuseppe Mazzotta, "The *Canzoniere* and the Language of the Self," *Studies in Philology*

75 (1978): 271–96. See also Greene's *Light in Troy*, 104–46, and Marguerite R. Waller, *Petrarch's Poetics and Literary History* (Amherst: Univ. of Massachusetts Press, 1980).

16. Eleanor Leach discusses Tityrus's experiences in terms of Roman customs of manumission (*Vergil's* Eclogues: *Landscapes of Experience* [Ithaca: Cornell Univ. Press, 1974], 120–32).

17. I have provided Paul Alpers's translation from *The Singer of the* Eclogues (Berkeley: Univ. of California Press, 1979). Subsequent English references are to this translation.

18. See Kennedy's discussion of Badius Ascensius's commentary on Eclogue I and its possible connections with Spenser's "September" ("Virgilian Legacies," 94–97).

19. For discussion of Mantuan's particular influence on *The Shepheardes Calender*, see Cullen's *Spenser, Marvell, and Renaissance Pastoral*; Nancy Jo Hoffman, *Spenser's Pastorals: The Shepheardes Calender and "Colin Clout"* (Baltimore: Johns Hopkins Univ. Press, 1977), 11–34.

20. Luborsky notes that the buildings in the "Januarye" woodcut are ones that readers would have associated with Rome ("The Illustrations to *The Shepheardes Calender*," *Spenser Studies* 2 [1981]: 24).

21. On the distinction between "hard" and "soft" pastoral, see Alpers, "The Eclogue Tradition and the Nature of Pastoral," *College English* 34 (1972): 352. See also Isabel MacCaffrey, "Allegory and Pastoral in *The Shepheardes Calender*," *ELH* 36 (1969): 88–109.

22. I regret that Anthony di Matteo's excellent discussion of Spenser and comments on the Virgilian Venus did not appear until after my manuscript had gone to press. Di Matteo provides a particularly useful summary of Venus's ambivalent interpretive history. The fact that two scholars examining the intertextual heritage of the same Spenserian passages come to different conclusions attests to the richness of the Neo-Latin commentary tradition. See "Spenser's Venus-Virgo: The Poetics and Interpretive History of a Dissembling Figure," *Spenser Studies* 10 (1989): 27–70.

23. *Seniles* IV.5, in *Opera quae extant omnia* (Basel: Sebastianus Henricpetri, 1581), 787. I have supplied the English translation by Aldo S. Bernardo et al., in *Francis Petrarch: Letters of Old Age, rerum senilium libri I–XVIII*, 2 vols. (Baltimore: Johns Hopkins Univ. Press, 1992), 1: 142. Petrarch repeats this allegorization of Venus as *voluptas* in *Rerum memorandarum libri*, ed. Giuseppe Billanovich, Edizione Nazionale delle Opere di Francesco Petrarca (Florence: Sansoni, 1953), III.50.

24. On the much disputed question of E. K.'s identity, see especially Jefferson B. Fletcher, "Spenser and 'E. K.,'" *Modern Language Notes* 15 (1900): 330–31; Raymond Jenkins, "Who Is E. K.?," *Shakespeare Association Bulletin* 19 (1944): 147–60; D. T. Starnes, "Spenser and E. K.," *Studies in Philology* 41 (1944): 181–200; Johnson, The Shepheardes Calender: *An Introduction*, 26–27.

25. R. Dodoens' *Nieuwe herball or historie of plantes*, trans. Henry Lyte (1578), II.lvi.217. Cited under "Carnation," *Oxford English Dictionary*, 1971.

26. McLane, *Spenser's* Shepheardes Calender, 52–53.

27. Barbara J. Bono, *Literary Transvaluation: From Vergilian Epic to Shakespearean Tragicomedy* (Berkeley: Univ. of California Press, 1984), 67–69; Donald Cheney, "The Circular Argument of *The Shepheardes Calender*," in *Unfolded Tales: Essays on Renaissance Romance*, ed. George M. Logan and Gordon Teskey (Ithaca: Cornell Univ. Press, 1989), 155.

28. For an alternate discussion of the relationship between "November" and "Aprill," see Johnson, The Shepheardes Calender: An Introduction, 128–32.

29. See Kennedy's discussion of this transition in "Virgilian Legacies," 83–85.

30. On the complexities of Chaucer's Renaissance reception, see Alice S. Miskimin, The Renaissance Chaucer (New Haven: Yale Univ. Press, 1975); A. C. Spearing, Medieval to Renaissance in English Poetry (Cambridge: Cambridge Univ. Press, 1985), 59–120. My understanding of the Renaissance Chaucer has been particularly enhanced by several studies of his relationship to Shakespeare. See especially the essays in Chaucerian Shakespeare: Adaptation and Transformation, Medieval and Renaissance Monograph Series II, ed. E. Talbot Donaldson and Judith J. Kollmann (Detroit: Michigan Consortium for Medieval and Early Modern Studies, 1983); Ann Thompson, Shakespeare's Chaucer: A Study in Literary Origins (Liverpool: Liverpool Univ. Press, 1978); E. Talbot Donaldson, The Swan at the Well: Shakespeare Reading Chaucer (New Haven: Yale Univ. Press, 1985).

31. Lydgate, The Fall of Princes, quoted in Chaucer: The Critical Heritage, ed. Derek Brewer, 2 vols. (London: Routledge and Kegan Paul, 1978), 1:57; Caxton, "Prohemye" to The Canterbury Tales (1484), quoted in Chaucer, ed. Brewer, 1:76.

32. Thomas Hoccleve, The Regement of Princes, quoted in Caroline F. E. Spurgeon, Five Hundred Years of Chaucer Criticism and Allusion: 1357–1900, 3 vols. (1925; New York: Russell and Russell, 1960), 1:22.

33. Stephen Hawes, The Pastime of Pleasure, quoted in Chaucer, ed. Brewer, 1:82.

34. Roger Ascham, quoted in Chaucer, ed. Brewer, 1:100.

35. Edmund Becke, Prefatory letter, quoted in Chaucer, ed. Brewer, 1:102. As Caroline Spurgeon notes, " 'Canterbury Tale' seems very early to have been used as a term of contempt, meaning either a story with no truth in it, or a vain and scurrilous tale" (Five Hundred Years, xxi). It is used in that sense both by Cranmer and Latimer.

36. John Harington, Preface to the translation of Orlando Furioso, in Elizabethan Critical Essays, ed. G. Gregory Smith, 2 vols. (Oxford: Clarendon Press, 1904), 2:215.

37. Francis Beaumont, quoted in Chaucer, ed. Brewer, 1:137.

38. John Burrow, see "Chaucer," in The Spenser Encyclopedia, ed. A. C. Hamilton et al. (Toronto: Univ. of Toronto Press, 1990).

39. Scholars have commented on Chaucer's interest in antithetical interpretations of human experience. See especially Paul G. Ruggiers, The Art of The Canterbury Tales (Madison: Univ. of Wisconsin Press, 1967), 30–41; Peter Elbow, Oppositions in Chaucer (Middletown, Conn.: Wesleyan Univ. Press, 1973); Stewart Justman, "Medieval Monism and Abuse of Authority in Chaucer," Chaucer Review 11 (1976): 95–111; Robert B. Burlin, Chaucerian Fiction (Princeton: Princeton Univ. Press, 1977); Richard Lanham, The Motives of Eloquence: Literary Rhetoric in the Renaissance (New Haven: Yale Univ. Press, 1976), 65–81.

For a previous consideration of how Spenser responds in his shorter poems to Chaucer's more ludic aspects, see Judith H. Anderson, " 'Nat worth a boterflye': Muiopotmos and The Nun's Priest's Tale," Journal of Medieval and Renaissance Studies 1 (1971): 89–106.

40. I am indebted throughout this section to previous discussions of the youth-age conflict in "Februarie" and "March" by Cullen, Spenser, Marvell, and Renaissance Pastoral, 125–29; Berger, Revisionary Play, 416–31; and Johnson, The Shepheardes Calender: An Introduction, 62–72. Johnson draws a particularly useful connection between "Februarie" and Chaucerian fabliau on the basis of their common concern with vengeance and retribution.

41. When Thenot proclaims that the shepherds will "paye . . . the price of [their] sur-quedrie, / With weeping, and wayling, and misery" (49–50), he may echo the opening lines of the Merchant's Prologue: "Wepyng and waylyng, care and oother sorwe / I knowe ynogh, on even and a-morwe" (1213–14). His impotent rage, his opposition to youth, and above all his contempt for love link him to the narrator of Chaucer's darkest comedy of disillusionment.

42. See Berger, *Revisionary Play*, 423; Johnson, The Shepheardes Calender: *An Introduction*, 64.

43. Thomas Cain, "Introduction," *The Yale Edition of the Shorter Poems of Edmund Spenser*, ed. William Oram et al. (New Haven: Yale Univ. Press, 1989), 55–56.

Chapter 4: From Roma Aeterna *to the New Hierusalem*

1. For discussion of Book I's relationship to the Protestant reception of the Book of Revelation, see John E. Hankins, "Spenser and the Revelation of St. John," *PMLA* 60 (1945): 364–81; Frank Kermode, *Shakespeare, Spenser, Donne: Renaissance Essays* (London: Routledge and Kegan Paul, 1971), 40–41; Florence Sandler, "*The Faerie Queene*: An Elizabethan Apocalypse," in *The Apocalypse in English Renaissance Thought and Literature: Patterns, Antecedents and Repercussions*, ed. C. A. Patrides and Joseph Wittreich (Ithaca: Cornell Univ. Press, 1984), 148–74.

2. Luther's comments in his "Lectures on Genesis" are typical: "In the historical accounts of the heathen there are certainly outstanding instances of self-control; of generosity; of love toward fatherland, parents, and children; of bravery; and of philanthropy. Yet we maintain that the loftiest thoughts about God, about the worship of God, and about the will of God are [to them] a darkness more than Cimmerian" (trans. George V. Schick, in *Luther's Works*, ed. Jaroslav Pelikan and Helmut T. Lehmann, 55 vols. [St. Louis: Concordia, 1955–86], 2:42).

3. Noted by Georgia B. Christopher, *Milton and the Science of the Saints* (Princeton: Princeton Univ. Press, 1982), 73. I am indebted throughout to Christopher's discussion of Protestant attacks on classical culture.

4. Lawrence Humphrey, *The Nobles, or of Nobilitye: The Original Nature, Dutyes, Right, and Christian Institucion Thereof* (London, 1563), sig. x.

5. "Grace and Free Will," in *The Folger Library Edition of The Works of Richard Hooker*, ed. W. Speed Hill et al., 6 vols. (Cambridge: Belknap, 1977–93), 4:103. See Dewey D. Wallace, Jr.'s discussion of the prevalence of belief in humanity's radical depravity throughout the period in *Puritans and Predestination: Grace in English Protestant Theology, 1525–1695* (Chapel Hill: Univ. of North Carolina Press, 1982).

John King provides a summary of the scholarly controversy over Spenser's religious partisanship in "Was Spenser a Puritan?" *Spenser Studies* 6 (1985): 1–35. In general, the debate centers more on Spenser's opinions on ecclesiastical discipline than on such fundamental Reformation beliefs as justification by faith. As David Norbrook notes, Spenser's doctrines were broadly based enough to appeal to both Puritans and loyal members of the Established Church (*Poetry and Politics in the English Renaissance* [London: Routledge and Kegan Paul, 1984], 60ff.).

6. John King, *Spenser's Poetry and the Reformation Tradition* (Princeton: Princeton Univ.

Press, 1990), 183–232. See also Michael Leslie, *Spenser's "Fierce Warres and Faithfull Loves": Martial and Chivalric Symbolism in* The Faerie Queene (Cambridge: D. S. Brewer, 1983); Anthea Hume, *Edmund Spenser: Protestant Poet* (Cambridge: Cambridge Univ. Press, 1984), 72–106; Alan Sinfield, *Literature in Protestant England, 1560–1660* (London: Croom Helm, 1983).

7. Paul Alpers, *The Poetry of* The Faerie Queene (Princeton: Princeton Univ. Press, 1967), 334–69.

8. For further discussions of tensions between Protestant and humanist concepts of education, see Andrew D. Weiner, *Sir Philip Sidney and the Poetics of Protestantism: A Study of Contexts* (Minneapolis: Univ. of Minnesota Press, 1978), 28–50; Gerald Strauss, *Luther's House of Learning: Indoctrination of the Young in the German Reformation* (Baltimore: Johns Hopkins Univ. Press, 1978), 216–21; Sinfield, *Literature in Protestant England*, 37ff.; John Morgan, *Godly Learning: Puritan Attitudes towards Reason, Learning, and Education, 1560–1640* (Cambridge: Cambridge Univ. Press, 1986).

9. John Shroeder, "Spenser's Erotic Drama: The Orgoglio Episode," *ELH* 29 (1962): 140–59; Isabel MacCaffrey, *Spenser's Allegory: The Anatomy of Imagination* (Princeton: Princeton Univ. Press, 1976), 161.

10. Judith Lee argues that Harington's modifications throughout his translation of the *Furioso* attempt to overcome Protestant anxieties about Ariosto's representations of the erotic and the fantastic ("The English Ariosto: The Elizabethan Poet and the Marvelous," *Studies in Philology* 80 [1983]: 277–99).

11. Alpers, *The Poetry of* The Faerie Queene, 160–99. For the alternative view that Spenser's reading of Ariosto was significantly mediated through his reading of the commentaries, see Graham Hough, *A Preface to* The Faerie Queene (New York: Norton, 1962), 116–23; Peter DeSa Wiggins, "Spenser's Use of Ariosto: Imitation and Allusion in Book I of the *Faerie Queene*," *Renaissance Quarterly* 44 (1991): 257–79. In general, the Ariostan commentaries, which were always printed either as prefaces or as appendices to Ariosto's text itself, lack the cultural authority of the major Virgilian commentaries, which were printed in the margins surrounding the *Aeneid*'s text.

12. The Virgilian subtext was first noted by John Upton in his edition of *Spenser's Faerie Queene*, 2 vols. (London, 1758). Shirley Clay Scott traces the descent of the arborification topos from Virgil through Ovid, Dante, Boccaccio, and other writers to Spenser in "From Polydorus to Fradubio: The History of a *Topos*," *Spenser Studies* 7 (1986): 27–57. As I argue in the text, Spenser particularly engages the conflict between Virgil's original version of the figure and Ariosto's parody. Anything in *The Faerie Queene* that might suggest the direct influence of Dante's Piero delle Vigne episode can be explained more plausibly in terms of Ariosto's mediation; nevertheless, see Maureen Quilligan's suggestive comparison of Spenser's and Dante's allegorical strategies in *The Language of Allegory: Defining the Genre* (Ithaca: Cornell Univ. Press, 1979), 101–21.

13. See Giamatti's discussion of madness in the *Furioso* ("Headlong Horses, Headless Horsemen: An Essay on the Chivalric Epics of Pulci, Boiardo, and Ariosto," in *Italian Literature: Roots and Branches*, ed. Giose Rimanelli and Kenneth John Atchity [New Haven: Yale Univ. Press, 1976], 292–304). See also Albert Ascoli, *Ariosto's Bitter Harmony: Crisis and Evasion in the Italian Renaissance* (Princeton: Princeton Univ. Press, 1987), 304–31.

14. See Benedetto Croce, *Ariosto, Shakespeare, e Corneille* (Bari: Laterza, 1920).

15. William Nelson, *The Poetry of Edmund Spenser: A Study* (New York: Columbia Univ. Press, 1963), 160–64.

16. On the concept of demonic parody as a structural device throughout *The Faerie Queene,* see Angus Fletcher, *The Prophetic Moment: An Essay on Spenser* (Chicago: Univ. of Chicago Press, 1971), 34–37, 98–106.

17. On the significance of Orgoglio's relationship to the Titans, see S. K. Heninger, Jr., "The Orgoglio Episode in *The Faerie Queene,*" *ELH* 26 (1959): 171–87.

18. Following an introductory discussion of the tripartite soul, Balbi appropriates Virgil's Aeolus episode as an allegory about the need to discipline passion with reason. See Girolamo Babli, *De civili et bellica fortitudine ex mysteriis poetae Vergilii nunc depromptus* (Rome, 1526), C3 ff. Boccaccio treats Homer's Aeolus as a type of the Christian God, restraining concupiscent impulse with divine love. See *De Genealogia deorum gentilium libri,* ed. Vincenzo Romano, 2 vols. (Bari: Laterza, 1951), 2:575.

19. Ernest Sirluck, "A Note on the Rhetoric of Spenser's 'Despair,' " *Modern Philology* 47 (1949): 8–11; A. C. Hamilton, *The Structure of Allegory in* The Faerie Queene (Oxford: Clarendon Press, 1961), 80–81; James Nohrnberg, *The Analogy of* The Faerie Queene (Princeton: Princeton Univ. Press, 1976), 151–55.

20. Richard Hooker, *Of the Laws of Ecclesiastical Polity,* in *The Folger Library Edition of The Works of Richard Hooker,* 1:118.

21. See Patricia A. Parker, *Inescapable Romance: Studies in the Poetics of a Mode* (Princeton: Princeton Univ. Press, 1979), 64–77.

22. See Antonio Minturno, *L'Arte Poetica* (Venice, 1563), 32–33; Cammillo Pellegrino, *Il Caraffa Ovvero Dell'Epica Poesia* (Florence, 1584), 138.

23. Hamilton, *Structure of Allegory,* 70–71.

24. See William Sessions's complementary account of how the Contemplation episode revises Aeneas's descent into the underworld ("Spenser's Georgics," *English Literary Renaissance* 10 [1980]: 235).

25. See King's discussion of how the House of Holinesse provides an "iconoclastic antidote" to Catholic practices and teachings (*Spenser's Poetry and the Reformation Tradition,* 58–65).

26. Augustine, *De Civitate Dei Libri XXII,* ed. B. Dombart and A. Kalb, 2 vols. (Leipzig: Teubner, 1928–29), 21.13.

27. Numquidnam oporptuerat te inter tanta dulcia poma mora etiam ponere tuaeque luculentae sapientiae funalia caligare? Ad haec ille subridens: "Si, inquit, inter tantas Stoicas ueritates aliquid etiam Epicureum non desipissem, paganus non essem" (*Expositio Virgilianae Continentiae Secundum Philosophos Moralis,* in *Fabii Planciadis Fulgentii V. C. Opera,* ed. Rudolf Helm [Leipzig, 1898], 103).

28. *The Aeneid of Thomas Phaer and Thomas Twyne: A Critical Edition Introducing Renaissance Metrical Typography,* ed. Steven Lally, The Renaissance Imagination 20 (New York: Garland, 1987), Gloss to VI.745.

29. *The Sixth Book of Virgil's* Aeneid, translated and commented on by Sir John Harington, ed. Simon Cauchi (Oxford: Clarendon Press, 1991), 83.

30. *Triplex purgatio. Fortassis alludit ad lustrationes funebres, . . . Item spargenda aqua, Item cremando* (Marginal gloss to lines VI.739 ff. in *P. Vergilii Maronis Opera, Philippi Melanchthonis illustrata scholiis* [Lyons, 1533]).

NOTES TO PAGES 107–115

31. On Spenser's reconciliation of the *vita activa* and the *vita contemplativa,* see Michael West, "Spenser and the Renaissance Ideal of Christian Heroism," *PMLA* 88 (1973): 1013–32.

32. Anna Cox Brinton summarizes Vegius's reception in her introduction to *Maphaeus Vegius and His Thirteenth Book of the* Aeneid: *A Chapter on Virgil in the Renaissance* (Stanford: Stanford Univ. Press, 1930), 29–30. While other poets, including Pier Candido Decembrio, Joseph Forestus, and the anonymous author of the "Analysis of the *Aeneid,*" also wrote continuations of the poem, Vegius's Thirteenth Book rose to prominence with its inclusion in Adam de Ambergau's Venetian *Virgil* of 1471. By the sixteenth century, Vegius's work had appeared in at least twenty Venetian editions and over half a dozen Parisian ones; it was printed at least once in Rome, Florence, Milan, Turin, Antwerp, Cologne, Nuremburg, Strasbourg, Zurich, and several other cities on both sides of the Alps. Badius, whose commentary on the *Aeneid* was a standard feature of most Renaissance editions of the poem, annotated Vegius in 1500. When Sebastian Brant published his sumptuously illustrated Virgil in 1502, he included the Thirteenth Book with woodcuts depicting the funeral of Turnus, Aeneas's marriage, and four other scenes.

In Britain, over a dozen editions of the *Aeneid* published before 1500 continued the saga of Aeneas with Vegius's additions. Even if Spenser did not know the Thirteenth Book in its original Latin, an unlikely possibility considering its widespread availability, he knew Gavin Douglas's *XIII Bukes of Eneados,* which concluded with a Scots translation of Vegius. Copland reprinted Douglas's translation in 1554; as K. Brunner has shown, several of the northernisms in *The Shepheardes Calender* suggest Spenser's direct knowledge of Douglas's translation (see *Variorum,* 7:616). By the time Thomas Twyne added a translation of the Thirteenth Book to Phaer's frequently reprinted *Aeneid,* English readers were familiar with a version of the story that included Aeneas's marriage.

33. Vegius, *De Perseverantia Religionis* (Paris, 1511), I.iiii.x. Trans. in Brinton, *Maphaeus Vegius and His Thirteenth Book of the* Aeneid, 28.

34. Latin references to Vegius are to Brinton's edition; I have supplied the Tudor translation by Thomas Twyne, from *The Aeneid of Phaer and Twyne.*

35. Hume, *Edmund Spenser,* 104–5; King, *Spenser's Poetry and the Reformation Tradition,* 197–99. See also Carol V. Kaske, "The Dragon's Spark and Sting and the Structure of Red Cross's Dragon-fight: *The Faerie Queene,* I.xi–xii," *Studies in Philology* 66 (1969): 609–38.

Chapter 5: Tempering the Two Didos

1. Much recent scholarship argues that a consciousness of the queen's paradoxical status as the female ruler of a patriarchal society underlies Spenser's revisions of modes and genres throughout *The Faerie Queene.* See especially Pamela Joseph Benson, "Rule, Virginia: Protestant Theories of Female Regiment in *The Faerie Queene,*" *English Literary Renaissance* 15 (1985): 277–92; Susanne Woods, "Spenser and the Problem of Women's Rule," *Huntington Library Quarterly* 48 (1985): 141–58; Maureen Quilligan, *Milton's Spenser: The Politics of Reading* (Ithaca: Cornell Univ. Press, 1983); Mary R. Bowman, " 'she there as Princess rained': Spenser's Figure of Elizabeth," *Renaissance Quarterly* 43 (1990): 509–28.

For more general discussion of the cultural contradictions posed by the Queen's gender, see Marie Axton, *The Queen's Two Bodies: Drama and the Elizabethan Succession* (London: Royal Historical Society, 1977); Louis Adrian Montrose, " 'Shaping Fantasies': Figurations of Gender and Power in Elizabethan Culture," *Representations* 1 (1983): 61–94.

2. Numerous studies document the early modern decline in women's social, political, and economic position. See especially Wally Secombe, "The Housewife and Her Labour under Capitalism," *New Left Review* 83 (1973): 3–24; Lawrence Stone, "The Rise of the Nuclear Family in Early Modern England: The Patriarchal Stage," in *The Family in History*, ed. Charles E. Rosenberg, Haney Foundation Series 17 (Philadelphia: Univ. of Pennsylvania Press, 1975), 13–57; Eli Zaretsky, *Capitalism, the Family, and Personal Life* (New York: Harper, 1976); Joan Kelly-Gadol, "Did Women Have a Renaissance?" in *Becoming Visible: Women in European History*, ed. Renate Bridenthal and Claudia Koonz (Boston: Houghton Mifflin, 1977), 139–64; Roberta Hamilton, *The Liberation of Women: A Study of Patriarchy and Capitalism* (London: George Allen and Unwin, 1978); Allison Heisch, "Queen Elizabeth I and the Persistance of Patriarchy," *Feminist Review* 4 (1980): 45–56; Merry E. Wiesner, "Spinsters and Seamstresses: Women in Cloth and Clothing Production," in *Rewriting the Renaissance: The Discourses of Sexual Difference in Early Modern Europe*, ed. Margaret W. Ferguson et al. (Chicago: Univ. of Chicago Press, 1986), 191–205.

3. Critics have often noted a general shift from sacred to secular concerns in the transition from Book I to Book II. A. S. P. Woodhouse states the case most emphatically in "Nature and Grace in *The Faerie Queene*," *ELH* 16 (1949): 194–228. Subsequent Spenserians have generally rejected Woodhouse's view that later books of the poem unfold solely on the order of nature. See especially Robert Hoopes, " 'God Guide Thee, *Guyon*': Nature and Grace Reconciled in *The Faerie Queene*, Book II," *Review of English Studies* 5 (1954): 14–24; A. D. S. Fowler, "The Image of Mortality: *The Faerie Queene*, II, i–ii," *Huntington Library Quarterly* 24 (1961): 91–110; Anthea Hume, *Edmund Spenser: Protestant Poet* (Cambridge: Cambridge Univ. Press, 1984), 107–44. While I agree with these scholars that grace still figures in the later books, I also maintain with A. C. Hamilton that Guyon's career nevertheless emphasizes how "natural man realizes the potentialities of his nature by ruling his passions through reason" (*The Structure of Allegory in* The Faerie Queene [Oxford: Clarendon Press, 1961], 91).

4. Scholars have often commented on the Belphoebe episode as a revision of Venus's appearance to Aeneas on the road to Carthage. See especially Edgar Wind, *Pagan Mysteries in the Renaissance* (New York: Norton, 1958), 76–80; Harry Berger, Jr., *The Allegorical Temper: Vision and Reality in Book II of Spenser's* Faerie Queene (New Haven: Yale Univ. Press, 1957), 157–58; Barbara J. Bono, *Literary Transvaluation: From Vergilian Epic to Shakespearean Tragicomedy* (Berkeley: Univ. of California Press, 1984), 71–74. Krier's account of how the episode jointly revises Virgilian and Ovidian paradigms of viewing a numinous being complements my discussion of how Spenser juxtaposes Virgilian and Ariostan effects (Theresa M. Krier, *Gazing on Secret Sights: Spenser, Classical Imitation, and the Decorums of Vision* [Ithaca: Cornell Univ. Press, 1990], 66–82). Anthony di Matteo shares my interest in the episode's relationship to Neo-Latin commentary on the Virgilian Venus ("Spenser's Venus-Virgo: The Poetics and Interpretive History of a Dissembling Figure," *Spenser Studies* 10 [1989]: 56–59).

5. See R. E. Neil Dodge, "Spenser's Imitations from Ariosto," *PMLA* 12 (1897): 184–85.

6. See Kathleen Williams's discussion of "the doubleness of effect" that Spenser achieves in presenting Belphoebe as both an agent of chastity and an object of desire (*Spenser's World of Glass: A Reading of* The Faerie Queene [Berkeley: Univ. of California Press, 1966], 48–51).

7. Merritt Y. Hughes (*Virgil and Spenser*, Univ. of California Publications in English, 2 [Berkeley: Univ. of California Press, 1929], 362), William Sessions ("Spenser's Georgics," *English Literary Renaissance* 10 [1980]: 228–29), and Thomas P. Roche, Jr. (*The Kindly Flame: A Study of the Third and Fourth Books of Spenser's* Faerie Queene [Princeton: Princeton Univ.

Press, 1964], 101–3) argue that Spenser read Venus's appearance to Aeneas as a manifestation of the Neoplatonic *Venus Urania*. The episode's general debt to Virgil has long been recognized. See especially Michael O'Connell's discussion in *Mirror and Veil: The Historical Dimension of Spenser's* Faerie Queene (Chapel Hill: Univ. of North Carolina Press, 1977), 101, 107–8.

8. Badius, in *P. Virgilii Maronis* Aeneida *Commentarium*, 176, verso.

9. "Nam si quis eam, qualis est cerneret, haud dubie nisu solo tremefactus aufugeret" (*Seniles*, IV.5; trans. in Bernardo et al., 1:142).

10. As Dodge has noted, several motifs link Braggadocchio to Mandricardo and Rodomonte just before Belphoebe appears ("Spenser's Imitations from Ariosto," 178–80). His boast never to bear a sword again unless it were that "which noblest knight on earth doth weare" (II.iii.17) echoes Mandricardo's vow to attain Orlando's sword Durindana. His theft of Guyon's horse recalls the thefts of Rinaldo and Astolfo's horses, and his terror at the sound of Belphoebe's hunting horn recalls that of several characters startled by Astolfo's magical *corno*.

11. By suggesting that Belphoebe's confrontation with Braggadocchio and Trompart engages Elizabethan anxieties about the commedia dell'arte, Maureen Quilligan raises yet another possible aspect of the episode's stigmatization of Italian culture ("The Comedy of Female Authority in *The Faerie Queene*," *English Literary Renaissance* 17 [1987]: 156–71).

12. See Berger's discussion of the episode's relation to the book's overall moral and poetic argument in *The Allegorical Temper*, 150–60.

13. John Upton noted the Virgilian source in his edition of *Spenser's Faerie Queene*, 2 vols. (London, 1758).

14. *Servii Grammatici qui feruntur in Vergilii Carmina Commentarii*, ed. George Thilo and Hermann Hagen, 3 vols. (1881–87; Leipzig: Teubner, 1923), 1:584. Servius concludes that the two Virgilian passages are not contradictory. He stresses that each statement must be understood as a response to a specific rhetorical situation rather than as a universal statement about death: *SED MISERA ANTE DIEM non est contrarium quod dicit in decimo stat sua cuique dies: nam, ut saepe diximus, secundum sectas loquitur; et hoc secundum alios, illud secundum alios dictum est.* ("But wretched before her day" does not run contrary to that which [the poet] says in Book X, 'Each has his day.' For, as we often say, one speaks according to parties; and this is said in accordance with some and that in accordance with others" [translation mine].)

Badius proposed an alternative solution based on a distinction between trespassing, or going beyond (*praeterire*), and anticipating, or coming before (*praevenire*), one's fated day. The *dies* of X.467 becomes an absolute limit: one cannot live beyond that date, but one can certainly die before it (*hoc est, constituisti terminos eius, qui praeteriri non poterunt sed bene praeveniri*). See *P. Vergilii Maronis* Aeneida *Commentarium*, 291, verso.

15. Thilo and Hagen 1:583. Since the longer Servian commentary ("Servius Auctus," or "Servius Danielis") was not published until 1600, Spenser would probably not have known this particular gloss. I include it to exemplify the kind of interpretive problems that medieval and Renaissance readers found in the final line of Virgil's Book IV.

16. Edwin Greenlaw was the first critic to propose the now commonplace view of Book II as an analysis of intemperance in its twin modes of concupiscence and irascibility ("A Better Teacher than Aquinas," *Studies in Philology* 14 [1917]: 196–217).

17. See James Nohrnberg's complementary characterization of Mordant as a type of the Pauline Adam (*The Analogy of* The Faerie Queene [Princeton: Princeton Univ. Press, 1976], 287–88).

18. See Hamilton's note to II.ii.3 in his edition of *The Faerie Queene* (Edmund Spenser, *The Faerie Queene*, ed. A. C. Hamilton [London: Longman, 1977], 182). See also Hamilton, "A Theological Reading of *The Faerie Queene*, Book II," *ELH* 25 (1958): 155–62; Fowler, "The Image of Mortality"; Kathleen Williams *Spenser's World of Glass*, 41–44; Nohrnberg, *Analogy*, 288; Hume, *Edmund Spenser*, 171–73. For alternative readings of the episode in terms of secular themes and sources, see Lewis H. Miller, Jr., "A Secular Reading of *The Faerie Queene*, Book II," *ELH* 33 (1966): 154–69; Carol V. Kaske, "The Bacchus Who Wouldn't Wash: *Faerie Queene* II. i–ii," *Renaissance Quarterly* 29 (1976): 195–209.

19. *Caxton's Eneydos, 1490*, ed. W. T. Culley and F. J. Furnivall, Early English Text Society (London: N. Trübner, 1890), 113.

20. For recent discussion of Acrasia as a type of Circe, see Nohrnberg, *Analogy*, 494–502. But as Douglas Bush has argued, Homer is hardly Spenser's only source for the Bower (*Mythology and the Renaissance Tradition in English Poetry* [Minneapolis: Univ. of Minnesota Press, 1932], 100–101). Krier's view that Guyon's later voyage to the Bower is closer in spirit to Aeneas's voyage than to Odysseus's corroborates my own sense of a dominant Virgilian influence on Spenser's characterization of Acrasia (*Gazing on Secret Sights*, 100–101).

21. Boccaccio called the historical Dido a "limb of Satan" because she was still a pagan, despite her natural virtue. He does not explicitly condemn her suicide (*De Claris Mulieribus*, trans. by Guido A. Guarino as *Concerning Famous Women* [New Brunswick, N.J.: Rutgers Univ. Press, 1963], 91).

22. See O'Connell's *Mirror and Veil*, 102–3.

23. Paul Johnson, *Elizabeth I: A Study in Power and Intellect* (London: Weidenfeld and Nicolson, 1974), 112–18; Christopher Haigh, *Elizabeth I* (London: Longman, 1988), 95–96.

24. See Roy Strong's discussion of the iconographical significance of the Siena-Sieve portrait in *Portraits of Queen Elizabeth I* (Oxford: Clarendon Press, 1963), 66–68. Doris Adler ("The Riddle of the Sieve: The Siena Sieve Portrait of Queen Elizabeth, *Renaissance Papers* [1978]: 1–10) and Lowell Gallagher (*Medusa's Gaze: Casuistry and Conscience in the Renaissance* [Stanford: Stanford Univ. Press, 1991], 123–40) interpret the portrait's allusion to Dido in terms of the controversy stirred by the French marriage negotiations. See also Stephen Orgel's discussion of the painting in "Shakespeare and the Cannibals," in *Cannibals, Witches, and Divorce: Estranging the Renaissance,* ed. Marjorie Garber, Selected Papers from the English Institute, 1985, New Series, 11 (Baltimore: Johns Hopkins Univ. Press, 1987), 40–66.

25. For an account of the Brant illustrations, see Anna Cox Brinton, *Maphaeus Vegius and His Thirteenth Book of the* Aeneid: *A Chapter on Virgil in the Renaissance* (Stanford: Stanford Univ. Press, 1930), 40–44; Eleanor Winsor Leach, "Illustration as Interpretation in Brant's and Dryden's Editions of Vergil," in *The Early Illustrated Book: Essays in Honor of Lessing J. Rosenwald,* ed. Sandra Hindman (Washington, D.C.: Library of Congress, 1982), 175–210. The Galle *Aeneid* engravings are in the Bodleian Library.

26. See G. W. Kitchen, ed., *Book II of the* Faery Queene (Oxford, 1887), 188; Hughes, *Virgil and Spenser*, 330–31.

27. *Macrobius: The Saturnalia,* trans. Percival Vaughan Davies, Records of Civilization: Sources and Studies, 79 (New York: Columbia Univ. Press, 1969), 159.

28. "Hic post mensam seria tractantur et ad erigendam rem publicam erigitur uirile robur; ibi ut luxuriae faueant fusis precibus inuitantur et numina," in *Joannis Saresberiensis Episcopi Carnotensis Polycratici, sive De Nvgis Cvrialivm et Vestigiis Philosophorvm Libri VIII,* ed. Clemens

C. I. Webb, 2 vols. (Oxford: Clarendon Press, 1909), 2:730d. I have supplied my own translation in the text.

29. "Immoderatio cibi et potus dispensatricem omnium officiorum temperantiam abigit. Ea impellente fit homo ad audiendum tardus, uelox ad loquendum et uelox ad iram; fit ad libidinem pronus et ad quaeuis flagitia praeceps," in *Polycraticus*, 2:727d.

30. William Nelson, *The Poetry of Edmund Spenser: A Study* (New York: Columbia Univ. Press, 1963), 181.

31. David Miller, *The Poem's Two Bodies: The Poetics of the 1590 Faerie Queene* (Princeton: Princeton Univ. Press, 1988), 164–214.

32. Maurice Evans, *Spenser's Anatomy of Heroism: A Commentary on* The Faerie Queene (Cambridge: Cambridge Univ. Press, 1970), 141.

33. See Theresa Krier's discussion of the episode as a fiction exploring the dynamics of self-consciousness (*Gazing on Secret Sights*, 157–59).

34. *The Boke Named The Governovr, deuised by sir Thomas Elyot, Knight* (London, 1580), I.ix. See A. C. Hamilton's note to II.ix.40 (*FQ*, 255).

35. Berger, *Allegorical Temper*, 77n; Jerry Mills, "Symbolic Tapestry in *The Faerie Queene* II.ix.33," *Philological Quarterly* 49 (1970): 568–69.

36. On the seductiveness of Dido's murals, see W. R. Johnson, *Darkness Visible: A Study of Vergil's* Aeneid (Berkeley: Univ. of California Press, 1976), 99–105; Krier, *Gazing on Secret Sights*, 37–41.

37. See Joan Rossi's "Britons moniments: Spenser's Definition of Temperance in History," *English Literary Renaissance* 15 (1985): 42–58. Mills offers a darker interpretation of the Chronicles' historical vision in "Prudence, History, and the Prince in *The Faerie Queene*, Book II," *Huntington Library Quarterly* 41 (1978): 83–101.

38. Edward Dowden, *Transcripts and Studies* (London, 1888), 287.

39. Herbert Grierson, *Cross Currents in English Literature of the Seventeenth Century: Or, The World, the Flesh & the Spirit, their Actions & Reactions* (London, 1929), 61.

40. Graham Hough, *A Preface to* The Faerie Queene (New York: Norton, 1962), 156–57.

41. Angus Fletcher, *Allegory: The Theory of a Symbolic Mode* (Ithaca: Cornell Univ. Press, 1964), 35.

42. Stephen Greenblatt, *Renaissance Self-Fashioning: From More to Shakespeare* (Chicago: Univ. of Chicago Press, 1980), 157–92.

43. Berger, *Allegorical Temper*, 212. See C. S. Lewis, *The Allegory of Love: A Study in Medieval Tradition* (Oxford: Oxford Univ. Press, 1936), 324–33; Isabel MacCaffrey, "Allegory and Pastoral in *The Shepheardes Calender*," *ELH* 36 (1969): 260; Nohrnberg, *Analogy*, 502. For the view of Carthage as a false Rome, see Mario A. Di Cesare, *The Altar and the City: A Reading of Virgil's* Aeneid (New York: Columbia Univ. Press, 1974), 2.

44. One might compare Putnam and W. R. Johnson's discussions of the *Aeneid* with W. B. Yeats's remarks on the Bower of Bliss in *Essays and Introductions* (New York: Macmillan, 1961), 370–74.

45. On the conflict between Alcinan and Logistillan views of Ariosto, see Albert Ascoli, *Ariosto's Bitter Harmony: Crisis and Evasion in the Italian Renaissance* (Princeton: Princeton Univ. Press, 1987), 122–35. Proponents of an Alcinan Ariosto include Croce; Attilio Momigliano, *Saggio sull'Orlando Furioso* (1928; Bari: Laterza, 1973); Francesco De Sanctis, "Ariosto," in *Storia*

della Letteratura Italiana, ed. M. T. Lanza, 2 vols. (Milan: Feltrinelli, 1964); and Donato. Those upholding a Logistillan Ariosto committed to his readers' education include the sixteenth-century allegorizers as well as Vincent Cuccaro (*The Humanism of Ludovico Ariosto: From the* Satire *to the* Furioso, L'Interprete 18 [Ravenna: Longo, 1981), and to an extent, A. Bartlett Giamatti, *Earthly Paradise and the Renaissance Epic* (Princeton: Princeton Univ. Press, 1966), 137–64.

46. Martha Craig, "The Secret Wit of Spenser's Language," in *Elizabethan Poetry: Modern Essays in Criticism,* ed. Paul J. Alpers (New York: Oxford Univ. Press, 1967), 464. The translation is from John Florio's *Queen Anna's New World of Words, or Dictionarie of the Italian and English tongues* (London, 1611).

47. See David Quint, *Epic and Empire: Politics and Generic Form from Virgil to Milton* (Princeton: Princeton Univ. Press, 1993), 249–53. As Quint argues, Tasso transforms the errant boat of romance into a vessel with an epic mission to fulfill. Spenser suppresses Tasso's assimilation of the romance motif to the epic idealization of *labor* in order to dismiss him as a writer solely of romance.

48. For a complementary account of Acrasia's murderous gaze, see Krier, *Gazing on Secret Sights,* 109–11.

49. Renaissance debates over the brutality of Turnus's death at Aeneas's hands provide yet another analogue to the controversy over Guyon's destruction of the Bower. For a discussion of these controversies and of Tasso's modification of the *Aeneid*'s conclusion in response to them, see Lauren Scancarelli Seem, "The Limits of Chivalry: Tasso and the End of the *Aeneid,*" *Comparative Literature* 42 (1990): 116–25.

Chapter 6: *"Diverse Folk Diversely They Demed"*

1. See Kate M. Warren, "Introduction" to her edition of Book III, quoted in *Variorum,* 3:311–14; R. E. Neil Dodge, "Spenser's Imitations from Ariosto," *PMLA* 12 (1897): 190–95; Josephine Waters Bennett, *The Evolution of* The Faerie Queene (Chicago: Univ. of Chicago Press, 1942), 138–53.

2. Thomas P. Roche, Jr., *The Kindly Flame: A Study of the Third and Fourth Books of Spenser's* Faerie Queene (Princeton: Princeton Univ. Press, 1964), 210. For earlier versions of this view, see Ernest de Selincourt, "Introduction" to his edition of *The Faerie Queene* (Oxford: Oxford Univ. Press, 1921), xliv–xlvii; Frederick M. Padelford, "The Allegory of Chastity in *The Faerie Queene,*" *Studies in Philology* 21 (1924): 367–81.

3. See Edmund Spenser, *The Faerie Queene,* ed. A. C. Hamilton (London: Longman, 1977), 300.

4. Malecasta's tapestries mark an important halfway point in the transformation of Verdant and Acrasia into Venus and Adonis, and of the Bower into the Gardens. See James Nohrnberg, *The Analogy of* The Faerie Queene (Princeton: Princeton Univ. Press, 1976), 491–502.

5. Fichter also sees Britomart's story as a revision of the *Aeneid*'s first four books. But he offers an alternative explanation for Spenser's Virgilianism in terms of the Christian *felix culpa* (156–65).

6. Donald Cheney links this particular incident to Ariosto's "comic disintegration of chivalric ideals" in *Spenser's Images of Nature: Wild Man and Shepherd in* The Faerie Queene (New Haven: Yale Univ. Press, 1966), 83–88.

7. As Lauren Silberman notes, the episode's comedy derives from its principal Ariostan

subtext, Bradamante's encounter with Fiordispina ("Spenser and Ariosto: Funny Peril and Comic Chaos," *Comparative Literature Studies* 25 [1988]: 23–32).

8. For discussion of Spenser's use of the *Ciris* as a subtext for Britomart's revelation of her love to Glauce, see Merritt Y. Hughes, *Virgil and Spenser*, Univ. of California Publications in English, 2 (Berkeley: Univ. of California Press, 1929), 348–54; Roche, *Kindly Flame*, 53–55; Nohrnberg, *Analogy*, 446–47.

9. *The Aeneid of Thomas Phaer and Thomas Twyne: A Critical Edition Introducing Renaissance Metrical Typography*, ed. Steven Lally, The Renaissance Imagination 20 (New York: Garland, 1987), gloss to VI.910ff. See also Harington's identification of Marcellus as Octavia's son, "wch yf yt had lyvde was lyke to have succeeded in the empyre" (*The Sixth Book of Virgil's Aeneid*, translated and commented on by Sir John Harington, ed. Simon Cauchi [Oxford: Clarendon Press, 1991], 59); Badius, 360 verso.

10. Hamilton's edition of the *Faerie Queene*, 334.

11. See Anderson, " 'In liuing colours and right hew': The Queen of Spenser's Central Books," in *Poetic Traditions of the English Renaissance*, ed. Maynard Mack and George deForest Lord (New Haven: Yale Univ. Press, 1982), 47–66; David Miller, *The Poem's Two Bodies: The Poetics of the 1590 Faerie Queene* (Princeton: Princeton Univ. Press, 1988), 224–35. For the more traditional view of Belphoebe as an unambiguously ideal embodiment of chastity, see Paul Alpers, *The Poetry of* The Faerie Queene (Princeton: Princeton Univ. Press, 1967), 390–91; Roche, *Kindly Flame*, 136–48. Michael O'Connell sees a pervasive ambivalence toward the court as a direct link between the Virgilian and Spenserian views of history (*Mirror and Veil: The Historical Dimension of Spenser's* Faerie Queene [Chapel Hill: Univ. of North Carolina Press, 1977]). According to O'Connell's analysis, both poets felt compelled to judge the cultures that they also praised.

12. Thomas Greene, *The Descent from Heaven: A Study in Epic Continuity* (New Haven: Yale Univ. Press, 1963), 125–29; Barbara Pavlock, *Eros, Imitation, and the Epic Tradition* (Ithaca: Cornell Univ. Press, 1990), 170–83. For further discussion of the Ariostan episode and its relation to classical antecedents, see Eduardo Saccone, "Cloridano e Medoro, con alcuni argomenti per una lettura del primo *Furioso*," *Modern Language Notes* 83 (1968): 67–99; Walter Moretti, "La storia di Cloridano e Medoro: Un esempio della umanizzazione ariostesca delle idealità eroiche e cavalleresche," *Convivium* 37 (1969): 543–51.

13. Harry Berger, Jr., also notes the homosocial character of Arthur's relationship to Timias and suggests that their separation throughout the episode illustrates the threat posed by heterosexual desire ("Kidnapped Romance: Discourse in *The Faerie Queene*," in *Unfolded Tales: Essays on Renaissance Romance*, ed. George M. Logan and Gordon Teskey [Ithaca: Cornell Univ. Press, 1989], 226).

14. On the relationship between literal and metaphorical wounding in the Timias-Belphoebe episode, see A. Leigh DeNeef, *Spenser and the Motives of Metaphor* (Durham: Duke Univ. Press, 1982), 163–65; Berger, "Kidnapped Romance," 227–31.

15. See Reed Way Dasenbrock's discussion of the Timias episode as a critique of Petrarchanism in "Escaping the Squires' Double Bind in Books III and IV of *The Faerie Queene*," *Studies in English Literature* 26 (1986): 25–45.

16. See the gloss to III.v.54 in Hamilton's edition of the *Faerie Queene*, 354.

17. Warren refers to the opening stanza of canto v as a "still finer statement of the same thing" that Spenser said previously in the first stanza of canto i (quoted in *Variorum*, 3:312).

The *Variorum* editors gloss III.v.i simply by referring their readers to their notes on III.iii.1 (3: 244).

18. See Alpers's fine discussion of the episode's comic basis in *Poetry of* The Faerie Queene, 379–80.

19. Harry Berger, *Revisionary Play: Studies in the Spenserian Dynamics* (Berkeley: Univ. of California Press, 1988), 154–71; Mihoko Suzuki, *Metamorphoses of Helen: Authority, Difference, and the Epic* (Ithaca: Cornell Univ. Press, 1989), 159–73.

20. For discussion of the episode's debt to Ovid, see Helen Cheney Gilde, "Spenser's Hellenore and Some Ovidian Associations," *Comparative Literature* 23 (1971): 233–39; Suzuki, *Metamorphoses of Helen*, 162–65.

21. For suggestions of other possible links between the Hellenore episode and the Merchant's Tale, see A. Kent Hieatt, *Chaucer, Spenser, Milton: Mythopoeic Continuities and Transformations* (Montreal: McGill-Queen's Univ. Press, 1975), 119. For discussion of the strategies through which Chaucer achieves a relatively sympathetic view of May at January's expense, see E. Talbot Donaldson, *Speaking of Chaucer* (New York: Norton, 1970), 30–45; Alfred David, *The Strumpet Muse: Art and Morals in Chaucer's Poetry* (Bloomington: Indiana Univ. Press, 1976), 170–81; Priscilla Martin, *Chaucer's Women: Nuns, Wives, and Amazons* (Houndmills, Basingstoke: Macmillan, 1990), 104–5.

22. See also Roche, *Kindly Flame*, 65.

23. See M. Pauline Parker, *The Allegory of the* Faerie Queene (Oxford: Clarendon Press, 1960), 40, 46; Roche, *Kindly Flame*, 202.

24. See Bernard, "Pastoral and Comedy in Book III of *The Faerie Queene*," *Studies in English Literature* 23 (1983): 8ff.; Theresa M. Krier, *Gazing on Secret Sights: Spenser, Classical Imitation, and the Decorums of Vision* (Ithaca: Cornell Univ. Press, 1990), 183–84. See also Nohrnberg, *Analogy*, 31; Alpers, *Poetry of* The Faerie Queene, 388; Donald Cheney, "Spenser's Hermaphrodite and the 1590 *Faerie Queene*," *PMLA* 87 (1972): 198.

25. See Northrop Frye, *Anatomy of Criticism: Four Essays* (Princeton: Princeton Univ. Press, 1957), 153.

26. See Jonathan Goldberg, "The Mothers in Book III of *The Faerie Queene*," *Texas Studies in Literature and Language* 17 (1975): 5–26.

27. See C. S. Lewis, *The Allegory of Love* (Oxford: Clarendon Press, 1936), 340–46; Roche, *Kindly Flame*, 72–88; Isabel MacCaffrey, "Allegory and Pastoral in *The Shepheardes Calender*," *ELH* 36 (1969): 107–11; Berger, *Revisionary Play*, 172–94.

28. Lauren Silberman, "Singing Unsung Heroines: Androgynous Discourse in Book 3 of *The Faerie Queene*," in *Rewriting the Renaissance: The Discourses of Sexual Difference in Early Modern Europe*, ed. Margaret W. Ferguson et al. (Chicago: Univ. of Chicago Press, 1986), 259–71.

29. Susanne Wofford, "Gendering Allegory: Spenser's Bold Reader and the Emergence of Character in *The Faerie Queene* III," *Criticism* 30 (1988): 14.

30. See Henry Gibbons Lotspeich, *Classical Mythology in the Poetry of Edmund Spenser* (Princeton: Princeton Univ. Press, 1932), 11. I am especially indebted to Leonard Barkan's discussion of the episode in *The Gods Made Flesh: Metamorphosis and the Pursuit of Paganism* (New Haven: Yale Univ. Press, 1986), 231–42.

31. Latin references are to *Metamorphoses*, ed. William S. Anderson (Leipzig: Teubner,

1977). English references are to Rolfe Humphries's translation (1955; Bloomington: Indiana Univ. Press, 1967).

32. For the history of Ovidian exegesis in the Middle Ages and the Renaissance, see Don Cameron Allen, *Mysteriously Meant: The Rediscovery of Pagan Symbolism and Allegorical Interpretation in the Renaissance* (Baltimore: The Johns Hopkins Press, 1970), 163–99; Clark Hulse, *Metamorphic Verse: The Elizabethan Minor Epic* (Princeton: Princeton Univ. Press, 1981), 244–51.

33. Arthur Golding, "Epistle," in *Shakespeare's Ovid, Being Arthur Golding's Translation of the* Metamorphoses, ed. W. H. D. Rouse (London: De La More Press, 1904), ll. 232–33.

34. "Inani epitheton est picturae, aut quia caret corporum quae imitatur plenitudine, aut quia nullius est utilitatis," in *Servii Grammatici qvi fervntvr in Vergilii Carmina Commentarii,* ed. George Thilo and Hermann Hagen, 3 vols. (1881–87; Leipzig: Teubner, 1923), 1:149.

35. Cheney, "Spenser's Hermaphrodite," 192–200. See also Berger, *Revisionary Play,* 191–94.

36. For further connections between Redcrosse's degradation and Amoret's "Sweete ravishment," see Lauren Silberman, "The Hermaphrodite and the Metamorphosis of Spenserian Allegory," *English Literary Renaissance* 17 (1987): 207–23.

37. For examples of the *Bildungsroman* approach to Spenser's characters, see T. K. Dunseath, *Spenser's Allegory of Justice in Book Five of* The Faerie Queene (Princeton: Princeton Univ. Press, 1968); Maurice Evans, *Spenser's Anatomy of Heroism: A Commentary on* The Faerie Queene (Cambridge: Cambridge Univ. Press, 1970). At one point, Evans explicitly compares Britomart to Tess of the D'Urbervilles (164). For further critique of this approach, see Jonathan Goldberg, *Endlesse Worke: Spenser and the Structures of Discourse* (Baltimore: Johns Hopkins Univ. Press, 1981), 74.

38. Susanne Wofford, *The Choice of Achilles: The Ideology of Figure in the Epic* (Stanford: Stanford Univ. Press, 1992), 259.

Afterword

1. "Dido," in *The Spenser Encyclopedia,* ed. A. C. Hamilton et al. (Toronto: Univ. of Toronto Press, 1990).

2. Hamilton glosses the Virgilian echo in his edition of *The Faerie Queene,* 558. For more recent discussion of Radigund's epic origins as a type of Dido, see Mihoko Suzuki, *Metamorphoses of Helen: Authority, Difference, and the Epic* (Ithaca: Cornell Univ. Press, 1989), 177–91.

3. Susannah Jane McMurphy, *Spenser's Use of Ariosto for Allegory,* Univ. of Washington Publications in Language and Literature 2 (1924): 35–36. Quoted in *Variorum,* 5:349.

4. Humphrey Tonkin argues that Spenser's ambivalence toward Calidore's truancy figures divergent assessments of the relationship between pastoral and heroic worlds (*Spenser's Courteous Pastoral: Book VI of* The Faerie Queene [Oxford: Clarendon Press, 1972], 294–300).

5. See Hamilton's discussion of romance motifs in the Pastorella story in *The Structure of Allegory in* The Faerie Queene (Oxford: Clarendon Press, 1961), 204–6.

6. I am indebted to Berger's discussion of this ambivalence in "*The Mutabilitie Cantos*: Archaism and Evolution in Retrospect," in *Spenser: A Collection of Critical Essays,* ed. Harry Berger, Twentieth-Century Views (Englewood Cliffs, N.J.: Prentice-Hall, 1968), 172.

INDEX

Alençon/Anjou, François Hercules, Duke of, 67, 79, 126
Apollonius, 18, 20, 22–24, 26, 47
Ariosto, Lodovico: and skepticism, 52–56, 94–103, 113; and *Faerie Queene* I, 94–99, 102–3, 114–19; and Virgilian ekphrasis, 133; and *Faerie Queene* III, 145–49, 152–53, 155–60, 162
—*Orlando Furioso*: early modern responses to, 1–4, 49, 56–58, 67, 94; the San Giovanni episode, 52–53; the Alcina episode, 53–56, 94–99, 102–3, 114–19, 136–37; the Angelica-Medoro episode, 156–60; Bradamante's fight with Marfisa, 176
Aristotle, 4, 134
Ascham, Roger, 83
Augustine, 30–31, 34–39, 43–44, 69, 105, 111, 142
Augustus (Octavian): antifeminism and xenophobia, 6, 9–11; and the *Aeneid*, 11–12, 14–17, 19–20, 24–28, 113; and Ren-

aissance patronage, 52, 62, 66–68; and dynastic vulnerability, 154–55
Authorship, theories of, 2–3, 38–41, 48–49, 62–64

Badius Ascensius, Jodocus, 49, 57, 71, 76, 82, 84, 105, 116, 170
Balbi, Girolamo, 49–50, 100
Beaumont, Francis, 83
Becke, Edmund, 83
Bembo, Pietro, 63
Bernard. *See* Silvestris, Bernard
Bible, 83, 90, 111, 144
Blackmore, Sir Richard, 1–2
Blake, William, 178
Boccaccio, Giovanni: and Dido, 50–52, 57, 82, 131; and didacticism, 52, 91, 98, 105, 125, 145, 151, 168
Boiardo, Matteo, 56
Boleyn, Anne, 78
Bononome, Gioseffo, 57, 94